Praise for
THE BERLITZ TRAVELLERS GUIDES

"Aimed at educated, experienced travellers, the [Berlitz Travellers] Guides capture the flavor of foreign lands."
—*Entrepreneur*

"Filling a needed niche in guidebooks ... designed to eliminate the cumbersome lists of virtually every hotel and restaurant .... Special out-of-the-way places are detailed. ... The books capture the personality and excitement of each destination."
—*Los Angeles Times*

"There's a different tone to these books, and certainly a different approach ... information is aimed at independent and clearly sophisticated travellers. ... Strong opinions give these books a different personality from most guides, and make them fun to read."
—*Travel & Leisure*

"Aimed at experienced, independent travellers who want information beyond the nuts-and-bolts material available in many familiar sources. Although each volume gives necessary basics, the series sends travellers not just to 'sights,' but to places and events that convey the personality of each locale."
—*The Denver Post*

"Just the right amount of information about where to stay and play."
—*Detroit Free Press*

CONTRIBUTORS

BERNARD SHARE, editor of Aer Lingus's in-flight magazine *Cara,* is the author of books on travel and Irish history as well as three novels. He is also a regular broadcaster for RTE-Irish radio and is the editorial consultant for this volume.

VINCENT CAPRANI, a lifelong resident of Dublin, is the author of *A View from the DART,* a best-selling book on travel in Dublin. He contributes articles on Dublin for travellers and residents to a number of magazines.

WILLIAM MAXWELL, for over 25 years the manager of press relations for Aer Lingus, is also a leading critic with Ireland's largest daily, the *Irish Independent,* and a contributor to many travel magazines.

SAM McAUGHTRY, a native of Belfast and the author of six books, including three collections of short stories, is well known as a radio and television scriptwriter and broadcaster both north and south of the border.

JOHN O'DONOGHUE has been a journalist covering culture for *The Irish Times* and for RTE, the Irish National Broadcasting System, for many years.

LORCAN ROCHE, a descendant of the Roches who arrived in Wexford in 1167, is a freelance writer and a drama critic for the *Irish Independent,* and has been associate editor of *Travel-Holiday* magazine in the United States.

LORNA SIGGINS is an Irish journalist who has contributed to numerous publications, and is now a staff reporter with *The Irish Times.*

COLM TOIBIN, formerly an editor of one of Ireland's leading news magazines, is also the author of the noted travel book *Walking Along the Border* and a novel, *The South.*

THE BERLITZ
TRAVELLERS GUIDES

THE BERLITZ TRAVELLERS GUIDE TO IRELAND 1992

ALAN TUCKER
General Editor

BERLITZ PUBLISHING COMPANY, INC.
New York, New York

BERLITZ PUBLISHING LTD.
Wheatley, Oxford

THE BERLITZ TRAVELLERS
GUIDE TO IRELAND 1992

Berlitz Trademark Reg U.S. Patent and Trademark Office
and other countries—Marca Registrada

Published by Berlitz Publishing Company, Inc.
257 Park Avenue South, New York, New York 10010, U.S.A.

Distributed in the United States by
the Macmillan Publishing Group

Distributed elsewhere by Berlitz Publishing Ltd.
London Road, Wheatley, Oxford OX9 1YR, England

Originally published as the Penguin Travel Guide to Ireland
by Viking Penguin, a division of Penguin USA Inc.

ISBN 2-8315-1758-3
ISSN 1057-4719

Designed by Beth Tondreau Design
Cover design by Dan Miller Design
Cover photograph by Jay Maisel
Maps by David Lindroth
Illustrations by Bill Russell
Fact-checked in Ireland by Catherine Pearson
Edited by Lisa Leventer

Printed in the United States of America
1 3 5 7 9 10 8 6 4 2

THIS GUIDEBOOK

The Berlitz Travellers Guides are designed for experienced travellers in search of exceptional information that will enhance the enjoyment of the trips they take.

Where, for example, are the interesting, out-of-the-way, fun, charming, or romantic places to stay? The hotels described by our expert writers are some of the special places, in all price ranges except for the very lowest—not just the run-of-the-mill, heavily marketed places in advertised airline and travel-wholesaler packages.

We indicate the approximate price level of each accommodation in our description of it (no indication means it is moderate in local, relative terms), and at the end of every chapter we supply more detailed hotel rates as well as contact information so that you can get precise, up-to-the-minute rates and make reservations.

The Berlitz Travellers Guide to Ireland 1992 highlights the more rewarding parts of the country so that you can quickly and efficiently home in on a good itinerary.

Of course, this guidebook does far more than just help you choose a hotel and plan your trip. *The Berlitz Travellers Guide to Ireland 1992* is designed for use *in* Ireland. Our writers, each of whom is an experienced travel journalist who either lives in or regularly tours the city or region of Ireland he or she covers, tell you what you really need to know, what you can't find out so easily on your own. They identify and describe the truly out-of-the-ordinary restaurants, shops, activities, and sights, and tell you the best way to "do" your destination.

Our writers are highly selective. They bring out the significance of the places they *do* cover, capturing the personality and the underlying cultural and historical resonances of a city or region—making clear its special appeal.

The Berlitz Travellers Guide to Ireland is full of reliable and timely information, revised and updated each year. We would like to know if you think we've left out some very special place. Although we make every effort to provide the most current information available about every destination described in this book, it is possible too that changes have occurred before you arrive. If you do have an experience that is contrary to what you were led to expect by our description, we would like to hear from you about it.

A guidebook is no substitute for common sense when you are travelling. Always pack the clothing, footwear, and other items appropriate for the destination, and make the necessary accommodation for such variables as altitude, weather, and local rules and customs. Of course, once on the scene you should avoid situations that are in your own judgment potentially hazardous, even if they have to do with something mentioned in a guidebook. Half the fun of travelling is exploring, but explore with care.

ALAN TUCKER
General Editor
Berlitz Travellers Guides

Root Publishing Company
330 West 58th Street
Suite 5-D
New York, New York 10019

CONTENTS

MAPS

THE
BERLITZ
TRAVELLERS
GUIDE
TO
IRELAND
1992

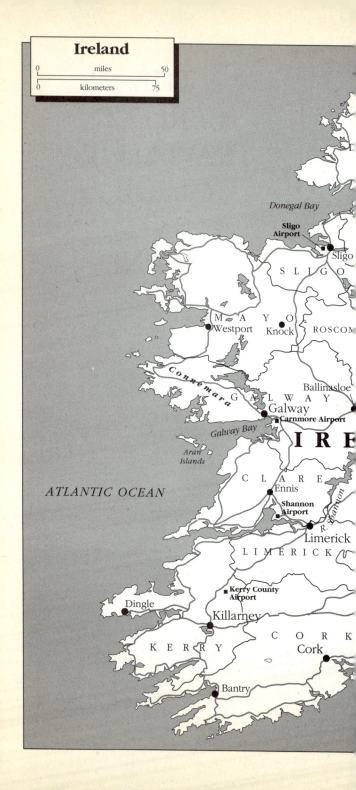

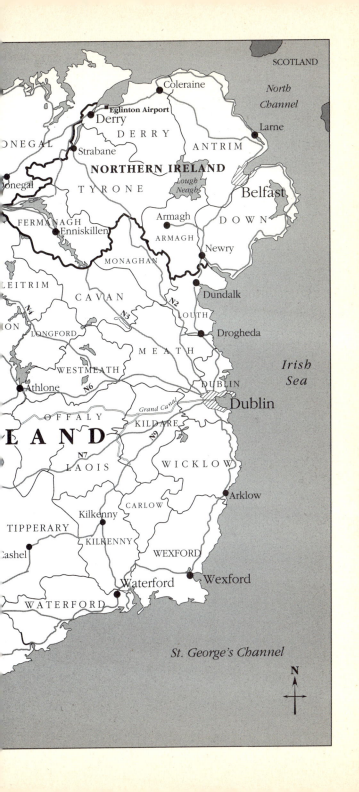

OVERVIEW

By Bernard Share

Bernard Share, the editor of Cara, *the in-flight magazine for Aer Lingus, also writes frequently on travel topics about Ireland. He is the author or editor of several books, including* Irish Traditions, *and lives in County Kildare.*

The image of Ireland: a green, somnolent land over which there linger the still-pungent odors of battles long ago; a self-regarding community that has somehow contrived to sidestep the grosser manifestations of modern affluence; a concatenation of tight-knit factions none of which will give an inch and from which the more harassed or more adventurous escape to zigzag round the globe with, as the poet Louis MacNeice put it a generation ago, "... a gesture and a brogue/And a faggot of useless memories."

Like all reflective images, it is to be read backwards. Ireland today produces as many electronic components as cattle, imports its potatoes, and sends its army to Lebanon and its elite rock groups everywhere. It is still green—a maritime location in the path of the Atlantic weather systems sees to that. And it is still, in spite of its membership in the European Community, the United Nations, and a clatter of other international conspiracies (always excluding military alliances), inward-looking. It is, its philosophers will tell their less percipient co-citizens, still in search of an identity. This in spite of having recivilized Europe in the Dark Ages by means of a shock wave of monks and having contributed again in this century through the impact of a pantheon of such major literary figures as Joyce, Yeats, Beckett, Synge, Wilde, and O'Casey. None of this the alert visitor will miss, as it is constantly being brought to the attention of a public that is probably, at any given time, more interested in the British soccer results, American TV soaps, or the price of drink. Should the visitor be from another English-speaking country, even if his name be Katzentraum or Ng, he will be automatically assumed to be of Irish descent, because the extended Irish diaspora is the one significant external factor this self-absorbed society will readily admit to. There are nevertheless many Irelands, some of them existing simultaneously in the same place, even in the same area of national consciousness, and the ones you will remember may not necessarily be those that your camera records.

The particular Ireland you choose to pursue in the space of a short visit will, of course, depend upon your individual taste and inclination; but this is a small and compact country, and you will not find difficulty in combining within the confines of a two-week vacation the Dublin theater with hill walking, genealogical research with canal cruising, the brooding Celtic past with the rocking present.

Excluded by geography from the simplistic appeal of a sun destination, Ireland has developed its own highly individualistic attractions that are governed not so much by the temporalities as by temperament. This is not to say that the weather is a negative factor: the succession of changes within the course of a single day may serve to illumine quite an ordinary event or introduce into even the best-laid plans a piquant element of challenge. The weather, you will discover, is a topic of diurnal speculation in a way it would never be in, say, San Francisco or Sydney. Some say that its rapidly changing moods account for the perceived volatility of the Irish character. You may make up your own mind on that.

Whatever you feel about the weather—and Ireland, in a good summer, can be hotter than Spain—you will probably discover in the Irish people a quality of individuality that has resisted the stereotyping imposed by concentrated urban living and the uneasy suspicion of one's fellow man that it engenders. Thus it is rare to pass someone on the road—whatever your mode of travel—without a greeting, which may vary from a curt nod or a hand salute from the wheel of a car (and the variation of gesture from county to county is a study in itself) to a "Grand evening" or more ample and leisurely exchange in a shop or a pub. People in Ireland talk to one another—on trains, in buses, in the street, at the racetrack—as a matter of course and because there is a perennial interest in other people's occupations and preoccupations. And that holds for the visitor as well. "The Irish are very fond of strangers," observed a French traveller in 1644—a conclusion to which the more commercial aspects of tourism have done little to give the lie.

In very simple terms Ireland is a flat saucer rimmed with modest mountains. The greatest concentration of population—and prosperity—is on the eastern seaboard and centered upon the county and city of Dublin, which accounts for nearly one-third of the total population of some 3.5 million. Administratively the island is divided into 32 counties, of which 26 constitute the Republic of Ireland ("The South") and six form the area of Northern Ireland, an integral part of the United Kingdom of Great Britain and Northern Ireland. These six counties also constitute six-ninths of the historic Province of Ulster, one of four (the others are Leinster, Munster, and, in the west, Connacht, also given as Connaught) that still, in spite of the political divide, play Gaelic and Rugby football against each other. There are many other ways in which the whole island of Ireland functions as an entity: both the Roman Catholic and Episcopalian (Church of Ireland) churches recognize no internal frontier. In many sports Ireland fields 32 county teams. The car rally known as the Circuit of Ireland is just that. And the Railway Preservation Society of Ireland, based just north of Belfast, sends its steam specials to any place on the island where the rails still run.

The partition of the island into Northern Ireland and the Republic occurred in 1922 as a result of the largely Protestant north opting out of a state that had achieved its independence from Britain after some 700 years of colonial rule. There were those who bitterly opposed and continue to oppose this solution to what used to be known as The Irish Question—hence what are euphemistically known as "The Troubles" that manifest themselves in the form of continuing civil strife in parts of Ulster. It must immediately be said, however, that as a visitor you may pass freely and safely in any part of Ireland, you will be welcomed by all regardless of your or their religious and political conviction, and you are more than likely to remain totally unaware of any military or paramilitary presence—unless, of course, you go looking for it. Northern Ireland, under the guidance of its tourist board, has developed the many natural and man-made attractions of the region to a level that at least equals and sometimes excels that of the rest of the country. Whatever the present political realities, *as a visitor you would be well advised to think of Ireland as one nation and to plan accordingly.*

Change is not something that this country is inclined to embrace for its own sake. Because of demographic and geographic constraints Ireland has always been slow to ape the initiatives of richer, more populous societies, and has thus preserved evidences of many eras of its history, from the prehistoric to the postbellum. There was, for instance, no Industrial Revolution here, and hence, in contemporary terms, no deserted wastelands, no gaunt-eyed factories, no—or very few—inherited urban slums. Ireland today is an industrial nation, but that industry is very much the creation of the last three or four decades. Its tools are electronic, its products high tech, its markets global.

Because there was no Industrial Revolution many of the old craft-based occupations survived to assume a new dimension in a push-button world. Many countries have developed craft industries under the impetus of the tourist trade, but some, structured more or less from scratch, have lacked the traditional resonance that gives them real validity. In the West of Ireland they still build—and use—*curraghs* (a form of rowboat) in the style of that which may have taken Saint Brendan to America in the sixth century. The Irish, it may be asserted with some confidence in the face of Scottish protest, invented whiskey. Aran sweaters, from the islands of that name off the west coast, were knitted in distinctive patterns to facilitate the identification of fishermen drowned at sea. There is frequently a story behind such traditional occupations, and usually someone willing to tell it . . . in English, the second official language. Irish, sometimes called Gaelic, is recognized as the nation's first tongue, and is taught in all the schools. You will hear it on the radio, on television, but infrequently as the common language except in the West, where it still thrives. It is said, however, that the largest Gaeltacht (Irish-speaking area) is now located in Brussels.

The oldest recognizable Irish civilization dates from around 3500 B.C. From that era onward the country saw a succession of invasions, each of which made its own distinctive contribution to the modern nation. The Celts, the Normans, and the British constitute the main streams, but Ireland has at different times given shelter and welcome to French Huguenots, Russian Jews, Chilean exiles, and Vietnamese boat people. So have many countries, but because the population of Ireland has always been small in relation to the number of its immigrants these later comers have created a more tangible impact than they might have done in a larger, more cosmopolitan society.

It is thus, in Ireland, possible to make giant leaps, both in time and in cultures, with a minimum of geographical displacement: from Neolithic monuments to Celtic churches to Medieval monasteries to Georgian great houses, from 17th-century battlefields to Europe's largest lead and zinc mines, all within, say, the modest counties of Louth and Meath. One of the prime attractions of the country is this ease of access, this possibility of doing something quite different every day of the trip without having to travel inordinate distances. There are some happenings, of course, that are at best annual events, as anywhere. But with a little careful reading of this book supplemented by informed inquiry of tourist offices it should be possible to include the Wexford Opera Festival, the Dingle Curragh Races, the Irish Derby, the Dublin Theatre Festival, Kilkenny Arts Week, the Ould Lammas Fair at Ballycastle, the Yeats Summer School, or whatever within your planned program and itinerary.

Some of these events, together with others you have heard about, you may *not* find in this book. To avoid the narrative becoming a mere catalog we have chosen to be selective rather than inclusive, leaving you a certain amount of discovering to do on your own. The omissions relate very generally to the area of the **Midlands**—across which it will be necessary in most cases to travel to reach, from Dublin, such well-documented places as Donegal, Connemara, Clare, and vice versa. The Midlands do not, thus, involve a special journey, and information on their specific attractions is readily available from the Irish Tourist Board and local tourist offices in Midland towns. The area embraces the River Shannon—but this appears in the text under several headings. Its towns of note and interest include Birr (Birr Castle); Edgeworthtown, home of the novelist Maria Edgeworth; Carrick-on-Shannon, a base for river cruising; and such relatively untrodden areas of natural beauty as the Slieve Bloom Mountains (between Birr and Port Laoise) and the Tipperary shores of Lough Derg. If there is one omission for which we might be arraigned it is that of **Clonmacnoise**, the ancient monastic settlement on the Shannon south of Athlone which, on account of both its dramatic siting (approach, if you can, by boat from downstream) and its historic significance, ought not, if at all possible, to be missed.

But to discourse further on what is *not* in this book is perhaps too close to a perversion of the metaphysics of George Berkeley, the 17th-century cleric, born in County Kilkenny, who spent three years in Rhode Island and left his mark on American philosophy and education. We suggest, therefore, eight main areas of interest, each with its own appeal, each a distinctively colorful piece of the patchwork that is Ireland.

Dublin is an obvious starting point, not only because it is a 1,000-year-old capital city with all that implies in terms of cultural, recreational, and historical attractions, but because in its corporate identity there are subsumed the many discrete elements of the wider Irish society: Norman and Gael, Catholic and Protestant, unrepentantly urban and but recently rural. With Dublin as a base it is easy to expand into the environs—**"The Pale"** that was historically the limit of the occupying power for several centuries. More than a hinterland, it embraces the evocative emptiness of the Wicklow Mountains, the Neolithic mega-monuments of the Boyne Valley, and many civilized pleasures in between.

Kilkenny, Ireland's jewel among Medieval cities, suggests an ideal center from which to explore the sunny **Southeast** ("sunny" usually being a relative adjective in Ireland, but here deployed with some confidence), with its rich Norman and Viking associations, good fishing, fine beaches, and a tapestry of intriguing little towns and villages.

From there it is a simple move to the wilder **Southwest** and **West**, through the cultured, quasi-Continental city of **Cork** with its lilting speech to the fjords and mountains of **West Cork** and **Kerry**. Come here to enjoy gourmet food, to hear Irish spoken and traditional music played . . . and to wonder at the landscape. Northward into Clare and Galway this latter changes as subtly as the speech.

In **Clare** there is, perhaps, the best traditional music anywhere—though this would be hotly contested from Kerry to Donegal—set against the stark backdrop of the Burren, a limestone plateau like a life-size model of the moon. **Galway City** has absorbed in its time many influences (not for nothing does it boast a Spanish Arch) but its eyes are to the west: to the **Aran Islands** and Irish-speaking **Connemara**, to the finest fishing lakes you'll find anywhere.

Northward again, **Mayo, Sligo,** and **Donegal,** all rugged, Atlantic-rimmed counties where life has never been easy, offer the kind of peace and easy-paced diurnalities that present an unspoken challenge to urban values. There is much to do in the **Northwest** (golf, pony trekking, fishing, eating, drinking, talking), but many will rejoice in the fact that there is also a lot *not* to do.

Our last two areas embrace the politically divided **Northeast**: Northern Ireland. For the visitor, however, the division will remain largely a line on the map—though Derry, Enniskillen, and, of course, Belfast, will make you aware of the alternative Irish tradition: Protestant and planter rather than Catholic and Gael. For a rich amalgam, try the **Border Counties**, where the national frontier disappears beneath the placid waters of Lough Erne, which glitter, happily, neither orange nor green. After this disarming baptism you will be all the more ready to appreciate the sharp contrasts, and sharper wit, of Antrim, Down, and Armagh, where the welcome will be at least as warm as anywhere else on the island and the wit, the "crack" . . . well, that we will leave you to discover for yourself.

Finally, a word on the travel itself—the mechanics, the pleasures, and, sometimes, the frustrations. Do not plan to drive from one side of the island to the other in a day, unless you really have to. In this country there are few long stretches of nothing, and, even where there are, the *néant,* or nothingness, possesses its own elusive appeal, as in the case of the Midland bogs. Do not confine yourself, if driving, to the major, N-class roads. Much of the hidden Ireland lies down the back roads: the pubs where, if you have a mind to, you will really meet the locals; the towns that rarely or never see bus tours and that you may thus observe as their people go naturally about their daily business. There are few of these places that do not boast some antiquity, often taken so much for granted by the natives that they are unable to account for it, or some claim to fame, if only for having nurtured a famous son. Take your time—an art not altogether lost in rural Ireland. Remember, too, that driving motor vehicles is not entirely the well-regulated business that it may be in other parts of the world, and that such matters as double yellow lines and other parking prohibitions, bus lanes, traffic lights, and the laws relating to drunken driving are more frequently honored in the breach.

The main-line trains, on the other hand, travel at an air-conditioned 90 m.p.h. And from the smallest village on the remotest peninsula you may call, if you have to, the other side of the world. You may fly by regular scheduled services to Dublin from four airports west of the Shannon: Knock, Galway, Shannon, and Sligo, as well as from Kerry and Derry. In Ireland it is true to say that you are never very far from anywhere else, distance being, in this context, as much a temporal as a linear measure. As a guest for an evening in an 18th-century mansion or sitting with a fishing line on the end of a deserted pier watching the sun going down over Galway Bay you will, if you are lucky, experience an otherness that few tourist destinations can still provide.

Ireland, it has been said, is a state of mind—a fact that has been acknowledged by visitors to her shores for at least half a dozen centuries. As the Irish writer Oliver Goldsmith put it in the 18th century: "The natives are peculiarly remarkable for the gaiety and levity of their dispositions; the English, transplanted there, in time lose their serious melancholy air, and become gay and thoughtless, more fond of pleasure and less addicted to reasoning." *Caveat viator!*

USEFUL FACTS

Getting There

By Air. Aer Lingus has the most comprehensive year-round schedule from New York, Chicago, and Boston to Shannon and Dublin. Delta serves Shannon and Dublin. The only direct flights from Canada are charters.

From Britain, Aer Lingus serves Dublin, Cork, and Shannon; British Midland Airways flies from London to Dublin; Ryanair flies from Luton and Stansted to Dublin; Ryanair also serves Knock Airport, Waterford, and Sligo; and Aer Lingus has daily commuter flights to Sligo, Knock, Farranfore (Kerry), Cork, Shannon, Galway, and Derry, all via Dublin. Passengers from European cities and beyond have a wide choice of direct flights on Aer Lingus, Air France, Lufthansa, and SAS; for details consult your travel agent.

By Sea. Ferry services operate from Dublin to Holyhead in Wales; Rosslare to Fishguard and Pembroke in

Wales; to Cherbourg, Le Havre, and Roscoff in France. As schedules change, passengers should consult a local travel agent.

Entry Documents
All visitors except British citizens require up-to-date valid passports. U.S., Canadian, and Australian citizens do not requre visas. Ireland has strict regulations regarding importation of livestock, foods, and agricultural produce, so check with your local airline or commerce department before you leave.

When to Go
The most abused facet of Ireland is its weather. It follows one of the best Irish euphemisms: "not too bad and not too good"—which means, bring a raincoat and a heavy sweater, even in summer, to cater to sudden changes. The best time to go is between April and October, but the Gulf Stream does have an effect year round: Ireland never gets heavy snowfalls, and it is not so much cold in the winter as damp from the rain—which, after all, keeps the grass green.

Local Time
Ireland, like Britain, operates on Greenwich mean time; western European time is one hour ahead of GMT. New York and Toronto are five hours behind GMT. Irish clocks move to daylight savings time for the summer months.

Telephones
The country code for the Republic of Ireland is 353; for Northern Ireland it is 44. The city code for Dublin is 01. When phoning Ireland from outside the country, drop the zero from all city codes.

Currency
The unit of currency in Ireland is the Irish pound, sometimes called the punt. The British pound sterling and U.S. dollars are accepted in many Irish stores, but other currencies should be converted at banks. Major credit cards—American Express, Diners Club, Visa, and Master-Card—are accepted almost everywhere.

The official currency in Northern Ireland is the pound sterling, although the Irish pound is generally accepted in border areas.

Electric Current

The standard is 220 volts, so North American appliances will require converters, and adapter plugs as well. Hotels and guesthouses usually have dual 220/110 sockets for razors and other portable electrical equipment.

Business Hours

Business hours are from 9:00 to 6:00, with late nights on Thursdays and Fridays. There is some Sunday shopping in Dublin, but you should check with your hotel. (Outside Dublin, shops almost always are closed on Sundays.) Banking hours are 10:00 to 12:30 and 1:30 to 3:00, Monday through Friday.

Health Care

E.C. visitors are entitled to medical care in Ireland under reciprocal agreement. U.K. travellers should pick up a brochure on their entitlements from local GP or Social Security offices before travel.

Staying in Ireland

Hotel and other accommodation rates are quoted on the basis of a single person sharing (or per person sharing, pps): For two people the price is roughly double. Single rates not-sharing work out to be higher. Rates do not include breakfast or other meals unless otherwise stated, although many of the smaller hotels and all bed & breakfast establishments include a full Irish breakfast in the price.

The term "high season" refers to the main tourist months, roughly June to the end of September, but it should be noted that public holidays, such as Easter and St. Patrick's weekend, rate as high season even though they fall outside this period, and specific local events (the Dublin Horse Show, Galway Races, etc.) attract high season rates.

Finally, prices quoted for 1992 are *projections* only. Always check on actual rates before booking.

Getting Around

The national transport service includes buses and trains. Dublin Bus serves the city, Bus Eireann serves the provinces, and Irish Rail runs the railways. Dublin City has the DART (Dublin Area Rapid Transport system), which provides a rail link around the city from Howth to Bray, with feeder buses linking in. Pick up a bus and train schedule from your local tourist office.

In Northern Ireland, Northern Ireland Railways operates the railways and Ulster Bus runs the bus service.

Taxis are supposed to be metered, and should not be used if they are not. Apart from local journeys to hotels or airports, taxi drivers are prepared to make extended trips, but of course you should consult them about the price before doing so.

All major car-rental companies—Avis, Budget, Dan Dooley, and Irish Car Rentals—have offices at airports and points of entry in Ireland. Rates should be posted publicly.

Ireland has two major inland waterways, the 210-mile-long River Shannon, which flows through County Cavan and County Limerick to the Atlantic, and the 80-mile-long Grand Canal, which links Dublin with the River Shannon and the River Barrow. You can cruise these scenic waterways by renting a cabin cruiser from one of nine outfits approved by the Irish Tourist Board. All of the boats have cooking facilities and showers, and they sleep from two to eight people. Operators must be at least 21 and prove they can handle the controls. Rates run from £300 to £1,700 a week, depending on the size of the craft and the season.

For rentals on the **River Shannon**, contact: **Carrick Craft**, P.O. Box 14, Reading RG3 6TA, England, Tel: (0734) 42-29-75; **Emerald Star Line Ltd.**, 47 Dawson Street, Dublin 2, Tel: (01) 679-8166, Fax: (01) 679-8165; **Athlone Cruisers Ltd.**, Shancurragh, Athlone, County Westmeath, Tel: (0902) 728-92, Fax: (0902) 743-86; **SGS (Marine) Ltd.**, Ballykeeran, Athlone, County Westmeath, Tel: (0902) 851-63, Fax: (0902) 854-31; **Silverline Cruises Ltd.**, Banagher, County Offaly, Tel: (0509) 511-12, Fax: (0509) 516-32; **Shannon Castle Line**, Dolphin Works, Ringsend, Dublin 4, Tel: (01) 60-09-64, Fax: (01) 68-90-91; **Derg Line Cruisers**, Killaloe, County Clare, Tel: (061) 37-63-64, Fax: (061) 37-62-05. Boats can also be rented for travel on **Lough Erne**, which links County Fermanagh with the River Shannon. See the Border Counties chapter for details.

To rent a boat on the **Grand Canal**, contact: **Celtic Canal Cruisers Ltd.**, Tullamore, County Offaly, Tel: (0506) 218-61, Fax: (0506) 512-66; or **Lowtown Cruisers**, Robertstown, County Kildare, Tel: (045) 604-27, Fax: (045) 603-72.

Irish Tourist Offices

These are exceptionally good in terms of providing literature, advice, and information on local events such as
theater, musical evenings, the best singing pubs, where to
go and what to do. The staff are courteous and will go out
of their way to be helpful. No visitor should fail to drop in
on them. They are located in virtually every town and are
extremely well stocked with free literature; books, cassettes, and records are for sale. Ask for a copy of their
illustrated guide to hotels and guesthouses, updated annually. In Dublin the Irish Tourist Board (Bord Failte) is
located at 14 Upper O'Connell Street; Tel: (01) 74-77-33.
In Belfast the Northern Irish Tourist Board is at 48 High
Street; Tel: (0232) 23-12-21 or 24-66-09.

Outside of Ireland you may contact offices of the Irish
Tourist Board at: 757 Third Avenue, New York 10017, Tel:
(212) 418-0800; 160 Bloor Street East, Suite 934, Toronto
M4W 1B9, Tel: (416) 929-2777; 150 New Bond Street,
London W1Y 0AQ, Tel: (03071) 493-3201; 36 Carrington
Street, 5th Level, Sydney NSW 2000, Tel: (02) 299-6177,
Fax: (02) 299-6323.

For information on Northern Ireland contact: Northern
Ireland Tourist Board, 276 Fifth Avenue, New York, NY
10001, Tel: (212) 686-6250, Fax: (212) 686-8061; British
Tourist Authority, 94 Cumberland Street, Suite 600, Toronto, Ontario M5R 3N3, Tel: (416) 925-6326, Fax: (416)
961-2175; Northern Ireland Tourist Board, 11 Berkeley
Street, London W1X 5AD, Tel: (03071) 493-0601, Fax:
(03071) 499-3731; and British Tourist Authority, Midland
House, 171 Clarence Street, Sydney NSW 2000, Tel: (02)
29-5464, Fax: (02) 262-1414.

—*William Maxwell*

BIBLIOGRAPHY

General and Literary

MAURICE CRAIG. *The Architecture of Ireland.* A comprehensively illustrated account from the beginnings to 1880.

CHRISTOPHER FITZ-SIMON. *The Irish Theatre.* From miracle
plays to Beckett and after. Illustrations include playbills,
productions, protagonists.

R. F. FOSTER. *Modern Ireland 1600–1972.* Incisive and
eminently readable.

PETER HARBISON. *Pre-Christian Ireland.* Incorporates the latest archaeological findings, with some interesting new theories and discoveries.

LORD KILLANIN AND MICHAEL V. DUIGNAN. *The Shell Guide to Ireland.* Revised and updated by Peter Harbison, this is an excellent one-volume guide with archaeological and historical emphases.

JOHN AND SALLY MCKENNA. *The Irish Food Guide.* Includes restaurants and good food stores nationwide.

JOHN FITZMAURICE MILLS. *The Noble Dwellings of Ireland.* The human faces behind the Palladian façades. Color illustrations.

FRANK MITCHELL. *The Irish Landscape.* From 2,000 million years ago to today. Comprehensive and highly readable.

T. W. MOODY AND F. X. MARTIN (EDS). *The Course of Irish History.* (Revised and enlarged ed., 1984.) The best one-volume account for the general reader.

JAN MORRIS. *Ireland—Your Only Place.* Evocative essay with superb photographs.

SEAN O'FAOLAIN. *The Irish.* A "character study" by the distinguished short-story writer and critic of social mores.

MICHAEL RICHTER. *Medieval Ireland: The Enduring Tradition.* A Continental scholar discusses the island's history and religious and intellectual life from the early years of the Christian Era to the founding of Dublin's Trinity College, in 1591, to show how the Learned Tradition of Ireland set it apart from England and the Continent for a millennium.

AIDRIAN ROOM. *A Dictionary of Irish Place Names.* With apposite background information on some 3,000 names.

KATHLEEN JO RYAN AND BERNARD SHARE (EDS). *Irish Traditions.* Essays by several hands on distinctive aspects of the Irish experience, from sports to suburbs, from Neolithic artifacts to neighbors. Color photographs.

DARAGH SMYTHE. *A Guide to Irish Mythology.* A competent and informative introduction to "forms more real than living men."

BRIAN AND CAROL WALKER. *Where Can I Eat In Ireland?* An excellent guide to vegetarian restaurants in Ireland.

ANTHONY WEIR. *Early Ireland: A Field Guide.* A site-by-site listing of everything worth seeing, with map references.

MICHAEL WYNNE. *National Gallery of Ireland: Fifty Irish Painters.* A succinct introduction to Irish art through three centuries.

Facts About Ireland. The official publication of the Department of Foreign Affairs will settle most arguments.

Gasaitéar na Léireann (Gazeteer of Ireland). An official bilingual listing of place names with linguistic and grammatical information.

The volume and richness of Irish literature must restrict us to a few general indications: For Dublin: the works of James Joyce, Brendan Behan, Sean O'Casey, Flann O'Brien (Myles na Gopaleen), James Plunkett, George Moore *(Hail and Farewell),* Oliver St. John Gogarty, Jonathan Swift's pamphlets. For Cork: Sean O'Faolain, Frank O'Connor; for County Clare: Edna O'Brien; for Kerry and the West in general: J. M. Synge, John B. Keane, Liam O'Flaherty, W. B. Yeats, Lady Gregory; for Donegal: Patrick McGill, Peadar O'Donnell; for the Midlands: John Broderick, John McGahern, Patrick Kavanagh; for the North: John Hewitt, Seamus Heaney, Sam Hannah Bell, Brian Moore, Forrest Reid. Browsing in the bookshops of Dublin, Cork, and Belfast will add many more, and Kenny's of Galway in particular offers excellent service to visitors. The magazine *Ireland of the Welcomes,* published six times a year by the Irish Tourist Board, is consistently interesting and informative.

Dublin and Environs
HENRY BOYLAN. *This Arrogant City: A Reader's and Collector's Guide to Books about Dublin.* An excellent guide to a wide range of further reading.

VINCENT CAPRANI. *A View from the DART.* Dublin and suburbs from the coastal rapid-transit system. Witty and informative.

CON COSTELLO. *Looking Back. Aspects of History, Co. Kildare.* Informative illustrated guide.

MAURICE CRAIG. *Dublin 1660–1860.* The authoritative architectural history of the city's golden age.

PAT LIDDY. *Dublin Be Proud.* Drawings of the city's more interesting details, with background information.

FRANK MCDONALD. *The Destruction of Dublin.* The ravages of the planners and "developers" in the recent past and the present and the threat to the future. Timely and caustic.

E. E. O'DONNELL. *The Annals of Dublin.* From 4.5 million years ago to date. A must for fact fanciers. Fine old photographs.

MICHAEL J. O'KELLY. *Newgrange: Archaeology, Art and Legend.* The definitive work on one of the most important and impressive prehistoric sites in Europe.

ALFRED P. SMYTH. *Celtic Leinster.* Life in the Pale and beyond, A.D. 500–1600. A fascinating perspective.

PETER SOMERVILLE-LARGE. *Dublin: The First Thousand Years.* The best one-volume social, political, and cultural history.

J. M. SYNGE. *In Wicklow and West Kerry.* An account of his travels rich in poetic insight and shrewd observation.

The Southeast

GERALDINE CARVILLE. *The Heritage of Holy Cross.* The history and restoration of 12th-century Tipperary Abbey.

R. H. HYLAND. *The History, Topography and Antiquities of the County and City of Waterford.* A compendious record first published in 1824 and still well worth consulting.

KATHERINE M. LANIGAN AND GERALD TYLER (EDS). *Kilkenny: Its Architecture and History.* A comprehensive account of the sixth-century foundation from a conservationist standpoint.

DERVLA MURPHY. *Wheels within Wheels.* The distinguished travel writer's childhood in County Waterford.

HUMPHREY O'SULLIVAN. *The Diary of Humphrey O'Sullivan.* A fascinating account of 19th-century life in County Kilkenny, written in Irish between 1827 and 1835.

RICHARD ROCHE AND OSCAR MERNE. *Saltees, Islands of Birds and Legends.* An account of these offshore islands, breeding ground for more than 200 species of birds.

Cork and Kerry

T. J. BARRINGTON. *Discovering Kerry.* The most comprehensive study of the kingdom's history, heritage, and topography available. Illustrations and maps. Exhaustive and exhausting.

T. CROFTON CROKER. *Legends of Killarney* and *Legends of the Lakes.* Rich local lore—to be taken with a grain of salt.

ROBERT GIBBINGS. *Lovely Is the Lee* and *Sweet Cork of Thee.* Headily atmospheric accounts adorned with the author's own fine woodcuts.

RICHARD HAYWARD. *Munster and the City of Cork.* Richly detailed and with sensitive pencil drawings by Raymond Piper.

DES LAVELLE. *Skellig—Island Outpost of Europe.* The two remarkable islands off the Kerry coast examined in detail, with the historical background.

MUIRIS MACCONGHAIL. *The Blaskets, A Kerry Island Library.* The definitive book on the area.

SEAN PETTIT. *The Streets of Cork* and *My City by the Lee.* Good walking guides.

PEIG SAYERS. *Peig.* Renowned autobiography, written originally in Irish, of life on the now-abandoned Blasket Islands.

CHARLES SMITH. *The Ancient and Present State of the County of Kerry.* The classic 1761 account.

PETER SOMERVILLE-LARGE. *From Bantry Bay to Leitrim.* A journey in the footsteps of O'Sullivan Beare on his retreat from the Battle of Kinsale in 1601.

JOAN AND RAY STAGLES. *The Blasket Islands.* The community that once formed "the next parish to America" in words and pictures.

Clare and Connemara

GEORGE CUNNINGHAM. *Burren Journey West.* The flora and fauna of the area.

RUTH DELANY. *By Shannon Shores.* Not just those of Galway and Clare, but the full length of the great waterway. Read this before you cruise the river.

JOHN M. FEEHAN. *The Secret Places of the Burren.* Observations of a perspicacious and disputatious traveller.

JAMES HARDIMAN. *The History of the Town and County of Galway*. First published 1820 but still a standard work.

BRIAN MERRIMAN. *The Midnight Court*. Ribald poem, originally in Irish, set in County Clare in the late 18th century. Frank O'Connor's translation is the best.

PEADAR O'DOWD. *Old and New Galway*. A comprehensive, illustrated reference.

RICHARD POWER. *Apple on the Treetop*. A novel based on a year among the Aran islanders.

TIM ROBINSON. *Stones of Aran*. A poetic journey with insights into the history and folklore of the islands; included are his two large-scale, annotated maps of Aran and the Burren.

COLIN SMYTHE. *A Guide to Coole Park, County Galway*. Lady Gregory's house, destroyed in 1941, was the "headquarters" of the Irish literary revival and the setting for several of Yeats's poems.

J. M. SYNGE. *The Aran Islands*. The islands were the source of much of Synge's achievement as a writer; with his own original photographs.

Donegal, Sligo, and Mayo

ROBERT BERNEN. *Tales from the Blue Stacks*. Stories by a New Yorker who settled on a derelict Donegal sheep farm in 1970.

BRIAN BONNER. *Our Inis Eoghain Heritage*. First of three books dealing with the life and traditions of the Inishowen Peninsula.

DESMOND FENNELL. *A Connacht Journey*. A fine contemporary travel narrative that probes the reality behind the myths of the West of Ireland.

T. A. FINNEGAN. *Sligo: Sinbad's Yellow Shore*. A prospect of Sligo and environs from the vantage point of Coney Island (the original one).

BENEDICT KIELY. *Yeats' Ireland*. A beautifully illustrated anthology.

SHEELAH KIRBY. *The Yeats Country*. The places associated with the life and writings of the poet.

H. T. KNOX. *The History of the County of Mayo*. Covers the period up to 1700 in absorbing detail.

T. O'RORKE. *The History of Sligo, Town and County.* A 19th-century work of scholastic devotion, but very readable.

LORD SLIGO. *Westport House and the Brownes.* Family history writ large: a lively account of 12 generations.

DOROTHY HARRISON THERMAN. *Stories from Tory Island.* Oral history from the islanders themselves.

DAVID THOMSON. *Woodbrook.* Life in a Sligo "big house" between the wars. Brilliant evocation of the end of an era.

The Border Counties
POLLY DEVLIN. *All of Us There.* A beautifully written evocation of a childhood on the shores of Lough Neagh in the 1940s and 1950s.

HENRY GLASSIE. *All Silver and No Brass.* The Christmas mummers of County Fermanagh and the authentic tang of Ulster speech.

EUGENE MCCABE. *Heritage.* Short stories dealing with the peculiar ferocity of the sectarian divide on the border.

MARY ROGERS. *Prospect of Fermanagh.* The history, archaeology, and folklore of the county, described with great enthusiasm and local knowledge.

————. *Prospect of Tyrone.* The history and legends of the county examined with the same affection.

COLM TOIBIN. *Walking Along the Border.* A journey by foot from Derry to Warrenpoint, crossing and recrossing the border.

Antrim, Down, and Armagh
J. C. BECKETT ET AL. *Belfast: The Making of a City.* A comprehensive and concise survey from the beginnings in 1800 to 1914.

JOHN BROOKS. *Ulster's Heritage* (Irish Heritage Series). A tour of the properties of the National Trust in Northern Ireland.

LYNN DOYLE. *An Ulster Childhood.* Growing up in County Down at the end of the last century.

ALAN GAILEY. *Ulster Folk Ways* (Irish Heritage Series). An introduction based on the collections of the Ulster Folk and Transport Museum, Cultra.

JOHN HEWITT. *Rhyming Weavers.* Country poets of Counties Antrim and Down. Includes samples of their styles.

MICHAEL J. MURPHY. *Mountain Year.* Life on the slopes of Slieve Gullion, County Armagh.

JOHN PEPPER. *John Pepper's Ulster Phrase Book.* A humorous guide to the intricacies of Ulster speech (Sotsotis— "the weather is very warm").

—Bernard Share

DUBLIN

By Vincent Caprani

Vincent Caprani, who was born in Dublin and has lived there all his life, is the author of numerous articles for Cara *(the in-flight magazine of Aer Lingus),* Books Ireland, *and other magazines. He is also the author of a number of fiction and nonfiction books, many of which are published in the United Kingdom and the United States as well as in Ireland. One of his books, a guidebook to Dublin, has been a best-seller in Ireland.*

If Dublin has, over the past quarter century, paid a high price for its efforts to become a modern industrial and commercial capital, it is nonetheless one of the few cities that is preferred by its citizens to any other. The natives remain—and the visitors come—for a variety of reasons:

- To immerse themselves in one of the great literary capitals of the world
- To take advantage of its location as the gateway to rural and ancient Ireland
- To sample a sporting town's wealth of golfing, fishing, and equestrian and aquatic pastimes
- To experience a sense of distant history as close as yesterday
- And to find quaint pubs, colorful characters— and even more colorful talk.

Above all, Dubliners are talkers and, by extension, writers. Dubliners have a constant need to "discuss" their city, as is evidenced by the annual output of about 25 books on Dublin written and published by Dubliners for the city's one million inhabitants, and the numerous albums and cassettes recorded by local ballad groups and

Dublin Suburbs

0   miles   2

0   kilometers   3

TO RUSH, LUSK
AND DONABATE

SWORDS

N2

**Dublin
Airport**

**Dunsoghly
Castle**

N1

**Dunsink
Observatory**

River Tolka

*Botanic
Gardens*

KIL

N3   *Royal Canal*

GLASNEVIN

DRUMCONDRA

Casino

MARINO

*Phoenix
Park*

D U B L I N

Collins Barracks

River Liffey

N4

ISLANDBRIDGE

**Trinity
College**

KILMAINHAM

*St. Stephen's
Green*

BALLSBRIDGE

SANDYMOUNT

RANELAGH

Grand Canal

DONNYBROOK

N7

RATHMINES

← TO NAAS

RATHGAR

N81

RATHFARNHAM

DUNDRUM

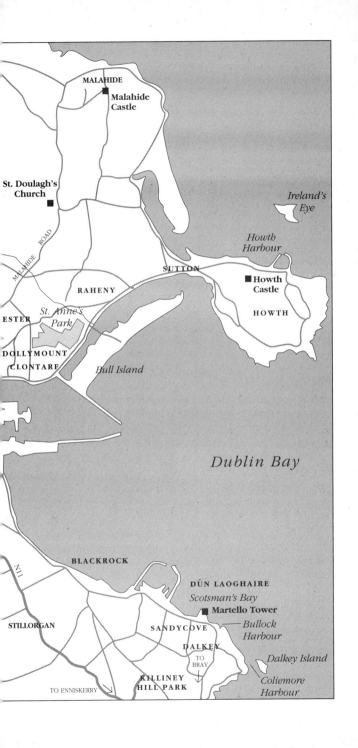

MALAHIDE

Malahide
Castle

St. Doulagh's
Church

Ireland's
Eye

MALAHIDE ROAD

Howth
Harbour

SUTTON

RAHENY

Howth
Castle

St. Anne's
Park

HOWTH

ESTER

DOLLYMOUNT
CLONTARF

Bull Island

Dublin Bay

BLACKROCK

N11

DÚN LAOGHAIRE
Scotsman's Bay

Martello Tower

STILLORGAN

SANDYCOVE

Bullock
Harbour

DALKEY

TO
BRAY

Dalkey Island

KILLINEY
HILL PARK

Coliemore
Harbour

TO ENNISKERRY

solo artists extolling the city's charms and culture. No other city has produced three Nobel Prize winners for literature (George Bernard Shaw, William Butler Yeats, and Samuel Beckett) and given modern literature its most famous day: June 16, 1904—Bloomsday, in James Joyce's *Ulysses*.

The citizens love chatting, writing, and singing about their city and its characters. Even the occasional disparaging note in their discourses and ditties contains an element of wounded pride or a backhanded compliment. Dubliners' humor is earthy, satirical, close to the cobblestones, and with a racy imperturbability that tends to deflate the pompous. Their songs are sentimental and nostalgic, covering an absurdly kind heart and a stern pride in the superiority of their town.

And Dubliners do have much to boast about. Their city—the country's capital and largest city in the Republic—occupies a beautiful site on the east coast of Ireland at the mouth of the River Liffey, with the broad sweep of Dublin Bay to the east, the Dublin Mountains to the south, and rolling plains extending to the west and north.

Dublin, with its many separate and overlapping districts, is a marvelous mix of the parochial and the cosmopolitan, the traditional and the modern. Many of its present problems stem from half-hearted efforts to contain an elegant 18th-century core within the rapidly expanding 20th-century sprawl of satellite towns, industrial parks, housing developments, and motorways that has almost entirely swallowed up the pleasant rural villages that formed the city's periphery less than a quarter of a century ago. Yet vestiges of these villages still remain because, above all, Dublin is still a place of contradiction rather than conformity. Its citizens revel in controversy, not consensus, in myth rather than method.

One such myth is that the city is more or less divided between wealthy, erudite, and sophisticated inhabitants south of the River Liffey, and shabby, impecunious, and unlettered denizens on the North Side. Statistical data certainly indicates a preponderance of the well-heeled south of the river, yet also shows that there are as many low-income families on the South Side as the north, and the latter area contains wealthy neighborhoods such as Howth, Sutton, Malahide, Glasnevin, and Clontarf, further confounding the issue.

So, if some form of demarcation is required, then it is

perhaps better to ignore the north–south argument and to plump for a more realistic east–west divide. A good rule of thumb is to seek the better-class districts close to the sea and more or less contiguous to the DART rail line. (With the advent of easy rail travel in the mid-Victorian era, Dublin merchant and professional classes hastened to the maritime suburbs for the cleaner air, hence a spread of upmarket housing adjacent to the railway. The trend has never really abated.) By the same token of contradiction, however, many of these rail lines today pass through enclaves of dingy streets and poor housing, and the newer and predominantly working-class locations lying in a vast semicircle to the west and north of the city are liberally dotted with fine old mansions, parklands, and modern villas.

Dublin is a place that can be evoked but rarely summed up, a solid harmony of granite, warm brickwork, harsh concrete, trees, canal water, wrought iron, macadam, cobblestones, bright sunlight, misty rain—in short, depicting it is as easy as capturing a few blobs of mercury with the prongs of a table fork. Like the vast majority of its citizens who so frequently criticize their mother town—and then immediately combine in argumentative opposition to the foreigner who has the impudence to agree with them—it is a contradiction.

It is also an adventure and a voyage of discovery. We cover ancient Dublin first, at the center—mostly on the South Side of the Liffey, where the visitor's major interests will tend to group. Then, after a foray into the southern suburbs and the South County beyond, we return to the North Side, move into the northern suburbs, and end in the North County.

MAJOR INTEREST

Dublin Castle
Marsh's Library
Trinity College (and Long Room, with the Book of
    Kells)
Merrion and Fitzwilliam squares and Georgian
    Dublin
St. Patrick's and Christ Church cathedrals
National Museum (Irish antiquities)
National Library (first editions of Irish writers)
National Gallery (Irish, English, and European
    masterpieces)

Municipal Gallery of Modern Art (Impressionists)

Irish Museum of Modern Art

Beatty Library and Gallery of Oriental Art (Egyptian papyruses)

Street life in the Liberties

Grafton Street shopping

The pubs of Dublin

The Martello tower at Sandycove (Joyce's *Ulysses*)

Malahide Castle

The city owes its existence to the Liffey. Viking and Danish pirates sailed up this river more than a thousand years ago (Dublin celebrated its millennium in 1988), liked what they saw, and decided to stay. That decision meant laying waste to the tiny Celtic settlement huddled about the ford of the river. Though few Dubliners today know where the ford stood, it is not too difficult to locate this cradle of early Dublin: about midway along Usher's Island (on the south bank of the river) and facing the spot where Blackhall Place exits onto the north bank of the river at Ellis Quay. Blackhall Place leads to Stoneybatter ("batter" comes from the Irish *bothar*, a road); this ancient thoroughfare was called *Bothar-na-gloch*, the road of stones, and was part of the second-century highway from the royal Hill of Tara to Wicklow. It crossed the Liffey near that early Celtic settlement known—as Dublin is still called in Gaelic—as *Baile Átha Cliath* (pronounced Ball-ya Aw Klee-a), or "town of the ford of the hurdles." Both the name and the settlement were quickly supplanted by the Norse *Dyfflin* (from the Irish *Dubh Linn,* meaning "black pool"). In time the tiny riverside Norse hamlet became a Norman fortress, then an Elizabethan citadel, then the elegant Georgian "second city of the Empire," before slipping back a little into a mixture of Victorian slums, factories, and warehouses surrounded by the suburban mansions and villas of its rich merchants. And that, in a sentence, is the history of Dublin.

Scandinavian Dublin

There are three spots where Dublin is reputed to have begun, all three with Scandinavian connections. Take your pick of (1) Wood Quay, lying in the riverside shadow of Christ Church Cathedral and the controversial modern "pepper-and-salt-canister" municipal buildings; (2) the high ground at the junction of Suffolk and Andrew streets and Church Lane near Trinity College, now occupied by St. Andrew's Church, which is built on the ancient mound of the Thingmote, where early Norse Dubliners held their great outdoor assemblies and crude parliaments; or (3) the little grass triangle at the northern side of Trinity College, just a truncheon's throw from the door of College Street police station—which, with typical Dublin idiosyncrasy, isn't actually in College Street but at the western end of Pearse Street. The stone ornament in the grassy triangle marks the position of the ancient Steyne, or great stone, around which those first Viking invaders beached their fearsome dragon-prowed longships.

In those days—more than a thousand years ago—the Steyne and the Thingmote stood well outside the little wattled hamlet of Dyfflin. From this embryonic Dublin the Norsemen made inland raids on their Gaelic neighbors, routing them and exacting tribute—the *nosegelt,* so called from the penalty for default, namely cutting off the offender's nose. Those early Norse Dubliners also traded in metals, skins, timber, fish, and wines with their kinsmen along the coasts of western Europe. Relics of this buried past may be viewed in the National Museum (discussed at greater length, below) in Kildare Street, the treasury section of which also contains priceless objects—jewelry, utensils, weapons, and so forth—dating from the Bronze Age culture that flourished in Ireland in the seventh century B.C., and fine examples of the vigorous and distinctive Celtic Christian art of the ninth and tenth centuries A.D.

Norman Dublin

There was a thriving and settled community at Dyfflin by the time the mail-clad Norman horsemen came riding down on the little township in the 1160s. Warlike, though cultured, the Normans under Richard de Clare (known as Strongbow) quickly took the town and the surrounding countryside and inaugurated profound changes in Irish life. The Norman method was to conquer, build stout and graceless defensive towers, have vassals and villeins work the captured land, and then make an endowment to the Roman church in thanksgiving to the Almighty for having blessed the bloody work of sword and longbow. Their architectural genius was expressed in immense grim castles and noble abbeys, giving Dublin three of its most ancient and impressive buildings: Christ Church Cathedral (1172), St. Patrick's Cathedral (1191), and Dublin Castle (1205). All three are inextricably interwoven into the story of Dublin, and all are within easy walking distance of one another and well worth visiting.

St. Patrick's Cathedral (in Patrick Street, several blocks west of St. Stephen's Green) once stood on an island encircled by two branches of the River Poddle, long since confined underground. A trace of the island is still discernible in the attractive little park adjoining the present cathedral, which dates from 1370 and was erected with many of the stones and on the site of the original cathedral of 1191. Visitors with a literary bent will undoubtedly recall Jonathan Swift's incumbency as dean of St. Patrick's from 1713 to 1745, and will be attracted to the Swift memorabilia here in the form of his pulpit, table and chair, a collection of his works, and his scroll as a freeman of the city. Swift's bust, epitaph, and tomb, "where savage indignation can no longer lacerate his heart," lies close by that of his beloved "Stella" (Esther Johnson) in the west end of the nave. There, too, is the Medieval Chapter House door with a curious hole cut in it. This is the "door of reconciliation," which gave the phrase "chancing your arm" to the English language. In 1492 the earl of Kildare cut the hole and through it stretched his arm to clasp the hand of his archenemy, the earl of Ormonde, who had taken refuge in the Chapter House. By this gesture, peace and reconciliation were restored.

For those interested in military history, there is a Roll of Honour containing the names of 50,000 Irishmen who fell in the First World War, and the sad tattered flags of the many Irish regiments who served on the battlefields of Europe and the British Empire still hang above solemn aisles where Cromwell's Roundheads contemptuously stabled their horses during the wars of the 17th century. The place abounds in memorials and monuments—from the black marble over the grave of the duke of Schomberg, who fell at the Battle of the Boyne in 1690 (the monument contains an inscription by Swift), to the impressive Baroque monument to the Boyle family erected by the first earl of Cork. The visitor should note the effigy of a little boy in the center of the lowest tier: It represents Robert Boyle (1627–1691), later a famous chemist and physicist. Today, St. Patrick's is the national cathedral of the Church of Ireland (Protestant).

(A general rule in the exploration of old churches: Where inscribed stones are found on the floor an actual tomb is indicated, but in the case of a wall tablet there may be a coffin or an urn of ashes underneath, or the wall tablet may be only a cenotaph, that is, a memorial to a person or persons buried elsewhere.)

Christ Church Cathedral, built at what is now the western end of Dame/Lord Edward streets on the site of the original wooden cathedral founded in 1038 by Sitric Silkenbeard, the first Christian king of the Dublin Norsemen, took more than 50 years to complete. In addition to its historical significance and fine architectural qualities, the cathedral—which since the Reformation has belonged to the Anglican Communion—stands as a kind of memorial to its founder, Richard de Clare, the Norman overlord who had Sitric's simple wooden structure torn down and then rebuilt in stone at the behest of Saint Laurence O'Toole, archbishop and patron saint of Dublin.

Christ Church's range of monuments, memorials, and memorabilia equals that of St. Patrick's, but to some Dubliners its greatest treasures are the heart of Saint Laurence O'Toole (died 1180), which is encased in an iron receptacle in a little chapel to the right of the high altar, and the crusader-like monument to Richard "Strongbow" de Clare in the south aisle. Incidentally, some authorities claim that the time-honored Dublin penchant for bestowing nicknames dates from the coming of the Normans and especially Strongbow. The dockside area of Ringsend (known generally as Raytown from the fish originally unloaded there) boasts that it is the world capital of nicknames. One of Raytown's pubs, the **Oarsman**, at the bridge, proudly displays on its barroom wall a chart listing more than 500 of the most colorful local nicknames.

The romance of **Dublin Castle** is a microcosm of the city's history since 1205, when Henry II wrote to his chief lieutenant in Ireland, Myler FitzHenry: "You are to erect a castle at Dublin, as well to curb the city as to defend it . . . and with strong fosses and walls. . . ." There was need of such a fortress in those days. The regular forays from the Wicklow Mountains of the hardy clansmen of the O'Byrnes and O'Tooles made life in Norman Dublin exciting, even precarious. The castle was quickly built and just as quickly besieged by the mountain marauders. By 1228 the archbishop of Dublin had to build

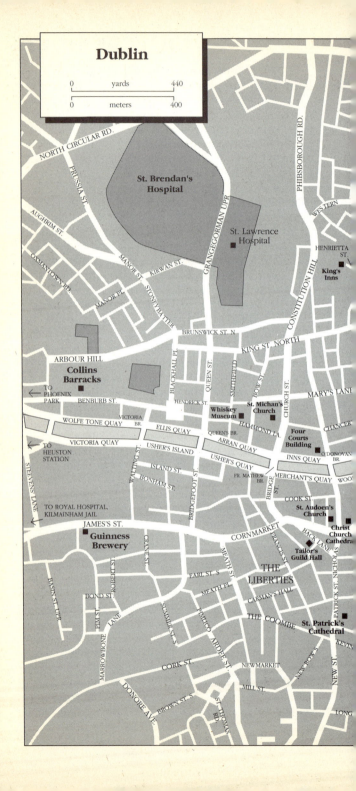

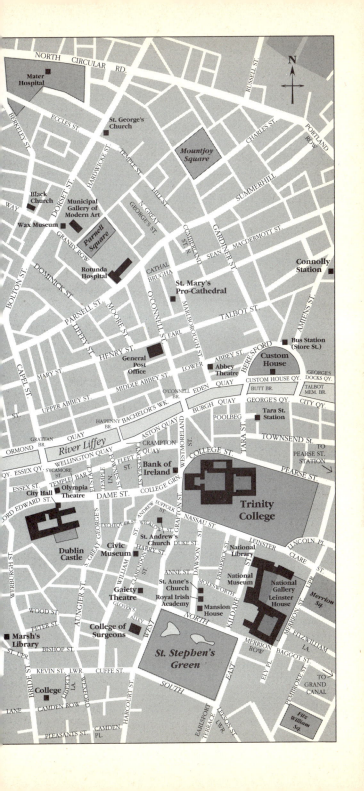

a bigger and better castle. There then followed bigger and better sieges. By 1361 the entire fortress had to be rebuilt.

Within the massive new walls were the Mint and the Courts of Justice. These latter saw the occasional "trial by ordeal," one as late as 1528, in which Teig MacGilpatrick O'Conner, charged with murder, and his accuser fought with sword and shield like gladiators of old. This "trial" took place before a distinguished assembly, and O'Conner was vindicated: He shortened the prosecutor's stature by lopping off his head and presented it ceremoniously, as proof of his innocence, to the lords of justice, by whom he was immediately acquitted. Perhaps the Irishman's distrust of "castle justice" was nurtured on such events. The main entrance today occupies the site of the old gate on which the heads of many rebellious Irish chiefs were exposed on spikes. To the leaden statue of Justice surmounting the entrance (the work of Van Nost, 1752), the political climate of the 18th century caused Dubliners to add the slogan,

> "Statue of Justice, mark well her station
> Her face to the Castle, her back to the Nation!"

At the commencement of the 1916 Easter Rising, a band of two dozen Irish Citizen Army men made an unsuccessful effort to capture the castle. Their surprise attempt to rush the Upper Yard was foiled by an elderly policeman, who managed to get the iron gate shut and locked just in the nick of time. The insurgents then occupied the nearby City Hall and other buildings opposite the castle entrance and, like their O'Toole and O'Byrne ancestors 700 years before, put up a fierce fight for three days before being repulsed with heavy casualties.

Less than six years later, on January 16, 1922, Michael Collins (as chairman of the new Irish Free State government) entered the castle's council chamber and presented a copy of the Anglo-Irish treaty to the last of Britain's viceroys, Lord Fitzalan. In return the castle was formally surrendered to the Irish government.

For Collins it was only his second visit to the castle. Two years before, with a price on his head, he had entered the castle in the guise of a grimy-faced coal-cart driver in order to make contact with his own agents inside.

The chapel in the Lower Yard dates from 1814 and is the work of Francis Johnston. It is a fine Gothic edifice with a ceiling of groined arches supported by beautiful pillars, and its stained-glass windows depict the coats of arms of all the viceroys from 1814 to 1922.

Dublin Castle also houses the sumptuous State Apartments, which, since 1938, have been the scene of the inaugurations of Ireland's presidents. Visitors are advised, however, to check in advance, because these offices and apartments are sometimes closed to the public.

The Liberties

Situated near the castle and the two cathedrals are a number of other historic buildings—St. Audoen's Church (1171), the Tailor's Guild Hall (1706), Marsh's Library (1702), and the Brazen Head Inn (1668). Life is lived lustily in this South Side district west of the castle, once the "Liberties of the Abbey of St. Thomas à Becket," then the domain of the earl of Meath—and thus largely outside the legal jurisdiction of the city's lord mayor and sheriff (hence, "the Liberties"). No trace of the abbey exists today. At the Reformation its lands and rights were granted to the earl of Meath. Dubliners visiting the Liberties do so rather as explorers, in a spirit of adventure, seeking some experience not readily obtainable elsewhere. They are lured by the old antiques and bric-a-brac shops in Francis Street and to the pubs, market stalls, and huckster shops. Not many of the Liberties people know or care how this place got its name and distinctive character, or that many of them are descendants of French Huguenot refugees and silk weavers who fled from Catholic persecution after the Edict of Nantes was revoked in 1685.

St. Audoen's Church, across from Christ Church and the oldest of Dublin's many parish churches, is named after the patron saint of Rouen, France, who was held in special veneration by the Normans. Three of the bells in the tower were cast in 1423 and are the oldest in Ireland. **St. Audoen's Arch** (1275) is the sole surviving gate of Medieval Dublin.

The **Tailor's Guild Hall**—open to the public, and entered from the narrow, cobbled Back Lane (off Nicholas Street near Christ Church) through a quaint stone archway dating from 1714—has been the headquarters of An Taisce (pronounced Un Tashk), the Irish National Trust since 1983. An Taisce is a voluntary watchdog organization concerned with environmental matters, the preservation of Ireland's historical and architectural heritage, and the restoration of buildings and sites that are within that category.

Despite inadequate funding and severe financial constraints, An Taisce has carried out much needed refurbishment to many buildings, such as the Tailor's Guild Hall. One example of the task confronting the organization involves the original marble fireplace in the guildhall's general assembly room. Some years ago, when the building was unoccupied and in a near ruinous condition, the fireplace was crudely ripped out of its setting by scavenging junk dealers and broken into four or five separate pieces, which wound up in a number of junkyards in different parts of the city. A small group of An Taisce enthusiasts tracked down the scattered portions and then painstakingly repaired, reassembled, and relocated the fireplace in its original setting.

Tailor's Hall is the last surviving guildhall in Dublin. Its assembly room contains a fine 18th-century musicians' gallery from which the patriots Wolfe Tone and Napper Tandy are known to have addressed the members of the revolutionary "Back Lane Parliament" with rousing speeches that helped kindle the flames of the subsequent 1798 Uprising. Also in Back Lane, and directly opposite Tailor's Guild Hall, is **Mother Redcap's Tavern.** Converted from a disused shoe factory, it provides lunches, midday snacks, and music most evenings; it's also something of a hangout for An Taisce activists, inner-city conservationists, ballad singers, and traditional reciters.

Just to the east of St. Patrick's Cathedral stands **Marsh's Library,** the oldest public library in Ireland. Bequeathed to the city by Archbishop Narcissus Marsh in 1702, it contains all his books and Edward Stillingfleet's vast and priceless collection of early printed books from the 15th century, rare manuscripts, and the autographs of many of the famous people from the 15th to the 17th centuries. The library fittings are still as they were in the 18th century (a major restoration of the interior funded by the American Irish Foundation was completed in 1986) with tiny reading cubicles, or cells, of decorative woodwork, the hefty and valuable tomes secured against possible theft by lengths of heavy chains. Also dating from the 18th century is the legend that the ghost of Dr. Marsh wanders from shelf to shelf each night in a vain search for some long-lost family document. The library is closed to visitors on Tuesdays and public holidays.

If all the foregoing historical names and dates require

the flavoring of the romance—and the liquid refresh-ment—of an ancient hostelry, then the visitor should explore the **Brazen Head** in Lower Bridge Street, just a few minutes' walk from Tailor's Guild Hall. There is nothing manicured or sanitized about the back streets of the Liberties, and this gem of a tavern is the sole survivor of the numerous inns that stood here in Norman, Tudor, and Stuart times, eras of lusty revelries and the brutal sports of cockfighting and bullbaiting. Though it is men-tioned in Joyce's *Ulysses,* and Brendan Behan was one of its habitués, visitors to the Brazen Head may be disap-pointed by its lack of literary memorabilia and the confession-box dimensions of its old taproom. This bar parlour nonetheless contains a motley collection of prints and mementos of Irish history; an upstairs room (open to visitors) contains a table, chair, and desk reputed to have belonged to the romantic and tragic young patriot Robert Emmet.

The Brazen Head served as a kind of unofficial head-quarters for the United Irishmen, some of whose leaders were arrested here in 1798. In addition to the 350-year-old oaken beams supporting the low ceilings and the upper portions of the inn, a small but interesting feature is the mid-18th-century graffito cut with a diamond ring into one of the original bottle-glass panes of the first-landing window. Impromptu but authentic ballad ses-sions by some of Dublin's leading traditional singers and musicians are a frequent occurrence here most Sundays at midday. But now a word on our pubs in general.

The Dublin Pub

There are about 700 pubs—give or take a few—in the greater Dublin area, and that doesn't include hotel and theater bars, army messes, or private "members only" sports clubs and the like. The pubs are liberally scattered about the city and suburbs and range from the grotty and unpainted to the brass-and-glassy glitter of Victorian em-poriums, such as the **Long Hall** in South Great George's Street and the **Stag's Head** in Dame Court, a little alley off the south side of Dame Street. The pub remains virtually unchanged since its gala opening in 1895. Practically all of the slicker type provide tasty pub grub of the soup-salad-hot-pot variety.

Many of the center-city pubs have in recent years mildly offended old-style Dubliners by dropping the traditional family name over the shop front in favor of tourist-slanted, though tenuous—or even spurious—associations with the city's historic and literary personages of the past; hence a plethora of the "Oscar Wilde," "Daniel O'Connell," "Robert Emmet" nomenclature on the fascia board.

Nearly all Dublin pubs are "winter" drinking holes rather than "summer" ones; that is, their decor is generally polished wood and suggests warmth rather than the coolness imparted by tiled patios or leafy beer gardens. Most have their own distinct type of loyal clientele—newspapermen, firemen, actors, sportsmen, students, or whatever—though all have the ubiquitous floaters and, periodically, the trendies who, like a swarm of chattering starlings, suddenly descend on the latest "in" place. Except for some of the latter, Dublin pub patrons have never acquired the habit of cocktails; regulars will tell you that the pint (by which they mean Guinness, though there are at least ten different brands of draught beers and lagers generally available) is the only true beverage.

A lot of Dublin's social life revolves around the pub scene, which helps nurture one's sense of priorities: convivial conversation, griping about politicians, gossiping about sports, and breaking into impromptu singsongs. Nightlife tends to reach its crescendo about pub-closing hours, maintaining the tempo through the last-bus curfew, and diminishing a little as the under-21s seek out the discos (weekends mainly) and the older crowd hits the Leeson Street nightclub strip.

Many of the pubs provide good music; *In Dublin* magazine regularly lists about 120 venues, from "trad" at the **Béal Bocht** (Charlemont Street, south of St. Stephen's Green) to jazz at **Slattery's** (Capel Street) and the **Waterfront** (Sir John Rogerson's Quay, east of City Quay) to Irish music and step dancing at **Hughes's** (Chancery Street). The music and the musicians vary greatly, as do the patrons and the venues—"Jazz when I'm happy, trad when I'm sad," seems to be a fairly good guide to Dublin preferences.

For the best in authentic traditional singing try **An Góilín** (pronounced Un Go-leen, which can be roughly translated from an old Mayo Gaelic dialect as either "an inlet" or "Have you been singing lately?"), an informal club that welcomes foreign folk singers and instrumentalists as well as natives. It meets on Friday evenings (9:00 P.M. September through July) in the back bar at the Brazen Head (see the previous section). But come early—it's always packed with enthusiasts; admission is one punt.

In addition to all kinds of music, many pubs display all manner of odds and ends: old prints, brass, framed news clippings, crockery, pewter, weird bottles, fancy mirrors—most of these items being authentically old, others specially manufactured for today's taverns. This is a gallant attempt to reverse the 1960s trend of plastic-and-veneer modernization and widespread discarding of the Victorian legacy of mahogany and brass fittings. Ironically, many of the very same pubs that modernized are now leading the way in restoring old-style qualities and craftsmanship to their premises, often turning them into mini-museums in the process. **Kitty O'Shea's** (Upper Grand Canal Street, near Lansdowne Stadium), named after Parnell's paramour and a favorite with rugby football fans—the pub, not the lady—has many items of Parnelliana displayed on its walls, while **The Bailey** (Duke Street) has Michael Collins's revolver, as well as the hall door rescued before the sad demolition of 7 Eccles Street, Leopold Bloom's fictional home and once a city landmark.

Almost every Dublin street has its own pub, if not several, and most have unique qualities of character or entertainment. And their resident characters, some of whom are only too willing to explain the particular pub's wall charts, mementos, pictures, historical bric-a-brac, or whatever. Of course, the more garrulous and "helpful" the character, the more he may expect to be treated to a pint for his trouble. (Later in this chapter, the section Bars and Nightlife provides a roundup of more Dublin pubs.)

But back to the area around the Brazen Head.

The North Quays

Normans, Huguenots, Flemings, Walloons—Dubliners have a varied ancestry. But what of those Dublin Norsemen so abruptly displaced by the Norman newcomers of the 1160s? Only a few paces from the Brazen Head stands the Father Mathew Bridge (formerly the Whitworth Bridge), which occupies the site of the ancient and sole bridge built by those Scandinavian Dubliners.

They were sent scurrying across their narrow wooden bridge by the arrival of the first Normans, vanquished and banished to the near north side of the river and the areas now known as Smithfield and Oxmantown (the latter deriving from Ostman, or Eastmen, a name given to all Scandinavians, Danes, and Norsemen originating from east of Dublin). As recently as the early 20th century— and despite nearly a thousand years of cosmopolitan admixture—residents of the Smithfield and Oxmantown areas retained to a remarkable degree the flaxen-haired and blue-eyed characteristics of their ancestors. Even to-day the astute observer can spot the occasional Scandina-vian type among the burly fruit porters and denizens of the Green Street market area.

The visitor with an ear finely attuned to the nuances of accent and remote dialect may also catch the odd word of an indecipherable argot that is neither Dublin slang nor a West of Ireland Gaelic importation. Throughout the year, on the first Sunday of every month, horse dealers throng into Smithfield (just in off Arran Quay and sandwiched between Queen Street to the west and Bow Street to the east), among them members of Ireland's itinerant or "travelling people" clans with their own secret language, Shelta. Shrewd judges of men, money matters, and mar-kets, the travelling people—an Irish equivalent of gyp-sies, though they are not a Romany breed—use a strange coded language when they wish to communicate among themselves in matters of horse dealing and cart buying.

Mysterious words like *vardy* (a caravan, or cart), *gath-kane* (pub), and *shades* (police) are whispered amid the palm-spitting, hand-slapping ritual of unwritten contracts and the clatter of horse hooves over the broad, elongated square of Smithfield—for centuries a hay market and in the 1960s the cinematic location for the Berlin Wall envi-rons in the Richard Burton film *The Spy Who Came in from the Cold.*

Smithfield is also the headquarters of the Irish Distill-ers Group. While once it boasted a half dozen distilleries, Dublin no longer has any, and nationwide only two re-main of the thirty-odd active distilleries of a century ago. Since the closure of the Jameson distillery in 1972, the old spirit store in Smithfield has been converted for use as the distillers group's administrative center, and an old warehouse has been adapted with imagination and care as an intriguing **Whiskey Museum**. On display are many articles associated with the old craft, a working model of the distilling processes, plus an audiovisual presentation and commentary. Here visitors are given a thoroughly enjoyable introduction to the subject of the "best whiskey in the world." Public tours are conducted Monday through Friday at 3:30 P.M.; Tel: (01) 72-55-66.

The origins of whiskey distilling are shrouded in the past, although the Irish boldly claim to have discovered it, subsequently exporting it along with Christianity and Gaelic music to the western isles of Scotland. The Scots dispute this, but they are content that their commercial product outstrips the Irish brand of whiskey on world markets. However, it is clear that the word "whiskey" is an English corruption of *uisge beatha,* the Gaelic for aqua vitae—the water of life. The Irish maintain that their version is the true source and that it dates to Tudor times, when invading English troops took a fancy to the local women and to the drink, but pronounced *uisge* as whiskey.

Just to the east of Smithfield are the ancient thorough-fare of Church Street and **St. Michan's Church** (founded in 1095), the oldest building on the north side of the river; the tower and some portions of the church are original. The vaults are celebrated for the antiseptic qualities of dry air, constant temperature, and chemical properties exuding from the limestone walls and the subterranean bog that contains the foundations. This combination operates wonderfully to preserve, in mum-mified form and in uncovered coffins, some 300-year-old corpses with features such as skin, fingernails, teeth, and veins clearly discernible.

Few places in Dublin more fully maintain the city's contrasting traditions than this area of largely run-down and derelict sites on and behind the north quays. The rough-and-ready monthly horse fair at Smithfield has its daily counterpart in the early morning bustle of the Dublin Corporation's **Fruit and Vegetable Market**, housed in a late-Victorian red- and yellow-brick building with its main entrance on Mary's Lane. A produce clearing center for the nation, the place is thronged from dawn light with vehicles bearing the exotica of imported fruits and the produce of Ireland's rich market gardens, orchards, and fields. This hurly-burly is in marked contrast to the late-morning pomp and dignity of the law at **Green Street Courthouse** (1797) north of the market and the **Four Courts** building at Inns Quay to the south, with judges and lawyers in their black robes and wigs toing and froing between chambers and courts.

Another Dublin idiosyncrasy: There were actually five

courts—Chancery, King's Bench, Common Pleas, Exchequer, and Rolls Court—originally housed in James Gandon's magnificent 18th-century building that fronts the river and splendidly counterbalances his other masterpiece, the Custom House (1792), three-quarters of a mile east down the quays on the same side of the river. Both buildings were extensively damaged during "The Troubles." In 1922 the Four Courts was seized by the Irregular (antitreaty) forces, who used it as their headquarters for two months during the uneasy peace that followed the evacuation of British troops from Ireland. Its shelling by the National (protreaty) army on June 27 of that year precipitated the Irish Civil War. An explosion set off by the Irregulars before surrendering almost completely destroyed the building's interior—along with the priceless documents, many of them public records dating back to 1174.

A similar thing happened at the **Custom House**, one of the chief centers of British administration in Ireland until the Dublin Brigade of the old IRA carried out its destruction in May 1921; here, too, the interior and a vast quantity of valuable books, records, and documents were destroyed.

Poor Gandon—all his fine interiors were either bombed, burned, or blasted in the cause of Irish freedom. The only one to survive is the dining room at the **King's Inns**, Gandon's final public building a few blocks north of the Four Courts on Henrietta Street. That dining room is still the venue for a 400-year-old custom whereby barristers-to-be, notwithstanding their successes at law studies, must partake of a certain number of dinners at the Inns before qualifying. The Society of King's Inns assumed that title in 1542—about the time lawyers were acquiring the land and property of the dissolved monasteries. Such legal centers were called "inns" because members took up residence there, and "inns of court" because of their ancient association with the judiciary.

Henrietta Street, Dublin's oldest Georgian thoroughfare, was once one of Europe's most elegant and fashionable streets. At the height of its fame in the mid-1700s it contained the residences of four bishops, a duke, four earls, a viscount, and an assortment of lesser knights and nobles. Luke Gardiner—who laid out many North Side streets on the sequestered lands of St. Mary's Abbey, and founded the Mountjoy and Blessington dynasty—had the German architect Richard Cassels design the houses, including Gardiner's own residence, number 10. Here the family resided for over a century, and here too was held "the grandest wake ever seen in Dublin" when, in 1814, the 103-year-old Countess of Blessington (said to have died as the result of a fall from an apple tree in the back garden of number 10) was laid out in state. The doors of the house were thrown open to all, and lavish fare to the tune of £4,000 was provided for any who cared to enter and pay their last respects. Moves are afoot for the preservation and renewal of Henrietta Street and North Great George's Street, another almost intact period street with several houses still used as private residences.

Phoenix Park

To the west of Smithfield lies **Collins Barracks** and then Phoenix Park. Formerly the Royal Barracks (and built in the year of Blenheim, 1704), Collins is believed to be the world's oldest military barracks built for that purpose in continuous occupation. At one time it was also the world's largest, accommodating a total of 5,000 British troops. Dubliners said of such garrisons that they were "useless in times of war and dangerous in times of peace."

West Dublin has in recent years become a crowded, sprawling region of suburban housing developments and industrial parks, but when the city had earlier put space aside for leisure and recreation it did so on the grand scale. Phoenix Park is Europe's largest enclosed urban park. Dublin being a city of misnomers, the park got its name, like whiskey, from another curious corruption of the Irish word *uisge,* in this case *fionn uisge,* meaning "clear water."

The then duke of Ormonde had the park walls erected in 1671 for the purpose of confining a deer herd within its precincts. Today some 300 fallow deer can be seen moving quite freely among the trees flanking the park's main thoroughfare. Always a popular place with Dubliners, the park contains, among other things, the People's Gardens, the official residences of the Irish president and the U.S. ambassador, the papal nunciature, the Irish Army general headquarters, a hospital, the lofty 205-foot Wellington obelisk, the typically misnamed Fifteen Acres (formerly the city's dueling ground and now an extensive plain of sports fields), and the **Dublin Zoo** (dating from 1831). The zoo has attracted worldwide attention for its success in breeding certain animals in captivity, most notably lions, one of which became the famous MGM motion-picture mascot.

Kilmainham

For the energetic walker wishing to return to the south bank of the Liffey, Islandbridge Gate is perhaps the best exit from the park. This leads across the river to Kilmainham with its Royal Hospital (1680) and Kilmainham Jail (1796). The long, tree-lined approach to the **Royal Hospital** gives an excellent view of Ireland's first classical building, the one that ushered in the architectural development of Dublin. It was originally an institution for wounded army pensioners and, as such, the first of its kind in the British Empire. Over the centuries the building has seen many uses but was permitted to fall into a near-ruinous state after it was closed in 1928. The efforts to restore it between 1980 and 1984 earned the prestigious European NOSTRA award for "distinguished contribution to the conservation of Europe's architectural heritage." Its magnificent apartments (open to the public on weekends) contain exhibits from the National Museum, most notably the silver collection; a new gallery of modern and contemporary art; and a permanent exhibition of Hogarth, Rembrandt, and Dürer engravings. In addition to offering various entertainments, exhibitions, and guided tours, the Royal Hospital also hosts many important state and private functions and is now the home of the new **Irish Museum of Modern Art**.

Ireland's first-ever museum of modern art was officially opened by the Irish prime minister, Charles J. Haughey, in May 1991 with the intention of presenting, through its permanent collections and temporary exhibitions, international and Irish art of the 20th century underpinned by a strong community and education program. Artists represented in the inaugural exhibitions ranged from Picasso, Miró, and Mondrian to LeWitt, Judd, Serra, Mullican, and Haacke, and from Jellet and Yeats to Doherty, Cross, Maguire and Lennon.

Plans for 1992 and beyond include IMMA's own growing collection of Irish and international works in regular rotation with temporary exhibitions and projects by Terry Atkinson: Grease Works; Duane Hanson: New Sculpture;

Gilbert and George: Cosmological pictures; Lee Jaffe: Recent Works; and a John Heartfield Retrospective.

Open hours are Tuesday through Sunday 10:00 A.M. to 5:30 P.M. The museum restaurant is open for lunch and refreshments from 10:00 to 5:00 every day. The Royal Kilmainham Bookshop, specializing in art, architecture, and design is open during museum open hours. Admission to the museum is free.

Nearby, on the corner of South Circular Road and Inchicore Road, and in stark contrast, stands **Kilmainham Jail**, Ireland's Bastille. The prison's story closely reflects the turbulent history of Ireland from the time it was founded just prior to the 1798 Rising until the end of the Civil War in 1923. Each succeeding generation of rebel and patriot provided guests for its dark dungeons and punishment cells—United Irishmen, Young Irelanders, Fenians, Land Leaguers, Parnellites, Sinn Feiners, and IRA men. Many were executed in its gaunt prison yard, including the Phoenix Park "Invincible" assassins of 1882 and the signatories of the 1916 Proclamation of the Republic, Padraig Pearse and James Connolly being among the latter. The very last prisoner to be held in Kilmainham (and not released until 1924) was Eamon de Valera, a leader in Ireland's struggle for independence who later became president of the Irish Free State (1932–1937), president of the Council of the League of Nations (1934–1935), Taoiseach (prime minister, pronounced Tee-shock) three times, and president of Ireland from 1959 to 1973.

In 1960 a group of voluntary workers began restoration work on the jail, and the resultant and ever-expanding museum reflects the Irish struggle for independence and the prominent part played by the various inhabitants of Kilmainham Jail in that struggle. This historical resource center provides half-hourly guided tours and audiovisual presentations from October through May on Wednesdays and Sundays (2:00 to 6:00 P.M.) and from June through September seven days a week (11:00 A.M. to 6:00 P.M.). Also featured during the summer months are various art and sculpture exhibitions related to the theme of Irish nationality and identity. Admission £2.25.

A little to the east of Kilmainham and across from Heuston Station—right back in the Liberties area, to be exact—lies a city within a city, the centerpiece of which is a tapering 150-foot tower crowned with a strange, onion-

shaped cupola visible for miles. This is no weird Musco-
vite importation but a massive windmill, now shorn of its
giant vanes, standing in the heart of the 230-year-old
Guinness Brewery.

Legend has it that the first Arthur Guinness acquired
the secret of his distinctive dark brew through the acci-
dental burning, or roasting, of some barley, and that the
popularity of this blackish beer among the hefty market
porters of the 18th century earned for it the name of
"stout porter" beer. Occupying 64 acres in the center of
Dublin, Guinness's is not only Europe's largest brewery
but is also the largest single beer-exporting company in
the world, with some 300 million pints annually shipped
abroad in the company's own tankers. But Dubliners, and
visitors for that matter, need not be alarmed at such a
huge drain on the lifeblood of the nation. The brewery is
capable of producing two and a half times that a year,
which is just as well considering the avidity with which
the Irish lower the stuff.

The brewery's former hop warehouse in nearby Crane
Street was completely refurbished in recent years, and it
is now used as an exhibition center. Open to visitors on
weekdays, the Hop Store provides a film presentation and
houses the brewery's extensive archival and museum
collections.

From Guinness's and St. James's Gate it is no more than a
brisk 20-minute stroll back to the city center in an almost
straight line past the Tailor's Guild Hall, Christ Church
Cathedral, and Dublin Castle—almost, because in Dublin
straight lines invariably contain a wobble or two. The
locals are fond of quoting such Irish bulls as "the farther
one walks a straight line the sooner one makes a detour."
The detours in this case are slight: perhaps a visit to the
foyer of the City Hall on Cork Hill (beside Dublin Castle)
or to the Olympia Theatre almost directly opposite it (and
on the western end of Dame Street), or a stroll through
the warren of old, narrow streets lying between Dame
Street and the river and known as the Temple Bar area,
Dublin's newly discovered and self-proclaimed Left
Bank—even though it is, in fact, the Right! (The Temple
Bar area and Olympia Theatre are discussed next.)

The **City Hall** may be worth a visit to see the frescoes,
mosaics, and sculptures that decorate its interior rotunda.
The hall, which was built as the Royal Exchange, dates
from 1769, and the Dublin City Council meets in what

were once the coffee rooms of the old merchant guilds that effectively ran the city back in the 18th century. The City Council has been somewhat facetiously and unfairly described as an "elected group of men with no money who meet each week to distribute it." In fact, the council handles an annual budget of over £330 million and governs a population of about 503,000; the combined population of both Dublin city and county is in excess of one million.

The mosaic on the floor of the City Hall's rotunda shows the city's coat of arms—three castles with flames issuing from their towers to symbolize the citizens' readiness to defend Dublin—and the city's motto *Obedentia Civium Urbis Felicitas,* which may be roughly translated as "Obedient citizens make for a happy city," a pious aspiration with which generations of disobedient and not-too-happy Dubliners have periodically taken issue.

Temple Bar

The **Olympia Theatre** is also worth viewing for those interested in genuine Victorian music-hall decor, 1870s vintage. If the Abbey Theatre (on the corner of Lower Abbey and Marlborough streets on the North Side; discussed below) is Ireland's national theater, then the Olympia may be termed the city's national playhouse, where everything from the Irish equivalent of vaudeville, dramatic works, and revues to concerts, one-man shows, and pantomime are performed. Deceptively diminutive from the outside, the Olympia has actually a hundred more seats than the better-known **Gaiety** (South King Street off St. Stephen's Green West), which, in addition to providing much the same type of theatrical fare as the Olympia, regularly asserts its superiority by hosting visiting repertory companies, ballet, and the Dublin Grand Opera Society's spring season (with important European stars in the leading roles).

While Dublin has had numerous theaters since the opening of the first one in Werburgh Street in 1637 and has produced a continuous supply of internationally acclaimed playwrights, actors, and actresses since William Congreve (1670–1729), Spranger Barry (1719–1777), and Peg Woffington (1720–1760), it has no readily identifiable theater district corresponding, say, to New York's Broadway or to London's West End. Its present-day professional theaters are dotted indiscriminately about the city: the

Gate on Cavendish Row (at the northern end of O'Connell Street, just past the Parnell monument), the Peacock, a downstairs adjunct to the more prestigious Abbey, the above-mentioned Olympia and Gaiety theaters, and about a dozen fringe theaters. Various other halls and venues are pressed into service for performances during one of the city's chief cultural events, the **Dublin Theatre Festival**, which is held annually around the end of September to early October.

For details of venues and times for all theater, cinema, concert, poetry reading, and art and photographic exhibitions, purchase the biweekly information magazine *In Dublin*.

For spotting actors and show-biz personalities—homegrown as well as visiting international stars like Eric Clapton, Sting, and Shirley Bassey in their moments of relaxation—perhaps there's no better place than **Bad Bob's Backstage Bar** at the corner of Sycamore and East Essex streets, virtually sandwiched between the Olympia's stage door and the Project Art Centre's 150-seat pocket playhouse. The Back Stage Bar provides live music seven nights a week—jazz, ballads, rock, or traditional—and its **Granary Buffet** restaurant, specializing in home-style food, is one of the most popular places for theater suppers. The bar is also a regular launching pad for events associated with the theater festival and the **Dublin Film Festival**, which follows about a week or two later in October each year.

Though facing out onto Dame Street, the modern **Central Bank** building (not to be confused with the nearby historic Bank of Ireland) more or less dominates Temple Bar, a district fast becoming a popular place for restaurants, crafts centers, recording studios, and theater workshops. Temple Bar is currently being developed as part of an extended pedestrian link through Crown Alley, then under Merchant's Arch—a favorite place for street musicians and buskers—and over the Ha'penny Bridge (Ireland's oldest metal bridge and formerly a toll bridge, hence its name) to a somewhat similar pedestrian shopping area on the North Side comprising Liffey, Henry, and Mary streets.

Dubliners hear much but see little of Ireland's financial market, and very few are aware of the location of the Stock Exchange in Anglesea Street. No spot in the city exhibits such a contrast in population as the picturesque streets surrounding the Central Bank. At noon on a week-

day it is a teeming hive, its pavements thronged, its narrow roadways reverberating with the buzz of traffic and
business activity; in the evening the same streets are given
over to leisurely promenaders and strolling lovers.

Similarly with **Coffers Restaurant** in Cope Street off
Anglesea, in an Old World building that is reputed to be
haunted by the benevolent ghost of its first tenant, a
Huguenot tailor of the 1730s. Coffers is a discreet midday
meeting place favored by bankers and stockbrokers and
an evening rendezvous for theatergoers, the intelligentsia, and discerning diners. They come for the moderately
priced wild Atlantic salmon in season, Irish meats and
steaks, fresh seafood and vegetables, and an interesting
wine list, in an intimate, family-owned restaurant made
cozy and warm by both the personnel and the original
Huguenot fireplaces.

Visitors may also fall for the illusion that they have
tiptoed a little into history and that they are guests not in
some center-city restaurant but rather in the private residence of an old gentleman tailor. The transformation
from the past to the 20th century has been remarkably
graceful here, and Coffers—certainly not the place to
grab a quick sandwich between shopping outings—is a
place to revel in a mode of living that died with the
Second World War.

College Green

College Green—not to be confused with "the Green,"
which to Dubliners signifies St. Stephen's Green, the
delightful center-city park—is the broad area in front of
Trinity College and the Bank of Ireland where lower
Grafton Street, Westmoreland Street, College Street, and
Dame Street converge.

Big business has its aristocracy, and this district is devoted to the upper circles of commerce. Clothes tend to
be more formal here; even the liveried bank porter has
not quite disappeared from this stronghold of wealth.
Because of the tendency of Dubliners to emphasize the
elegance of their Georgian streetscapes and squares, Dublin's Victorian buildings are often overlooked or even
criticized. Take, for example, the row of banking and
insurance offices on the south side of College Green and
facing the Bank of Ireland. While the overloaded detail of
some of these buildings—mock turrets and conical
towers—may be displeasing, many of the individual con-

ceptions repay examination, particularly the interior ceiling work and decor of the Northern Bank building.

To be seen to best advantage, the **Bank of Ireland** would probably require an elevated site and some surrounding gardens or parkland, but even in its low-lying, mid-city situation it is still a magnificent building. It was built in 1739, but over the following 60 years all the leading architects of the era—Lovett Pearse, James Gandon, Robert Parke, and Francis Johnston—at various times had a hand in its design. It was formerly the House of Parliament, unique perhaps among the world's parliaments in that it was the only one ever to vote itself out of existence, and famed for its learned debates and the oratorical skills of such men as the patriot Henry Grattan (his statue on College Green is the one displaying a raised, declamatory hand).

After the Act of Union in 1800, the building was adapted by Francis Johnston for the sole use of the bank; the cannon and sentry boxes outside date from that time, when it was deemed necessary to form a militia guard for the bank's protection.

During normal business hours the bank's old House of Lords, displaying the speaker's mace and two large 1735 tapestries illustrating the Battle of the Boyne and the Siege of Derry, is open to the public and worth visiting.

Trinity College

If the Bank of Ireland is one great showpiece in College Green, then Trinity College's west front is the other.

There are three universities in Dublin, each enjoying a particular prestige and position: Dublin University (Trinity), University College, Dublin (a constituent college of the National University), and the new Dublin City University—the latter two located in the suburbs. Of these three, Trinity has the most atmosphere, which is another way of saying that it has an older and greater tradition. That tradition can be detected in the campus meetings, conversations, clubs, some 200 societies, two pubs, writings, acting, and debate—a kind of liberal (and Protestant) ethos, which until about 20 years ago was so frowned upon by the Catholic hierarchy that members of the flock had to seek special permission from Dublin's archbishop to study there. And it is probably for that reason that this 40-acre, open-to-the-public oasis of gardens, playing fields, cobbled quadrangles, and old buildings has until quite recently retained a slightly forbidding air of "excommunication" for Dublin's predominantly Roman Catholic population.

The cultural and recreational pursuits of Trinity's 7,000 students can be gleaned from the myriad posters on the notice boards at the College Green and Nassau Street entrances, many of which invite the participation of the general public. Undergraduate life is particularly festive and raucous on occasions such as the annual Rag Week and Trinity Ball in May.

Founded by Queen Elizabeth I—the carved royal arms of Good Queen Bess near the exit of the library is the only remaining relic of the original building—Trinity is Ireland's oldest university. Most of its present buildings, however, date from the early-18th century, though the sense of antiquity within its precincts is heightened by the ancient cobblestones, the cast-iron bollards and lamps, and a leisurely Old World air that gives no hint of the turmoil that marked the college's early history.

In 1643 the college had to pawn its silver, and most of the fellows were expelled by Cromwell's officers; subsequently, others were excluded in a tit-for-tat reprisal by the monarchy; and all—fellows and students alike—were sent packing when James II turned the place into an army barracks in 1689. The following century witnessed periodic town-versus-gown riots.

Yet those centuries also witnessed an age of ardent learning and wide-ranging scholarship that produced such Trinity men as Ussher the biblical scholar, Marsh the Orientalist, Dodwell the historian, and Stearne, who founded the Irish College of Physicians. Most of the outstanding Irishmen of the 18th century, including Molyneux, Berkeley, Grattan, Tone, Burke, and Goldsmith—the last two commemorated by fine statues outside the main entrance—were Trinity men, and the influence of their alma mater is discernible in their writings and speeches. Also educated here were writers such as Jonathan Swift, Oscar Wilde, and Samuel Beckett, and scientists such as Rowan Hamilton of quaternions fame and E. T. S. Walton, who won the Nobel Prize for his work on the atom. The college further distinguished itself by admitting female students to degrees as early as 1903.

To appreciate the wealth and variety of Trinity, a detailed guidebook and ample leisure are required, but if you are pressed for time a visit to the old library should suffice. Its famous **Long Room** on the first floor (for

North Americans, second floor) is said to be the largest single-chamber library in Europe. Its 200,000 volumes and 5,000 manuscripts—Greek, Latin, Egyptian papyruses, etc.—are the college's oldest and most-prized possessions. Among its principal treasures are eighth- and ninth-century Irish ecclesiastical manuscripts—the books of Durrow, Dimma, and Armagh, and the magnificently illuminated copy of the Gospels, the **Book of Kells**. Since 1801, under various copyright acts, the college has been entitled to receive one copy of every work published in Britain and Ireland, so it now requires seven additional buildings, and a half-mile increase in bookshelves every year, to contain a collection exceeding two and a half million volumes.

The Provost's House (1760)—to the left of the main entrance and facing onto lower Grafton Street; not open to the public—is the oldest continuously inhabited house in Dublin. Of its many prominent tenants perhaps the most colorful was Dr. John Mahaffy, professor of Greek, sportsman, social snob, and wit. "In Ireland the inevitable never happens, but the unexpected often occurs," is one of his better-known quips. Mahaffy impressed on the young Oscar Wilde the importance not of being earnest but of making bons mots and the right social contacts. It was Mahaffy who, on being shown a sample of Joyce's work, snorted contemptuously, "the inevitable result of extending university education to the wrong sort of people." It need hardly be added that Joyce was a graduate of University College, Dublin, not of Mahaffy's beloved Trinity.

Grafton Street

Dublin's main shopping area lies along and near O'Connell and Grafton streets, which run north and south through the city center across the Liffey, O'Connell being north of the river, Grafton south—although almost every side street and outlying suburb has its boutique, antiques store, or craft shop. Dubliners like to hint or boast of little places in the quieter districts where all sorts of bargains supposedly can be unearthed; these places are not closed or out of bounds to the visitor—he or she has only to find them.

Grafton Street, which is closed to automobile traffic, and the side streets, interconnecting lanes, shopping malls, and alleys linking it with South Great George's

Street to the west and Dawson Street to the east, is *the* shopping strip in Dublin. The side streets contain everything from the Westbury hotel, **Casper and Giumbini's** restaurant (excellent traditional food, including Irish stew), the Hibernian Shopping Arcade, the Civic Museum, and the **Bruxelles Music Pub**, to Lord Powerscourt's 200-year-old town house, where a delightful enclosed courtyard and balcony have been converted into a modern shopping center, the **Powerscourt Townhouse Centre**, with everything from designer shoes and handbags to Irish linen and lace.

Grafton Street's leading department stores, **Switzers** and **Brown Thomas**, almost rival the nearby bookshops of **Waterstone**, **Hodges Figgis** (both on Dawson Street), and **Fred Hanna** (Nassau Street) in their encyclopedic range, while the neighboring streets are havens for print and antiques shops and boutiques. Shoppers here should concentrate on the Irish products of exceptional quality, such as Belleek china, Waterford and Galway crystal, woollens, and tweeds.

The **Sweater Shop** (Wicklow Street) is tops for Aran hand-knits, kilts, lamb's-wool sweaters, and the like, and **Weir's** (Grafton Street) gives good value for leather, gold, and silver items, and offers one of the finest selections of Claddagh rings, those distinctive "hands-clasping-a-crowned-heart" old Irish wedding tokens. At the top of Grafton Street—where it ends in a kind of dramatic flourish opposite the Fusiliers Arch (a memorial to the officers and men of five battalions of the Royal Dublin Fusiliers who died in the Boer War)—stands Ireland's largest retail development, the St. Stephen's Green Centre, opened in the summer of 1988 (discussed below).

Westward from O'Connell Street on the North Side runs Henry Street, a busy shopping area with popular department stores such as Arnotts, Roches, the modern ILAC (Irish Life Assurance Company) Centre, and the famous Moore Street butcher shops and stall holders. **Moore Street** provides one of the briskest scenes of general barter in the city. Fruit, vegetable, and fish stalls crowd the pavements, and nowhere are the vendors more pressing in their invitations to buy. Keen bargain sleuths who are not averse to poking through tatty junk piles laid out on the sidewalks of seedy North Cumberland Street (a few minutes' walk to the east side of O'Connell Street's northern end, taking the first right after the Gresham Hotel into Cathal Brugha Street) may occasionally unearth treasures from among the oddments of china-ware, pottery, brasswork, old picture frames, coins, military bric-a-brac, old household appliances, rusty garden implements, carpet scraps, and toys found here. The **Cumberland Market** is a once-a-week, Saturday morning affair—very early, six to seven—in a very unprepossessing area. (Shopping throughout Dublin is covered later in this chapter.)

Dawson Street
and St. Stephen's Green

Back to the Trinity College area: Trinity's Lincoln Place gate leads southeast to Merrion Square, its Nassau Street gate south to Dawson Street and the Green. St. Anne's Romanesque-fronted church, the Royal Irish Academy, and the Mansion House are cheek by jowl in Dawson Street.

It has been said that Dublin almost rivals Rome in the number and variety of its churches. A sprinkling of Jewish, Greek Orthodox, and Moslem congregations augment all the Protestant denominations in the minority religions category in this city whose population is about 90 percent Roman Catholic and which has, in addition to its secular clergy, well over a hundred separate religious orders of priests, nuns, monks, and brothers.

St. Anne's is one of the most beautiful of these churches, and it is known to a small group of Dubliners of all religious persuasions for the excellent lunchtime musical and cultural activities that take place here every Thursday. Visitors to St. Anne's should note the wooden "bread" shelves behind the altar. In the 1720s one of St. Anne's first parishioners made a bequest of £13 per annum in perpetuity to provide weekly loaves of bread for the poor of the parish. The custom of laying out loaves for distribution has continued to the present day, although the original handsome bequest must now be supplemented by donations.

The Royal Irish Academy, next door to St. Anne's, publishes major reference works of Irish interest—its library contains an extensive collection of ancient Irish manuscripts—and holds a leading place among the learned societies of Europe, but it is not open to the public. Nor is the Mansion House, except for group visits by prior arrangement. The Mansion House—essentially a town house of the Queen Anne period (1710) with later Victorian embellishments added—has been the official residence of the lord mayor of Dublin since 1715 and thus predates its London counterpart by about 30 years. Its principal interior apartment is the Round Room, built expressly for the reception of George IV in 1821 but much better known as the assembly room of the first Dáil Eireann—the parliament of the Irish people—where, in 1919, in defiance of Westminster, the Declaration of Independence was ratified.

The clean atmosphere of the Irish capital is doubtless largely due to its proximity to the sea and the mountains, and also due to its many fine parks and open spaces. One of these, **St. Stephen's Green**, is everything a center-city park should be. An air of subdued holiday spirit pervades its wooded walks (it's a mile-long walk around its four sides), formal lawns, fountains, and duck ponds. It also contains a bandstand, a pavilion, a children's playground, and 15 monuments and statues. Lord Ardilaun (Sir Arthur Edward Guinness) had the park laid out in its present form in the 1880s and established a decoy pond for wildfowl, a source of much entertainment to generations of Dubliners and visitors.

The buildings surrounding the Green include (south side) Iveagh House, now the Department of Foreign Affairs, and University Church with its narrow, fussy entrance leading into the nearest thing Dublin has to a Byzantine-type church; (west side) the Unitarian Church, containing a striking collection of stained-glass windows—French, Flemish, English, and the main window, a splendid example of the revived Irish style—the College of Surgeons (1806), and the St. Stephen's Green Centre (Ireland's largest retail development), which opened in 1988 at a cost of £60 million plus and contains a wide range of Ireland's most exclusive department stores; and (north side) the Adam Salesrooms and the Shelbourne Hotel. The College of Surgeons was built on the site of an old Quaker cemetery, and when it was extended by William Murray in 1825 care was taken to retain the two narrow lanes (Goat Alley and Glovers Alley) that flank the building that originally facilitated the nocturnal activities of the body snatchers—known locally as "Sack 'em up men"—whose business it was to discreetly deliver their macabre bundles to the college's dissecting room. During the 1916 Rising the college was commandeered by the Irish Citizen Army led by Michael Mallin and with the colorful and tempestuous Constance Markievicz as second-in-command.

The north side was the former "Beaux Walk," the 18th-century center of fashion and dandyism, and the haunt of such notorious rakes as the inveterate gambler Buck Whaley, who once walked to Jerusalem and back to win a bet, and "Sham Squire" Francis Higgins, who, for 1,000 pounds, betrayed his friend, the patriot Lord Edward Fitzgerald, to the authorities before the 1798 Rising. To-day, what remains of Victorian and Edwardian club life still flourishes on this side of the Green.

The **Adam Salesrooms** on this side provide a happy hunting ground for dealers and collectors interested in period furniture, paintings, glass, silver, porcelain, china, books, manuscripts, and wine. To witness an auction here is first-class entertainment. Not that there is much visible excitement. An air of laid-back ennui appears to prevail as first editions and rare documents go under the hammer and change hands, often for considerable sums. Dublin-ers, from plebeian ex-tenement dwellers to shabby gen-teel suburbanites and a few faded remnants of the Anglo-Irish ascendancy class, have in recent years taken to rummaging through their attics and cellars for forgotten valuable heirlooms or quaint family bric-a-brac to sell at the salesrooms.

The **Shelbourne Hotel**—known to upper-class globe-trotters of every continent—dates back to 1824 and pos-sesses the hallmark of approval of royalty and nobility, as well as millionaires, literary personalities, and stars of stage and screen. Thackeray stayed here in 1842, describ-ing it as a "respectable old edifice" and exclaiming over its "copious breakfasts," and George Moore wrote parts of his novels *A Drama in Muslin* and *The Bending of the Bough* in a front bedroom commanding a splendid view of the Green. The late Princess Grace of Monaco appreciated its elegance and the fact that she could take quiet early morning walks in the Green away from the usual hordes of international press photographers and reporters. The Irish Constitution of 1922 was drafted in Room 112, now called the Constitution Room. The Shelbourne's Lord Mayor's Lounge—with leaf-green silk-lined walls, swag and tail drapes, and a splendid chandelier—is a toney reflection of the leisurely Victorian age and the perfect setting for relaxed morning coffee and the 150-year-old tradition of "afternoon tea." Like the famous Horseshoe

Bar, this celebrated tearoom is popular with discerning Dubliners and visitors alike as an ideal place to meet or to relax after shopping or sightseeing forays. (The Shelbourne Hotel is discussed further in the Accommodations section, below.)

Directly opposite the Shelbourne's front entrance, which is illuminated at night by a brace of lanterns held aloft by statues of two nubile slave girls with fettered ankles, stands a modern commemorative statue to the patriot Wolfe Tone. Tone's statue, against a background of giant granite plinths, was no sooner unveiled when some Dublin wag christened it "Tone-henge" (the nicknaming of the city's statues being something of a traditional pastime).

Georgian Dublin

Few European cities offer the same scale and scope of 18th-century elegance as the area of Dublin bordered by Trinity College and the east side of St. Stephen's Green on the one side, and the Mount Street and Leeson Street bridges of the Grand Canal on the other. Its Georgian buildings give it nobility; its bosky squares, tree-lined canal, and broad thoroughfares (as far back as 1768 the city had a special Wide Streets Commission to give muscle to its plan for spaciousness) all make it a district of openness, light, and air. It is also the district of museums, art galleries (public and private), little parks, historic houses, government offices, nightclubs (Leeson Street), and even the occasional fine restaurant or ballad pub. Though the interiors of what were formerly residences have largely been converted into offices, consulting rooms, and private apartments, there is still something of the sober austerity of old-style Anglo-Irish Protestantism about these buildings, an overall unity of design relieved by the constant variety of detail in doorways, fanlights, and ornamental balconies.

The Anglo-Irish—a rather loose term for all those well-to-do Protestants who, over about three centuries, owed their cultural and even political allegiance to London and to their British cousins—haven't really had a very good press in recent years. This generic term usually refers to someone who isn't Gaelic, Catholic, or Nationalist in background and outlook, though like everything else in Ireland there are contradictions and notable exceptions.

The original Norman invaders of 800 years ago, aristocratic in their ambitions at least, had little difficulty in assimilating with a native Gaelic order that itself was inherently aristocratic in character. By the time of Elizabeth I these Hiberno-Normans (or "Olde English," as the London court termed them) had become more Irish than the Irish themselves, and the Virgin Queen considered it most politic to plant "New English" in the rich pasturelands of Munster and the Pale.

Elizabeth's successor, James I, went much further when he literally sowed the entire province of Ulster with Scottish Protestants after the exodus of the Gaelic chiefs in 1603. The subsequent wars and the political ferment of the 17th century brought new strains of Englishness. Cromwellian troopers were rewarded with vast tracts of land, and, similarly, William of Orange, after he became William III of England, Scotland, and Ireland in the Revolution of 1688, paid off many of his English and Dutch officers by creating a new landed gentry on the forfeited estates of those who had sided with his Catholic rival, James II. The less turbulent years of the 17th and 18th centuries saw the peaceful infiltration of many English and Scottish merchants into the life of the country. Out of this essentially Protestant and British oligarchy grew the term "Anglo-Irish."

If history can accuse this class of having perfected the art of skimming the cream off Ireland, then it can also credit the same people with having created the Augustan era of Georgian Dublin and of having laid the groundwork for much that is elegant and erudite in Ireland today. In addition to producing everything from profligate rakes, cruel landlords, proud soldiers, gentle scholars, and altruistic women, the Anglo-Irish class has provided Ireland with such names as Swift, Berkeley, Goldsmith, Burke, Shaw, Wilde, and Yeats, together with patriots such as Grattan, Emmet, Butt, Davis, and Parnell.

The Georgian district also contains a famous collection of institutions devoted to educational, artistic, and scholarly interests. In **Kildare Street**, parallel to and east of Dawson Street, the National Museum and the National Library, as well as the National College of Art, flank the forecourt and "town house" façade of Leinster House, the seat of Dáil Eireann (House of Representatives) and Seanad Eireann (Senate).

The **National Library** entrance hall frequently displays small exhibitions—Irish bookbinding, prints, political tracts and posters, famous Irish letters, etc.—while the

Reading Room (scene of the literary debate in Joyce's *Ulysses*) preserves a representative collection of first editions and works of such Irish writers as Swift, Goldsmith, Yeats, Shaw, Joyce, and Beckett. The library's need for additional space for its ever-increasing collection of books, maps, and newspapers led to the recent acquisition of the adjoining Kildare Street Club premises, a Venetian-style brick "palazzo" at the northern, or Trinity, end of the street that now houses the Heraldic and Genealogical Museum—of particular interest and help to those tracing ancestral roots.

The **National Museum** houses an outstanding collection of Irish antiquities, some of which are among the finest examples of early Christian art in Europe. Exhibits cover a period from roughly 6000 B.C. to modern times, with everything from costumes, silver, medals, and weapons to photos, letters, and military memorabilia of the 1916 Rising.

The museum's **Treasury Gallery** is inspired by the great cathedral galleries of Europe and illustrates the pagan pre-Celtic and Celtic background of early Christian Irish art, including stunning gold masterpieces—gorgets, torques, lunulae—from pre-Celtic times as early as 1800 B.C., and from the Celtic pre-Viking zenith. An audiovisual presentation explains the historical and archaeological context of the exhibition and gives guidance on how to appreciate the major masterpieces. This is presented in a specially designed theater with informal tiered seating and selected exhibits, including sculptures, which are linked to the on-screen program. Centerpieces of the display itself include the eighth-century A.D. **Ardagh Chalice** and **Tara Brooch, St. Patrick's Bell,** the **Cross of Cong,** and the **Moylough belt shrine,** together with book shrines, croziers, crosses, and other priceless items. To these are added the fruits of intensive collecting over the past decade, including the recently discovered "Derrynaflan hoard" and six other recently acquired silver hoards from the Midlands containing over 30 kilograms of silver objects. An exquisitely worked chalice is the most important item among the eighth- and ninth-century religious artifacts in the Derrynaflan hoard, discovered in February 1980 near a ruined fifth-century abbey in County Tipperary.

The **Music Room** contains some 70 musical instruments, mostly Irish made, with *uilleann* pipes, harps (one ascribed to the great Carolan), pianos, harpsichords, and experimental stringed instruments. The Art and Industrial Division comprises Irish glass, furniture, costumes, coins, stamps, ceramics, and medals. In addition to Greek, Roman, Egyptian, and Oriental antiquities, the museum's Ethnographical Collection contains much material originating from Captain Cook's voyages of discovery.

The **National Museum Annexe**—around the corner in Merrion Row, just past the Shelbourne Hotel—contains numerous Viking artifacts discovered during the almost continuous excavations between 1962 and 1981 in the city's Christchurch Place, Winetavern, and Wood Quay sites, among Europe's largest and richest urban digs. Exhibits on display here include 11th-century bone-and-antler combs and carrying cases, iron swords, polished bone pins, scales for weighing precious metals, hundreds of lead weights all conforming to units based on the Carolingian ounce, and an iron saw shaped to resemble a Viking longboat and used to cut antler and bone.

Both the library and the museum are open to the public, as is Leinster House when the parliament is not sitting. **Leinster House** (1745) was originally the town house of the duke of Leinster, who, on being reminded of the folly of building his mansion in what was then rural countryside when the fashionable side of the city was clearly on the north side of the Liffey, declared that fashion would follow him across the river. The accuracy of his forecast was quickly proven.

The opposite side of this sprawling educational and legislative complex is on Merrion Square and contains the National Gallery and the Natural History Museum. Like their Kildare Street counterparts, they flank Leinster House, in this case the rear, "country house" façade, with its lawn and obelisk commemorating the founders of the Irish Free State: Arthur Griffith, Michael Collins, and Kevin O'Higgins, a tragic triumvirate, all of whom died within five years of each other, the last two by bullets.

The **Natural History Museum** holds a valuable collection of the remains of extinct and prehistoric animals and birds, together with mounted and preserved representatives of the world's fauna.

Outside the entrance to the **National Gallery** are statues of George Bernard Shaw, who claimed that he owed his education to the gallery and bequeathed a third of his estate to it, and the Irish railway pioneer William Dargan, who was the prime mover in its establishment. One of the best "small" galleries in Europe—Irish painters, Dutch masters, English watercolorists, 17th-century French, Italian, and Spanish schools, and French Impressionists, amounting to more than 2,000 works on view—the building also houses an extensive art reference library, lecture theater, and one of Dublin's most popular and inexpensive restaurants.

In all there are about 40 galleries in the center-city area—a dozen of them in the Merrion-Fitzwilliam-St. Stephen's Green district—and every Saturday and Sunday an ongoing open-air exhibition takes place in **Merrion Square** park (opposite the National Gallery), with paintings, prints, drawings, and lithographs festooning the park railings and clustered about the Rutland Fountain (1791). The park, once the scene of distressed and starving hordes surrounding the soup kitchens of the famine era (1845–1847), is now one of the most beautiful and most popular of center-city retreats. Plaques on the walls of the surrounding mansions recall famous occupants— the Wildes, Daniel O'Connell, W. B. Yeats, George Russell (AE), and Sheridan Le Fanu—and the view from the south side of the square, looking toward Upper Mount Street and crowned by the "pepper canister" cupola of St. Stephen's (1825), offers what is possibly the finest Georgian vista in the city. **Fitzwilliam Square** to the south, on the other hand, is the smallest, latest (1825), and best preserved of Dublin's Georgian squares.

Dublin's Canals

Just as Londoners born within hearing of Bow Bells are said to be the true Cockneys, so too are the "rale Dubs," or Jackeens, said to be born within the confines of the city's Royal and Grand canals.

The Liffey divides old Dublin into two nearly equal portions, the North Side and the South Side. Until the advent of the railways—and, indeed, for almost a century after, it might be argued—the river acted as a kind of natural frontier between North Siders and South Siders. Well into this century, and in addition to the separate and distinct classes of citizens based on social and religious differences, there was this geographic division too. To the majority of North Siders the south city and its environs were almost as foreign as the Sahara and Timbuktu; and north of the river, as far as most South Siders were concerned, might well have been Ultima Thule or Alaska.

Villages such as Irishtown and particularly its sister parish of Ringsend (then almost entirely surrounded by the waters of the Liffey, the River Dodder, and the sea) were remote and distinct places. The building of the canals in the late-18th century added a further clannish frontier on both sides of the Liffey: Everyone outside the canals was said to be a "hazeler," so-called from the hazel sticks the rural drovers used to guide their cattle into the Dublin markets.

The South Side **Grand Canal** was constructed in 1772 to provide a passenger link between Dublin, the midland towns to the west, and the River Shannon. (Its most attractive urban setting is the tree-lined stretch between Leeson Street Bridge and the picturesque Huband Bridge at Upper Mount Street, near the "pepper canister" church.) Tens of thousands of passengers travelled annually along this 90-mile stretch prior to the introduction of the railways in the 1850s. Thereafter passenger traffic deteriorated, but freight barges continued working the canal right up to the middle of the present century.

Like so many things in Ireland, the building of the rival North Side **Royal Canal** grew out of personal pique and a subsequent feud. John Binns (there's a canal bridge named after him in Drumcondra) quarreled with his fellow directors on the Grand Canal board, resigned, and angrily vowed to build a bigger and better canal on the opposite side of the city. He commenced the Royal Canal in 1790, but, alas, lack of sufficient passengers and freight kept his venture only limping along until the advent of the steam locomotive. It was the extensive network of Ireland's 19th-century railways (with their ability to transport many more passengers and much more freight and mail in far quicker time, and at cheaper rates, over all manner of boggy lowland and hilly terrain) that ushered in the steady decline of the slower, more leisurely canal traffic.

The Royal Canal's subsequent fate accurately mirrored that of its South Side rival: It was closed to traffic in the early 1960s. In 1986 the Office of Public Works was vested with ownership and both canals are now entering a new era as sites for water cruising. Today it is the canals (plus the Trojan efforts of a handful of waterway enthusiasts, who have painstakingly rebuilt old lock gates and removed debris, silt, and weeds) that provide a "romantic" and slower mode of inland exploration with the provision of leisure and pleasure craft.

The South Side Suburbs

A suburb may have its charm no less than a historic city center. East of St. Stephen's Green along Baggot Street, or east of Merrion Square along Mount Street/Northumberland Road, **Ballsbridge**—containing the Berkeley Court and Jury's hotels, most of the foreign embassies, the Royal Dublin Society (R.D.S.) Showgrounds, and the Chester Beatty Library—stands for elegance, even luxury. A century ago it was the Belgravia of Dublin. At the time, the residents of Ballsbridge regarded themselves as more than members of Dublin's respectable Victorian society—they *were* that society. Their rules of behavior were not formulated in written codes, their social regulations being governed by nothing more than an innate awareness that things were either "done" or "not done." This sense of refinement still exists and is displayed in a succession of tints: neat rectangles of lawn fringed with flowers, painted wrought iron, the mica-glint of granite on steps and lintels, broad leafy avenues, and sturdy mansions.

Topography confines Ballsbridge to the district that is bounded on the north by the Grand Canal, on the south by Donnybrook, on the west by Ranelagh, and on the east by Sandymount. Socially, however, it may be said to extend much farther afield and to include most of its bordering districts. Although the professions and business interests have secured a footing in Ballsbridge, the area is still mainly occupied by the wealthy and the fashionable. Superior hotels, high-class restaurants, and diplomatic missions are interspersed among luxury apartments, suburban villas, and mansions. The centerpiece is undoubtedly the extensive R.D.S. Showgrounds. The **Royal Dublin Society**—the first of its kind in Europe, and with over 250 years of promoting improvements in agriculture, veterinary science, and stock breeding—is renowned worldwide for its two great annual events: the **Spring Show** (May) and the **Dublin Horse Show** (August). The former is primarily an agricultural produce/machinery/livestock exhibition and includes equestrian events; the latter is devoted to premier show jumping competitions. The Dublin Horse Show still attracts the best jumpers in the world to compete for the supreme equestrian prize, the Aga Khan Trophy. The society's Simmonscourt Extension is the venue for many indoor exhibitions, concerts, and shows throughout the year.

Nearby, in Shrewsbury Road—a delightful, wooded road—is the **Chester Beatty Library and Gallery of Oriental Art**. There is not a student of the Near and Far East in the world today who does not owe something to Chester Beatty, a New Yorker who roughed it in the mining camps of the Wild West as a mining engineer with a six-gun strapped to his waist. A millionaire at 40, he took to wintering in Africa to ease the chronic chest ailment brought on by silicosis, the miners' respiratory disease. The African continent brought him into contact with the world of ancient Egyptian manuscripts written on papyrus. Over the next 50 years he sought, acquired, and assembled the most remarkable collection of papyruses and Oriental art in the world. In 1950 Beatty came to live in Dublin, bringing his priceless collection with him. When he died in 1968 he bequeathed his vast collection to the Irish nation. Highlights include items dating back as far as 2500 B.C., biblical papyruses, Persian and Turkish paintings, Qur'ans, Japanese and European wood-block prints, and Chinese jade books.

Ireland's Jewish community numbers only about 2,000 members but has contributed in no small measure to the cultural and business life of the city since the arrival of the first group of Jews about 300 years ago. This contribution is well recorded in an absorbing collection of Jewish and Dublin memorabilia on display in the **Irish Jewish Museum**, in what was once the old Walworth Road Synagogue off Victoria Street in the Portobello district bordering on the Grand Canal. Israel's then-President Chaim Hertzog—himself a "Dub" who once lived in nearby Bloomfield Avenue—officially opened the museum.

SOUTH COUNTY

DART (Dublin Area Rapid Transport) runs from Howth (North Side) through the city center to Bray (South Side), a distance of about 25 miles. For the visitor the DART is best travelled from the city center southward (with the exception of an excursion to Howth and neighboring Sutton), where the stretch of line from Merrion to Dún Laoghaire seems to run almost along the sands and offers a panoramic view of Dublin Bay. En route, high walls front the public bathing places at Blackrock and Salthill, a legacy of Victorian prudery and railway stipulations preventing "such bathing places and the persons bathing therein from being exposed to the view of passengers on the said railroad." The final southern stretch of the DART line—exiting from the Dalkey hilltop tunnel and running through Killiney to Bray—possesses a touch of the Mediterranean. The view of the bay and the gentle curve of Killiney beach is said by many to rival the glories of Naples and Sorrento. Some, in fact, would claim that the bay is a gentler, prettier, less cluttered, and more nearly perfect crescent than its better-known rival. (The weather is a different matter.)

Dún Laoghaire

Dubliners "discovered" Dún Laoghaire (formerly Kingstown) with the coming of the railways in the 1830s and the simultaneous introduction of the world's first suburban railroad.

The place still retains a certain 19th-century charm along with its modern shopping complex, humble artisan dwellings, busy harbor, resort-type hotels and boardinghouses, regal promenade, and quaint side streets. Gothic church spires punctuate the predominantly horizontal rows of solid, comfortable bourgeois terraces (groups of row houses). Here and there the stately exclusiveness of some of its tree-lined avenues suggests the superiority of a minicapital city. Dún Laoghaire is unashamedly Victorian, a vivid expression of the twin 19th-century virtues of business acumen and social respectability.

Yet for all its "gem of the period" Victoriana, the township retains a salty tang. Dún Laoghaire is preeminently a sailors' town, for more than 150 years the exit and entry point for the main sea route between Ireland and Britain. It is still the home port of a busy commercial sea fishery, the mail boat terminal, the Sealink car ferry service terminal, the base for Irish lightships, and Ireland's premier yachting center, the site of such famous and ancient clubs as the Royal St. George, the Royal Irish, the National, and the Motor Yacht Club alongside one another on the harbor front. It also is headquarters for the Irish Yachting Association and the National Maritime Museum, the latter housed in what used to be the Mariner's Church.

Dún Laoghaire is well supplied with restaurants and cafés, the most notable being **Restaurant na Mara**, located at the DART station and overlooking the harbor. *Na mara* means "of the sea" in Gaelic, and, as the name suggests, the place specializes in seafood (Tel: 01-280-6767 or 01-

280-0509). Also on the seafront, at Windsor Terrace, are **Steers Steak House** (Tel: 01-280-6535) and **Digby's** (Tel: 01-280-4600), both offering fresh seasonal food. The **Salty Dog** at 3A Haddington Terrace (Tel: 01-280-8015) prepares Indonesian as well as European dishes.

Sandycove

A brisk 20-minute walk from Dún Laoghaire's east pier around the rim of Scotsman's Bay takes you to Sandycove and the **James Joyce Museum**. The museum is housed in a Martello tower, one of the 20-odd squat military fortifications resembling foreshortened butter churns that dot County Dublin's coast. These towers, modeled and named after a similar defensive tower at Cape Mortella in Corsica, were built in 1804 to withstand a Napoleonic invasion that never materialized.

Joyce set the opening chapter of *Ulysses* in the Sandycove tower, where he lived for a week in 1904 with his friend Oliver St. John Gogarty, whom he later immortalized and mercilessly portrayed in his masterpiece as the flippant Buck Mulligan. Sandycove has since become a mecca for Joyce enthusiasts, and today the ever-growing collection of Joycean memorabilia at the tower—letters, manuscripts, paintings, photos, rare and early editions of the author's work, his guitar, piano, waistcoat, and walking stick—is viewed by thousands of visitors each year.

Like many places on this stretch of coastline, Sandycove is a popular spot for windsurfing, canoeing, and water-skiing. Year round there are frequent aquatic displays of a different sort at the renowned Forty Foot bathing place, a secluded and picturesque seawater retreat for hardy swimmers. The Forty Foot was until quite recently the exclusive preserve of male bathers, many of whom enjoy swimming and sunbathing in the nude. The advent of the feminist movement, however, inevitably brought a determined invasion of this bastion of male chauvinism by some activists.

Dalkey

Dalkey, farther down the coast from Sandycove, is a place of weathered old stones, a village with a Continental flavor because of its narrow streets and fine villas. The old stones are evident in the main street at **Archibold's Castle**, a reminder that Dalkey was once a walled Medieval town designed to persuade the warlike O'Toole and O'Byrne clansmen outside that the garrison inside was stronger in number than it really was. Across the street from the castle is a restored 16th-century castellated stone house that is now the Town Hall. Then there are the stones of the seventh-century **St. Begnet's Church** on Dalkey Island, an example of early Irish ecclesiastical architecture; the massive shards of granite that hem in and seem to dwarf tiny Coliemore Harbour; and the stones of neighboring Bullock Harbour and castle. On the slopes of Dalkey Hill—great views here of the entire sweep of Dublin Bay, Dublin, and distant Howth—is **Torca Cottage**, where Shaw resided as a boy. (He claimed later that he was "a product of Dalkey's outlook.") Dalkey Hill is connected by a saddleback ridge to nearby Killiney Hill, both laid out as a public park complete with nature trail, the remains of an ancient church, and the prehistoric arrangement of stones known as the Druid's Chair. Killiney Hill affords similarly fine views of Killiney Strand, Bray Head, and, inland, the Dublin and Wicklow mountains.

Small boats are available at Bullock and Coliemore harbors for the sea angler. Off Dalkey Island and the Muglin rocks (where, at one time, the bodies of pirates hung in chains and clanked their ominous warning to other nautical lawbreakers) there is fishing for coalfish, pollack, tope, skate, and conger. Farther out, on the Burford and Kish banks, blond and thornback ray, turbot and brill, plaice and dab are among the more common species taken on the hook. In fact, the whole coastal area from Dún Laoghaire (where fishing from the rocks and piers is free) to Killiney and the County Wicklow resort town of Bray (where boats may be hired) abounds in bass, flounder, codling, and sea trout.

Bray

The massive promontory of **Bray Head** covers the southern extremity of Dublin Bay. Behind it lies the wild moorlands of the Wicklow Mountains, below it one of Ireland's premier seaside resorts, Bray. From Bray Head the views of the mountains inland, or back toward Killiney, Dalkey Island, and across the bay to Howth, are among the most spectacular on the east coast, while the narrow cliff walk around the shoulder of the Head—precipitously high above the single track of main-line railway, it is not a hike for anyone suffering from vertigo—offers breathtaking views of misshapen crags, coves, and rocks carved out by the eternal tides.

The town of Bray itself is a conglomerate of tiny fishing harbor, holiday resort, shopping center, elegant Victorian and Edwardian terraces and squares, lowly cottages, restaurants, boardinghouses and hotels, ballrooms, discos, and fast-food joints—a hodgepodge of the graceful and the garish, redeemed by a stony beach under a stout sea wall and a broad, mile-long esplanade. Bray is perhaps too near Dublin to be considered a part of County Wicklow (which of course it is), and that proximity to the capital has always made it popular with Dubliners.

Inland from this coastal area—in a rough arc from east to west—lie the mountain hamlets and wooded hills of southern County Dublin, an area of numerous nature trails, forest walks, pony-trekking centers, picturesque golf courses, and secluded picnic sites. All are within an hour's bus journey of the city center (see Getting Around, below).

DUBLIN'S NORTH SIDE

With a few notable exceptions, the city area north of the Liffey offers little of interest in comparison with the South Side. The shift of fashion south across the river inaugurated by the duke of Leinster was followed by a general exodus of the nobility in the wake of the Act of Union (1800), when London became the legislative and social hub of the British Isles. The inevitable result was that the fine Georgian terraces surrounding and radiating from places like Rutland (now Parnell) and Mountjoy squares soon degenerated into Victorian slums, a condition that lasted well into this century. Even today the area has a seedy, run-down appearance despite the best efforts of Dublin Corporation to revitalize it with attractive housing and miniparks.

The area's—and the city's—main street is the north-south **O'Connell Street**, Ireland's best-known thoroughfare. It is the venue for parades, political rallies, and kindred demonstrations, which usually take place outside the historic and impressive **General Post Office**. This building (1816) is, of course, hallowed as the improvised headquarters of the insurgents at the time of the 1916

Rising. It was from the post office portico that Padraig Pearse first read out the words of the Proclamation of the Irish Republic.

O'Connell Street is reputed to be one of the widest main streets in Europe. Statues of famous local sons—Catholic emancipator Daniel O'Connell, labor leader Jim Larkin, temperance monk Father Mathew, parliamentarian Charles Stuart Parnell, et al.—line the center of the thoroughfare, and, together with Clery's department store, Eason's bookshop, British Home Stores, the Gresham and Royal Dublin hotels, and a few remaining Victorian façades, enhance a street that has more or less given up the struggle in the rearguard action against the ravages of hamburger bars, jukeboxes, and fast-food joints. The street's newest statue—a 1988 Millennium presentation to the city by well-known local businessman Michael Smurfit—is an elongated female figure representing the mythical river Liffey and reclining in a bubbling fountain; the wags quickly christened it "the floozie in the Jacuzzi."

The other statues on the street are also not without interest. The quartet of buxom angels seated at the corners of the O'Connell monument contain visible bullet holes in breast, arm, and neck—grim reminders of the 1916 Rising and the fierce street fighting that occurred then and during the subsequent Civil War of 1922 to 1923. At the opposite, or northern, end of the street stands the triangular obelisk of polished Galway stone commemorating Parnell. Emblazoned on the obelisk are Parnell's oft-quoted words, "No man has a right to fix the boundary to the march of a nation," and as one arm of his life-size effigy appears to be pointing directly at the Rotunda Maternity Hospital, the irony of the words is not lost on those Dubliners who are aware that their city has one of the fastest-growing populations in western Europe.

The **Rotunda Hospital** (1752), the first purpose-built lying-in, or maternity, hospital in Europe, was the brainchild of Dr. Bartholomew Mosse, a barber-surgeon who also practiced what was then considered to be the lowly profession of midwifery. Concerned about the high rate of infant mortality and childbirth deaths, Mosse funded his venture by organizing everything from fancy dress balls to concerts and recitals (the premiere of Handel's *Messiah* in the Fishamble Street Music Hall was one such) and by opening first pleasure grounds behind the hospital and later the Rotunda Room (which gives the hospital its popular name) and the Assembly Rooms as income-generating entertainment centers.

Although technically under the same roof, the modern hospital and the former Assembly Rooms are now separate entities—the latter housing the now-closed Ambassador Cinema in the Rotunda Room, the old circular assembly room, and the Gate Theatre in what was the adjoining assembly supper room. The hospital chapel is an exquisite example of Austrian-style Baroque craftsmanship and as such represents Ireland's only essay into that flamboyant rococo genre on such a grand scale, making it one of Dublin's most unusual places of worship. It is open to the public at reasonable hours.

The Rotunda Room was the site of the formation of the modern Irish resistance movement in November 1913, when 4,000 men enrolled at the inaugural meeting of the Irish Volunteers. Little remains of the former pleasure grounds except the excellently maintained Garden of Remembrance (1966), which was built to honor the memory of all those who died in the struggle for Irish independence. Its location has a kind of poignant appropriateness: close to the Rotunda, site of the Volunteers' foundation, and directly on the open space where many of the same volunteers, as rebel prisoners, were stockaded overnight following the surrender that marked the end of the 1916 Rising.

A focal point of the garden is a bronze sculpture by the Irish artist Oisin Kelly, which shows four human figures being transformed into swans (a link with the mythological Children of Lir), symbolizing rebirth and victory. Enclosed by a marble wall at the rear, the Garden of Remembrance contains attractive sunken walkways and a shallow pool. Visitors should note the mosaic of blue-green waves interspersed with weapons from Ireland's Heroic Age (300 B.C.–A.D. 300) at the bottom of the pool; the broken spears recall the ancient Celtic custom of discarding weapons and throwing them into water at the cessation of hostilities.

Close by are the Municipal Gallery of Modern Art (Parnell Square, north side) and the **National Wax Museum** (just around the corner in Granby Row), featuring wax figures of personalities from over 200 years of Irish history: writers, statesmen, sportsmen, and many contemporary world figures.

Charlemont House (1762), the former town house of

the earl of Charlemont, was once regarded as the show-piece of the fashionable Dublin that the duke of Leinster wrenched southward to the Merrion fields. It is now the **Municipal Gallery of Modern Art**, converted to such use in 1908 largely through the generosity of Sir Hugh Lane, a wealthy collector who perished when the *Lusitania* was torpedoed in 1915. Lane's collection of French Impressionists forms the nucleus of the gallery's display, which also includes many 20th-century Irish and European masters, but because of a compromise resulting from a disputed codicil to his will his pictures alternate between galleries in London and Dublin.

Within easy walking distance to the north of the Municipal Gallery is Temple Street and Hardwicke Place, site of **St. George's Church**, which features what is thought by many to be the city's most beautiful and elegant spire (1814). It was at St. George's in 1806 that the duke of Wellington—after a protracted and lackluster engagement—married Kitty Pakenham. The Iron Duke deprecated his Dublin birthplace and denied his Irishness with the remark, "Being born in a stable doesn't make one a horse"—which probably accounts for O'Connell's description of the blunt and unbending old soldier as possessing "all the qualities of a poker except that of its occasional warmth."

Also within easy walking distance—a minute or so from the Wax Museum—is the **Black Church** (St. Mary's Place off Dorset Street), where Dublin urchins, up until the 1960s, ran the "gauntlet of youthhood" by sprinting around its high-railed perimeter on the stroke of midnight, at which hour one was supposed to encounter Satan in person. That deliciously terrifying sprint was mercifully of short duration because the Black Church—like its contemporaneous "pepper canister" cousin St. Stephen's in Mount Street—is built on what might be described as a traffic island. Local lore has it that these Protestant churches of the 1820s were designed and situated this way so that their congregations could easily turn them into defensive fortresses in the event of a popular Catholic uprising. A glance at the high, narrow, musket-slit windows and the slender main door, said to be built to permit the entrance of only a single mounted rider bearing siege provisions, would seem to support the legend. The Black Church, no longer in use as a place of worship, earns its name not from any association with the devil but from the calp stone from which it was built and which turns a blackish hue in the rain.

It is curious that Dublin, arguably the most Catholic capital in Europe, does not possess a Roman Catholic cathedral per se. **St. Mary's Pro-Cathedral**—meaning a kind of stand-in or substitute cathedral—dates from the pre-Catholic Emancipation era of 1815 to 1825, when such churches were generally confined to back streets in a desire to avoid offending the Protestant powers that be with too great a display of confidence or ostentation. To this day, no Roman Catholic archbishop of Dublin has petitioned the pope to revoke the cathedral status of Christ Church, which has belonged to the Church of Ireland, or Anglican Communion, since the Reformation.

The design for the pro-cathedral (in Marlborough Street, which runs parallel to and just to the east of O'Connell Street) was submitted by a brewer named Sweetman who had no formal training as an architect and who worked on its detailed plans in Paris while serving 18 years of political exile for his part in planning the events leading to the 1798 Rising. In 1902 the pro-cathedral's famed Palestrina Choir helped launch the singing career of John McCormack, the tenor who subsequently toured the world and became one of the richest and most successful recording artists of the early phonograph era. The choir can be heard any Sunday morning at the 11:00 mass.

South along Marlborough Street toward the Liffey, at the corner of Lower Abbey Street, stands Ireland's national theatre, the **Abbey**. Opened in 1904 by such stalwarts of the Irish literary and cultural revival as Yeats, Lady Gregory, and Edward Martin, and famous for its production of their early plays and the launching of Sean O'Casey's "triptych" of early 20th-century Dublin revolutionary working-class dramas, *The Plough and the Stars, Juno and the Paycock,* and *The Shadow of a Gunman,* the Abbey's original building was destroyed by fire in the early 1950s. The present plain but ultramodern structure dates from 1966.

The other notable buildings on this side of the Liffey, both on the quays, are Gandon's Custom House and the city's first skyscraper, Liberty Hall, on the former site of the Northumberland Chop House, later headquarters of "Larkin's Union" and the place where the Proclamation of the Irish Republic was printed on the eve of the 1916 Rising, and where the Irish Citizen Army assembled for battle on Easter morning, 1916.

The **Custom House** is partially obscured by the ugly

Loopline railway bridge and is best viewed from George's Quay on the opposite, or south, bank of the river. It stands today almost as much a memorial to political chicanery and property speculation, on the grand 18th-century scale, as to the architectural genius of James Gandon and the sculptural skills of Edward Smyth.

When in the 1770s John Beresford (chief commissioner of revenue) and his landholding crony Luke Gardiner set about wrenching the commercial axis of Dublin from the castle and Capel Street district to the new area in and around the present O'Connell Street, they used the arguments favoring the building of a new customhouse as the means of doing so. There was immediate opposition—parliamentary petitions, complaints, even mob violence—which was just as suddenly replaced by guffaws when it was realized that the Beresford-Gardiner clique had the harebrained scheme of erecting their massive edifice on a quagmire of river mud. But Gandon conceived an ingenious and innovative method of constructing the building's foundations on a vast raft of fir planks. The plan worked, establishing Gandon's reputation beyond all doubt. The decoration of the Custom House also established the reputation of the hitherto unknown Dublin sculptor Edward Smyth, who until then had spent his talents on nothing more exciting than modeling ornaments for chimneypieces and the odd tombstone.

The greatest of all Smyth's achievements (his later work can be seen in the statues surmounting the pediment of the General Post Office and the stone carvings on the Casino in Marino) is reckoned to be the riverine heads, the river gods of Ireland, used as keystones for the arches of the Custom House. There are 14 in all, each emblematic of a major Irish river—though one of them is curiously entitled "The Atlantic"—and distinguishable by means of the produce of their various riverbanks. The Liffey, as Anna Livia Plurabelle, is the only female head. (In Joyce's *Finnegans Wake,* Earwicker's wife, Ann, is symbolized in a dream as Anna Livia Plurabelle, signifying her beauty and plurality, containing the essence of all rivers and all women.)

The Custom House is the gateway to Dublin's dockland and harbor to the east—or, rather, what's left of the old dockland in an age of container traffic and jet travel. The stevedores, bargees, crane drivers, and lightermen have virtually disappeared, and the 27-acre site of derelict warehouses at the Custom House and St. George Docks is the site of the city's most significant development of this century. With 450,000 square feet currently under construction and another 750,000 earmarked for further phases, development of Dublin's International Financial Services Centre is ahead of schedule. To date more than 150 companies have applied to set up in the IFSC, and many senior foreign financiers are already in Dublin to set up an eventual pool of 2,500 banking, brokerage, and insurance executives and an expected total workforce of about 7,000 people. The accompanying salaries and lifestyles—and the commercial and cultural activity emanating from such an influx—is expected to have a considerable impact on many aspects of Dublin life, and, by regenerating the use of prime, serviced land on the north quays, to reverse decades of neglect and decay. In addition to the huge financial service center and offices the site will include apartments, shops, an art gallery, a riverfront luxury hotel, and a multipurpose convention center-cum-leisure area. Some existing cranes, hoists, capstans, cobbles, cut stone segments, and brickwork will be retained to maintain the original character of the district.

Dublin's extensive harbor dates from the 18th century, when a "ballast of stones" was built to confine the sprawling river and create today's quays. In 1800 Captain William Bligh, of *Mutiny on the Bounty* notoriety, carried out a detailed survey of the mouth of the river and made certain valuable recommendations.

The North Side Suburbs

Dublin's North Side inner suburbs contain the Botanic Gardens (Glasnevin), the Casino (Marino/Donnycarney), St. Anne's Park (Raheny/Dollymount), and Bull Island.

The **Botanic Gardens** date from 1795, a time when the curative properties of many plants were recognized by the medical profession and accordingly cultivated. The gardens' layout is formal and orderly, with 20,000 different varieties of plants, rare shrubs, and trees (the giant California redwood is one). There are separate gardens for roses and vegetables as well as individual sections for dwarf conifers, cacti, Oriental shrubs, houseplants, and so forth. The magnificent curvilinear range of glasshouses dates from the mid-19th century, when the gardens shared in the great discoveries brought back from voyages to every corner of the globe, and when Dublin's Botanic Gardens were noted for such fine achievements as the earliest reported attempt to raise orchids from seed. Take bus 13 or 19 (from O'Connell Street), 34 or 34A (from Middle Abbey Street).

The **Casino** (1762–1771; restored in 1984) is acknowledged to be one of the finest examples of Palladian architecture in Europe. Lord Charlemont, an aesthete who (in Macaulay's words) "gave the tone to the Society of the age," returned from his grand tour of Europe determined to build a palatial villa with a gallery to house his priceless collection of paintings and to have its accompanying gardens set off with a temple, or "casino," such as he had seen in Italy. The design was entrusted to Sir William Chambers, the leading Palladian expert of the day.

The result was a delightful masterpiece containing a subtle optical illusion: Viewed from a distance the Casino seems small, pretty, and one-roomed, whereas in fact it has three stories, 16 rooms, and such trick features as balustrades concealing the upper windows and classical urns serving as chimneys. The cost of building the Casino—and also that of the now demolished Marino House, of which the masons estimated each carved stone at "the value of a townland"—crippled Lord Charlemont's estate. Visitors journeying by bus to the Casino should take an upstairs right-hand window seat to try to catch a glimpse, too, of Marino Crescent, at the corner where the bus turns from Fairview into the Malahide road. Once known locally as "Ffolliot's Revenge," the crescent was built by a painter of that name, who, having some disagreement with Lord Charlemont, built this row of houses in order to effectively shut out the view of the sea from Marino House. Ffolliot's masterstroke of spiteful revenge was to build the rear of the crescent-shaped terrace of houses—and therefore the view presented to Lord Charlemont's outraged eye and aesthetic sensibilities—as a terrible hodgepodge of asymmetrical chimneys, crooked roof lines, unaligned windows, and jutting and irregular outhouses. Take bus 42 or 43 (Beresford Place, opposite the Custom House lawn) or 20A, 20B, or 24 (Eden Quay).

St. Anne's Park, formerly owned by the Guinness family, has a mile-long, tree-lined drive leading to the spot on which the Guinness mansion once stood. There are now playing fields, wooded walks, a pond, a number of "follies" (those 18th- and 19th-century minitowers, obelisks, temples, and gazebos with which the aristocrats and nouveau riche of the era vied with each other), and an internationally renowned rose garden. Take bus 29A or 30 from Lower Abbey Street.

Bull Island (or Dollymount Strand, as it is popularly known), with its miles of sand dunes and gently sloping beach, is the seaside area most frequented by Dubliners. In 1981 UNESCO designated it Ireland's first Biosphere reserve (one of only 220 such nature reserves in the world, along with places such as Yellowstone National Park in the United States and La Camargue in southern France). Greater Dublin, in fact, is probably unique among the metropolitan areas of western Europe in that it includes within its boundaries two extensive wildlife sanctuaries, Bull Island and the much smaller South Side **Booterstown Marsh**. These provide roosting areas for thousands of birds that use the mud flats of Dublin Bay as a source of food, and have one of the greatest densities in Europe of overwintering waders and wildfowl. Bird watchers are at their busiest in the winter months, when about 30,000 birds of various species settle on the mud flats after migrating from the Arctic.

Bull Island—actually a constantly growing, low-lying sand spit of about 3,469 acres—is linked to the mainland by an 80-year-old open-latticework wooden bridge, and, a kilometer (half a mile) north of it, a modern four-lane causeway road. A new interpretive and exhibition center on the island end of the causeway road acts as a kind of watchtower for the region and, in addition to providing information leaflets, videos, and exhibitions, has facilities for the study of the flora and fauna of the island. Here, less than 3 km (2 miles) from the center of a modern capital city, are more than 30 types of grass and vegetation, almost every form of indigenous salt-marsh and sea creature, plus mainland animals such as the rabbit, hare, rat, field mouse, and the occasional fox, stoat, pygmy shrew, and badger. Many land birds—owls, kestrels, sparrow hawks, peregrines, and raptors—can also be seen, with increasing frequency.

NORTH COUNTY

North of Phoenix Park is the **Dunsink Observatory** (1785), one of the world's oldest astronomical/meteorological research centers, with a small collection of exhibits relating to astronomy and famous personalities of the astronomical world, including William Rowan

Hamilton (1805–1865). As Astronomer Royal of Ireland he was its first director and the first-ever Foreign Associate of the American National Academy of Sciences (1863). The observatory is open on the first and third Saturday of each month from September to March. Admission is by ticket only; for information, Tel: (01) 38-79-11 or send a note specifying the date you want to visit and a stamped, self-addressed envelope to the Secretary, Dunsink Observatory. (There is no charge.) Take bus 40A from Parnell Street.

Continuing in a rough west-to-east arc: The **Boot Inn**, behind Dublin Airport, has a skull-scraping low ceiling and old oak bar and, outside, the ancient mounting stone where bygone boozing pals helped the highwaymen Jack Clinch and Collier the Robber into the saddle. Claiming to be Ireland's oldest inn (1604), it's still a fine pub, with good grub. Take bus 60 from Eden Quay.

About 2 km (1 mile) to the north, on the main Belfast motorway, is **Swords**, the overnight resting place of the slain Brian Boru after the Battle of Clontarf, with its 13th-century castle and its round tower slap up against the square tower of a 14th-century Norman church. Take bus 33, 41, or 41B from Eden Quay. Farther north is **Lusk** (more round towers, plus a "rural life" museum) and the seaside resort of **Rush** with its Good Old Days exhibition bringing alive the folk life of the last century. Take bus 33 from Eden Quay). Finally, at Donabate, there's the stately **Newbridge House** (1740s), with its ornate Red Drawing Room (unaltered in furnishings, paintings, and drapes since 1820), its magnificent kitchen displaying the full range of cooking and household appliances of three centuries, and its courtyard exhibiting a representative selection of horse-drawn carriages, including Lord Chancellor "Black Jack" Fitzgibbon's magnificent state coach of 1790. Take bus 33B from Eden Quay or the outer suburban train from Connolly Station.

Southeast of Donabate on the sea about 16 km (10 miles) from the city center is the pretty village-cum-dormitory suburb of Malahide, and to the south and at the head of Dublin Bay just east of Bull Island is the Howth Peninsula. The former, a wildlife sanctuary, features a sea estuary providing excellent and safe sail training; the latter has steep old streets and a fair-sized harbor. Both possess perfectly preserved and romantically storied castles. The outer suburban railway runs from the city center to Malahide, Donabate, and points farther north, such as the steadily developing dormitory suburbs growing up around the former rural and fishing villages of Rush, Skerries, Gormanston, and Balbriggan. DART goes from the center up to Howth.

Malahide

The oldest part of **Malahide Castle** dates from about 1174, when the surrounding countryside was seized by the Norman knight Richard Talbot in the second wave of the Norman invasion of Ireland.

First as a graceless defensive tower, then with the additions of battlemented walls and turrets to awe the natives and to command a wide view of the sea, and later as a stately mansion with a mock-Gothic porch, Malahide Castle remained in the continuous possession of Richard Talbot's heirs and descendants for 800 years (the last Lord Talbot died in 1973). It is everything a castle should be: impressively old, picturesque, historic—and haunted. The spectral form of Puck (a dwarfish Medieval family retainer) roams the castle's passageways, and in the past his nocturnal appearances were said to presage a death in the Talbot family. A somewhat more romantic ghost is that of the White Lady, who is reputed to step out of her portrait in the great hall and to glide about the dark corridors at night.

In the 1640s the castle was briefly occupied by Oliver Cromwell and his Roundhead officers, and it figured prominently in the later Williamite wars. The castle, which was acquired by the state and which now houses the **National Portrait Gallery**, possesses a wealth of historical, architectural, and artistic items. The splendid Banqueting Hall dates from 1475, the wainscoted Oak Room from the 17th century, the Small Drawing Room from about 1750, and the Large Drawing Room from the early 19th century. The castle is set in some 260 acres of picturesque wooded grounds. The castle parklands also contain the Fry Model Railway (a large working model), exotic gardens, and a cottage museum maintained and staffed on a voluntary basis by members of the Old Malahide Society. The museum's exhibits include numerous artifacts from local archaeological digs, including the second-oldest stone axhead ever discovered in Ireland, dating from 2000 B.C.

About 5 km (3 miles) south of Malahide (on the main

Dublin road) is **St. Doulagh's,** a charming, stone-roofed ninth-century church claiming to be the oldest still in use in Ireland (take bus 42 or 43 from Beresford Place, opposite the Custom House lawn).

Howth

The area of Howth, southeast of Malahide, is a treasure house of legend, myth, and history. At the dawn of Irish history, the Parthalons and the Firbolg peoples lived on this peninsula, mining for copper, until they were conquered over the course of the fifth to first centuries B.C. by the Celtic Gaels, who, with their great iron swords, were not long in hacking through the light copper-made weapons of the Firbolg. Criomthain, the first Gaelic chieftain of the locality (a cairn on the summit is said to cover his remains), had his fortress near the site of the present Bailey lighthouse. From here he sailed with his warriors to Roman Britain to pillage and to do battle, returning with vessels laden with plunder and slaves. Finn mac Cumhail's band of Celtic warriors, the legendary Fianna, ever on the lookout for approaching war vessels, had a military post here in ancient times; the summit commands an extensive view not only of Dublin Bay and the Wicklow Mountains but also of the peaks of the Mournes more than 60 miles to the north and, in favorable conditions, the distant Welsh mountains across the Irish Sea.

From this summit were first glimpsed the dreaded Viking longships of the eighth century. For more than two centuries these northern pirates plundered Ireland and in the process established their colonies along the coast in places like Howth. They in turn watched fearfully as the mail-clad Norman horsemen rode out from Dublin—a new breed of ruthless adventurers, aristocratic in their pretensions, skilled in the arts of the new warfare—led by the fearless Sir Almeric Tristram. With his men-at-arms and bowmen, Sir Almeric slaughtered the Norsemen of Howth near a brook on the hillside that still bears the awesome name of the Bloody Stream. When the lands of Howth, thus acquired by the sword, were confirmed by England's King John, Sir Almeric thereupon assumed the surname St. Lawrence, the name borne by his descendants at Howth to this day.

The splendid **Howth Castle** of his descendants, 15 minutes from the DART station or the number 31 bus stop, is a Norman keep consisting of battlements flanked by towers with some 18th-century additions and modifications. Its armory contains Sir Almeric's massive two-handed sword, an 800-year-old weapon he brought from a shrine in Normandy for the purpose of wresting half an Irish county from its war-like inhabitants. The grounds of the castle—famous for their 2,000 species of rhododendrons—are equally a reminder of Howth's turbulent past. A dolmen there is said to be the burial place of Aideen, who died of grief when she learned of the death of her princely husband, Oscar, slain in battle in A.D. 248. And because the gates of the castle were once locked against the Gaelic pirate-queen Grace O'Malley (who sought shelter and sustenance after a stormy sea voyage from England), she later kidnapped the son and heir of the St. Lawrences and held him prisoner until the lord of Howth gave a written pledge never to close the gate again at suppertime. This condition was observed faithfully by generations of St. Lawrences for more than 200 years, and then was modified by the present custom of always setting an extra place at the dinner table for any "unexpected guest."

The castle's present occupant, Christopher Gaisford St. Lawrence, is a descendant in the female line of the original Sir Almeric and thus represents the present generation of a family that has played a central role in the history of the Howth Peninsula for more than 800 years. He has opened up the estate—but not the castle—to the public with a 31-room hotel, the **Deer Park**, and an 18-hole golf course, both in picturesque settings and offering magnificent views out over the isle of Ireland's Eye toward the Mountains of Mourne. (See Accommodations, below, for more information on the Deer Park Hotel.)

A mile northeast of Howth Harbour—and forming a natural breakwater—lies the picturesque and uninhabited island of **Ireland's Eye**, about 60 acres of rocky, mountainous land mostly covered by tall ferns and with only two buildings: a deserted Martello tower and the ruins of Saint Nessan's sixth-century monastic church. Boat trips from Howth Harbour to the island in summertime have always been popular with day visitors from the city, as has been fishing from the harbor piers or waiting for the herring boats to come in with their catch on Thursday evenings.

The footprint of King George IV can still be seen on the jetty at the end of Howth's west pier, where he landed unexpectedly in 1821, much to the surprise of the local fisherfolk—and to the chagrin of the civic dignitaries and populace of Dún Laoghaire, on the southern side of Dublin Bay, who had been expecting him and who had provided a brand-new royal slipway, a band, a pavilion, a guard of honor, and countless flags and buntings. (He made amends a month later at the conclusion of his visit by departing from Dún Laoghaire, allowing the citizens to rename their harbor village Kingstown and to erect a George IV Testimonial Obelisk, which Thackeray later described as "hideous . . . an obelisk stuck on four fat balls and surmounted with a crown on a cushion . . . the latter were not bad emblems perhaps of the monarch in whose honor they were raised." The obelisk can still be seen at Dún Laoghaire, minus one of its balls, the result of a Republican bomb attempt to remove this royal reminder.)

Musts in Howth are: the fishing fleet (Thursday evenings); the new Marina and Yacht Club House; the cliff walks from Balscadden to the Bailey lighthouse; Howth's Tram and Transport Museum (Howth Castle Estate; for information contact M. Corcoran, Tel: 01-47-56-23, or Liam Kelly, Tel: 01-48-08-31); boats for hire and fishing parties, Laurence Hudson, East Pier, Tel: 32-42-55; and the **Abbey Tavern**, Abbey Street, with its warm turf fires, original stone walls, flagged floors, and gaslights. The Abbey Tavern specializes in fish dishes and traditional ballad entertainment nightly. Reservations are essential; Tel: (01) 39-03-07.

St. Mary's Abbey (14th century) in Howth Village, though roofless, is still a reasonably well-preserved ruin containing the altar tomb (1462) of Sir Christopher St. Lawrence and his wife, Anne. The abbey was once also used by smugglers for storing their contraband.

GETTING AROUND
Simple—just walk.

Not from Dublin Airport or the ferry terminals, of course; there are bus and train link services to those two Dublin gateways from the city center. There is bus service between the center and Dublin Airport approximately every 25 minutes from Busaras, the central bus station in Store Street. The 41A Dublin city bus service also runs between Eden Quay (off O'Connell Street on the north bank of the river) and the airport. There is taxi service, but unfortunately it can be a shock to the purse when you look and sound like a foreigner fresh off the plane. Any taxi you use should have a meter. The fare from the airport to the city center should be about £10 to £12.

Though the city center is best seen on foot, you can also travel by public transport, rent a car, or rent a bicycle—the last for the city area, perhaps, and a car when you intend to move farther afield into the countryside. You can get details of both from tourist information offices. Car-hire (rental) firms, as usual, have desks at the airport. Note that signposting in Dublin city leaves a lot to be desired, so drive with a navigator and a good map.

CIE (Coras Iompair Eireann) is the umbrella semi-state body for three transport companies: **Dublin Bus** (serving Dublin; Tel: 01-73-42-22), Bus Eireann, a.k.a. **Irish Bus** (serving provincial areas from Dublin; Tel: 01-36-61-11), and **Irish Rail**, including DART suburban rail (Tel: 01-36-62-22). Hours for all three information offices are 9:00 A.M. to 7:00 P.M. weekdays and 10:00 A.M. to 7:00 P.M. on Sundays and holidays. Timetables, including details of money-saving commuter tickets, can be purchased from newsagents and bookshops.

Bus drivers won't be too impatient if you don't have the exact change on entry, or if you aren't sure where you are going. However, look closely at the numbers on the stop and ask someone in line, if possible. Destinations (and numbers) are usually written in Irish and English on the bus itself. Don't rely on the service running on time; it won't. Depending on your destination, the fare will range between 50p and 95p, although these fares are expected to increase in the near future.

The efficient DART suburban rail service, which runs from 6:30 A.M. to 11:30 P.M., goes overland around Dublin Bay, linking Howth on the North Side to Bray on the South Side, via the city center. A special Dublin Explorer ticket that leaves you change out of a £10 note offers unlimited bus and rail (including DART) transport in Dublin city *and* county within a 20-mile radius. Special concessionary tickets on bus and train services are worth inquiring about at the Dublin Tourism Office, 14 Upper O'Connell Street (Tel: 01-74-77-33), as terms and rates can vary from year to year. Opposite the tourism office at 59 Upper O'Connell Street is the Dublin Bus office, where you can make reservations for city or south and north Dublin coastal tours that run in open-deck buses during the summer (Tel: 01-73-42-22). If you intend to travel out of the city, the Irish Rail/Irish Bus Rambler ticket is a very good value, allowing you unlimited travel by rail, express buses, and local services for £75 for 8 days or £110 for 15 days.

Getting out of Dublin

Apart from the DART and coastal commuter train stations—Connolly Station (Amiens Street), Tara Street, and Pearse Street are the main ones—the two main railway stations linking Dublin to the rest of the country are **Heuston Station** off Parkgate Street in the west and, again, **Connolly Station** on Amiens Street.

There are interconnecting buses between Connolly and Heuston stations, and from the latter to the city center (by O'Connell Bridge) or to Busaras, the central provincial bus station in Store Street. For special excursions and weekend tours, inquire at the Dublin Tourism Office on Upper O'Connell Street or phone Irish Bus and Irish Rail (see above for the numbers).

ACCOMMODATIONS

A well-known London art critic came over to Ireland a few years ago to give a lecture in Trinity College, Dublin. An Irish friend recommended that she and her husband stay in the Royal Hibernian Hotel in Dawson Street, as she was on an expenses-paid trip. Later the friend asked her what she thought. Her reply was ecstatic—not because of the luxurious rooms, the silver service, or the fact that her presence was mentioned in the Social and Personal column of *The Irish Times* the following day. Rather, what tickled the art critic was the advice that she and her husband received when ordering sandwiches at midnight. The obliging waitress offered a choice of ham, cheese, beef, or chicken. "Oh, and there's turkey," the young woman added. The couple ordered turkey, and the waitress protested. "You see," she explained to them, "if you order chicken, you are going to get turkey anyway. And chicken's a lot cheaper."

It's that sort of thoughtful touch that has given Irish hospitality a good name abroad. Sadly, the Royal Hibernian Hotel has been demolished and Dublin has taken on some of that impersonal air that you might find in any European city. *Some,* anyway. Dublin accommodation may be expensive, but it still has a charming informality about it.

Basically there are two types: hotels and guesthouses. Hotels, generally providing meals as well as sleeping quarters and bar service, are graded by Bord Failte, the Irish Tourist Board, into A*, A, B*, B, and C. Guesthouses vary from the purpose-built to the period-style residences, their main attraction being the personal attention and informal atmosphere therein. Bord Failte also grades guesthouses into A, B*, B, and C. To find out precisely what these gradings mean, consult the *Guest Accommodation* guide published annually by Bord Failte, which can be purchased from most of their information offices or direct from Bord Failte, Baggot Street Bridge, Dublin 2, Ireland; Tel: (01) 76-58-71 or 61-65-00. This guide, which is simply a list, not a critical review, also gives rates for those hotels and guesthouses that offer room only or bed-and-breakfast, while reserving another section for a scale of maximum charges for overnight and inclusive accommodation.

Two things to note: There is in general a big jump between first- and third-class hotel accommodation. Staying in Dublin can be expensive, by European standards at least. Lack of competition here, especially during off-season, can be blamed for the fact that even less-central premises will happily charge you £40 a night, and more.

Bord Failte has a Central Reservation Service for booking accommodations at the Dublin Tourism Office at 14 Upper O'Connell Street, Dublin 1 (Tel: 01-74-77-33; Telex: 32462; Fax: (01) 78-62-75—for bookings with Access, MasterCard, and Visa). Bord Failte also has a desk at Dublin Airport, and there are regional tourism offices throughout the country. **The Hidden Ireland** is a private organization offering accommodations in private country houses that possess architectural character and merit (and, they say, owners to match); Tel: (01) 68-64-63; Fax: (01) 68-65-78. You may also book directly or through your travel agent, of course, or through the nearest Irish Tourist Board office in your country.

First of all, decide where you want to be: Dublin is not a sprawling city, and the suburbs are within easy reach. Therefore, if you have a car or if you yearn for more relaxed surroundings, there are a number of competitively priced hotels and guesthouses out there.

Note that the South Side area is in demand during the Royal Dublin Society's Spring Show in May and the Horse Show in August; weekends of international rugby matches can also be hectic.

Tipping is low in Ireland, at 10 percent. Before booking, check that your hotel doesn't run discos and conferences too frequently for your comfort. And be prepared for the hearty Irish breakfast of juicy pork sausages and

rashers (bacon), fried eggs, and tasty black pudding—
and good strong tea that you could trot a horse and four
over.

The hotels and guesthouses discussed below are generally presented from the most expensive to the least. Note
that the rate ranges given here are *projections* for the low
and high seasons in 1992; for up-to-the-minute rate information it is always wise to telephone before booking.
Unless otherwise indicated, rates are per person sharing
and do not include meals or service.

City Center and Immediate Environs

Within the city center itself, the **Shelbourne Hotel** on St.
Stephen's Green has to be one of the most elegant
accommodations—and most expensive. Looking out
onto landscaped parkland that was donated to the capital
by the Guinness family, it is within a few minutes' walking
distance of shops, theaters, and the important sights. Politicians fresh from Dáil Eireann down in Kildare Street
frequent the bar; it has a fine restaurant, and afternoon
tea in the high-ceilinged parlor overlooking the Green is
an experience.

27 St. Stephen's Green, Dublin 2. Tel: (01) 76-64-71;
Telex: 93653; Fax: (01) 61-60-06. £75.

The **Hotel Conrad** on Earlsfort Terrace, off St. Stephen's Green, is part of the Hilton group and priced
accordingly. It's convenient to city center, and the National Concert Hall is within whistling distance.

Earlsfort Terrace, Dublin 2. Tel: (01) 76-55-55; Fax:
(01) 76-54-24; in U.S., (800) HILTONS; in Canada, (800)
268-9275. £71.50–£75.

The **Westbury Hotel**, in Clarendon Street, west of
Grafton Street, is one of the city's most luxurious hotels,
with spacious bedrooms of mahogany and brass. Its elegant upper foyer of marble, wood paneling, and Chippen-
dale leads to bars and a restaurant, and is the haunt of
public-relations consultants promoting blockbuster
authors—but even they may find the room rates a mite
expensive.

Grafton Street, Dublin 2. Tel: (01) 679-1122; Telex:
91091; Fax: (01) 679-70-78; in U.S., (212) 838-3110 or
(800) 223-6800. £72.50.

Or perhaps the tree-shaded **Berkeley Court** in Lansdowne Road, Ballsbridge—haunt of film stars, rock stars,
and any other stars that shoot into Dublin—beats the
Westbury to it. This hotel attracts interesting and affluent

guests and is ten minutes away from the center-city bustle in the business and diplomatic area of Dublin. It also has its own restaurant, grill, and bar.

Lansdowne Road, Ballsbridge, Dublin 4. Tel: (01) 60-17-11; Telex: 30554; Fax: (01) 61-72-38; in U.S., (212) 838-3110 or (800) 223-6800. £72.50.

Similarly high on the reputation and price list are **Jury's Hotel and Towers**, which moved from College Green in the heart of the city to Ballsbridge in 1972 and has recently undergone an impressive extension, and the luxurious **Burlington Hotel**, with its brash façade looking out onto Upper Leeson Street. Both—like the Berkeley Court—are south of the Grand Canal and in what in Dublin are called the suburbs, though still within walking distance of the center. They are also expensive, but with special deals for tourists. Both have cabarets in the summer season. The bar at Jury's is very popular among Dubliners, and its 23-hour coffee shop is a regular haunt for night-owls with an appetite.

Jury's Hotel and Towers, Pembroke Road, Ballsbridge, Dublin 4. Tel: (01) 60-50-00; Telex: 93723; Fax: (01) 60-55-40; in U.S., (800) 843-6664; in Canada, (800) 268-1133; in London, (081) 569-5555 or (071) 937-8033; in U.K., (0345) 01-01-01. £60–£87.50. Burlington Hotel, Upper Leeson Street, Dublin 4. Tel: (01) 60-52-22; Telex: 93815; Fax: (01) 60-84-96; in U.S., (212) 593-4220. £45–£54.

Blooms Hotel in Anglesea Street, within spitting distance of Trinity College and behind the Central Bank, is convenient and comfortable. Less expensive than the aforementioned, it is still up there in the "A" category. It has a popular restaurant, and its noisy bar attracts a young after-work clientele on Fridays.

Anglesea Street, Dublin 2. Tel: (01) 71-56-22; Telex: 31688; Fax: (01) 71-59-97; in U.S., (212) 545-2222 or (800) 223-0888. £50–£55.

The **Gresham Hotel** on O'Connell Street on the North Side, also central, has been graced by the likes of Ronald Reagan, General Eisenhower, Elizabeth Taylor, Marlene Dietrich, and Danny Kaye. Founded in 1817 and rebuilt after damage in the 1916 Rising, it retains some Old World style, despite recent refurbishment.

23 Upper O'Connell Street, Dublin 1. Tel: (01) 74-68-81; Telex: 32473; Fax: (01) 78-71-75; in U.S., (800) 221-4832. £50–£55.

Buswell's, close to the Irish parliament in Molesworth Street south of Trinity College, is very cozy and genteel, with a loyal political clientele and a family-run atmosphere.

25–26 Molesworth Street, Dublin 2. Tel: (01) 76-40-13; Telex: 90622; Fax: (01) 76-20-90. £39–£41.

The **Clarence Hotel** on Wellington Quay, overlooking the Liffey, has been a favorite with Irish visitors to the capital for many years. Within sight of the Ha'penny Bridge, it has a Regency air and a friendly atmosphere. Not what you would call elegant or luxurious, but homey. It has two restaurants and bars and is very close to the Olympia Theatre and the Project Arts Centre behind.

6–8 Wellington Quay, Dublin 2. Tel: (01) 77-61-78; Telex: 90710; Fax: (01) 77-74-87. £32, breakfast and service included.

The **Harcourt Hotel** on Harcourt Street is close to St. Stephen's Green and the city center. Reasonably priced, it is popular with jazz aficionados on Sunday evenings.

60 Harcourt Street, Dublin 2. Tel: (01) 78-36-77; Fax: (01) 78-36-77. £27.50, breakfast and service included.

The **Mount Herbert** on Herbert Road, Ballsbridge, and the **Kilronan House Hotel** on Adelaide Road, near the National Concert Hall south of St. Stephen's Green, are also well regarded. Both are less expensive than center-city competitors. The Mount Herbert was once the home of a lord and is popular with visitors from Northern Ireland during Horse Show Week and during international rugby matches in the Lansdowne Road stadium just around the corner.

Mount Herbert, Herbert Road, Ballsbridge, Dublin 4. Tel: (01) 68-43-21; Fax: (01) 60-70-77. £16–£21. Kilronan House, 70 Adelaide Road, Dublin 2. Tel: (01) 75-52-66; Fax: (01) 78-28-41. £26–£30, breakfast included.

Such are Dublin hotel price rates that it is good to know about such less expensive alternatives as hostels. **An Oige's Dublin International Youth Hostel** at 61 Mountjoy Street on the North Side (Tel: 01-30-17-66) has cheap dormitory-style accommodations. From £8.50 for IYHA members to £9 for non-members, breakfast included. The **Dublin Tourist Hotel** at 2–5 Frenchman's Lane, also on the North Side, is next to the central bus station at Store Street, and offers dormitory-, double-, or single-room accommodations in a converted wine warehouse at very low rates. £4.75–£12. Tel: (01) 36-38-77. **Kinlay House** at 2–12 Lord Edward Street, on the South Side just up from the Olympia Theatre and close to Christ Church Cathedral and Viking Dublin, offers hostel-style

bed-and-breakfast and is highly recommended. Tel: (01)
679-6644; Fax: (01) 679-7437. £7.

Farther Out

The **Orwell Lodge Hotel** in Orwell Road, in the leafy,
middle-class suburb of Rathgar (south of St. Stephen's
Green but too far to walk to the city center), is competitively priced, with a good restaurant. You can stroll along
the River Dodder nearby, and it's only a short bus ride
into town.

77 Orwell Road, Rathgar, Dublin 6. Tel: (01) 97-72-56;
Fax: (01) 97-99-13. £24, breakfast included.

Overlooking Dublin Bay, the suburb of Dún Laoghaire
on the South Side has some fine hotels and guesthouses—
as befits its former name of Kingstown—such as the **Royal
Marine Hotel**, which combines Victorian elegance with
20th-century comforts. It commands an imposing view of
the ferry port and the yachting activity. There's plenty of
walking out on the extensive piers, built by convicts to
shelter the 240-acre harbor.

Marine Road, Dún Laoghaire, County Dublin. Tel: (01)
280-1911; Fax: (01) 280-1089. £40–£45.

Howth Harbour, the North Side fishing port, is similarly blessed with the DART suburban railway service and
excellent walks. The comfortable **St. Lawrence**, facing
onto the fishing harbor, and the intimate **Howth Lodge
Hotel** are two good hostelries here.

St. Lawrence Hotel, Harbour Road, Howth, County Dublin. Tel: (01) 32-26-43; Fax: (01) 39-03-46. £31, breakfast
included. Howth Lodge Hotel, Howth Road, Howth,
County Dublin. Tel: (01) 39-02-88; Fax: (01) 32-22-68.
£22.50–£35, breakfast included.

For golfers, the **Deer Park Hotel and Golf Courses** is a
must, a comfortable, modern hotel overlooking Howth
Castle, on extensive grounds. Many of its rooms have
stunning views—on clear days—of the island known as
Ireland's Eye and, beyond, of Lambay Island.

Howth, County Dublin. Tel: (01) 32-26-24; Fax: (01) 39-
24-05. £24.50–£29, breakfast included.

Sutton, with its crossroads at the neck of Howth, is on
the DART route and has the comfortable **Marine Hotel**,
within reach of Bull Island bird sanctuary and—like
Howth—several golf courses. Sutton Cross is famous for
one meteorological statistic: It is said to be one of the
driest points in the country.

Sutton, Dublin 13. Tel: (01) 32-26-13; Fax: (01) 39-04-42. £37–£40, breakfast included.

—Lorna Siggins

DINING

Travel and travellers have been the savior of the Irish restaurateur. Without both, the Irish would still be completely oblivious to the delight of good food. For, apart from the time of the famine that decimated the Irish population in the last century, food has always been plentiful, and we do not really appreciate or, some say, know how to cook the plentiful materials that are around us. But there's still nothing like brown soda bread; the Irish breakfast of bacon, eggs, and sausages is a hearty one; and traditional dishes, when cooked properly, are something to be proud of. That's not just Irish stew and bacon and cabbage.

For all that, Dublin has no shortage of restaurants, but eating out is not cheap. Note that "full licence" entitles the restaurant to provide a full range of alcoholic drinks, while "wine licence" means just that alone. New legislation is extending full licensing to more restaurants.

We've taken Dublin by area, rather than by type of cuisine—but you can get a taste of everything here, from Italian to Japanese.

O'Connell Street/Westmoreland Street Area

For breakfast, lunch, or brunch, the **Café Kylemore** on the corner of O'Connell Street and North Earl Street on the North Side has a somewhat Parisian aspect—with bentwood chairs, marble-top tables, large windows, and lots of brass—but with plainer cooking. **Bewley's Oriental Café** on Westmoreland Street on the South Side is one of the three famous coffeehouses in the city center founded by the Quaker Bewley family. It serves a hearty breakfast from 8:15 A.M. Once frequented by James Joyce, it has wood-paneled walls and marble-top tables and is popular with the literati, but it has undergone a few changes since its opening in 1916. Open from 8:00 A.M. to 6:00 P.M. Monday through Saturday and from 10:00 to 5:00 on Sundays. **Middays** in the Peacock Theatre (below the Abbey Theatre) in Lower Abbey Street is a popular self-service lunchtime restaurant, ideal if you are in the area to buy theater tickets. The homemade fare has a healthy vegetarian emphasis. No credit cards.

Off Westmoreland Street, across the Liffey, Temple Bar

(an extension of Fleet Street, past Bewley's side entrance) is the home of two good lunchtime/evening restaurants. The **Pizzeria Italia** at 23 Temple Bar fills up quickly when it opens at noon, and at night the waiter will take your name and point you toward the local pub while you wait. A small high-stool, checkered-tablecloth establishment, it is relatively cheap. Closed Sundays. No credit cards. The **Elephant & Castle**, a little farther up the street, is an American-style restaurant renowned for its healthy portions—the Caesar salad would feed a Roman army! The restaurant is clean, the staff friendly and efficient, the coffee good, and the prices reasonable. Breakfast is served from 8:00 A.M.

College Green West to Christchurch Hill

Behind the Central Bank on the South Side there is a warren of little streets running down to the Liffey, crossing Temple Bar, with lots of interesting shops and places to eat. The **Bad Ass**, 9–11 Crown Alley, has pizzas ranging from "Barely Anufio" to "Muchio Freshio." Loud music, simple decor, bright lights, and very lively.

Rudyards Restaurant and Wine Bar at 15–16 Crown Alley is colonially Kiplingesque, a jazz venue on Saturday nights, and very busy at both lunch and dinner because of its good value. The spinach-stuffed pancakes are in popular demand. **Coffers** at 6 Cope Street is intimate, reasonable—and good for the best of Irish beefsteaks. It's got a "business-lunch" type ambience. (Cope runs parallel to Temple Bar and connects Fownes and Anglsea streets.) For a contrast, try the lunchtime **Well-Fed Café** at the Dublin Resource Centre, 6 Crow Street, adjoining a worker's co-op. Vegetarian fare, including soups, salads, lasagne, and quiche. Cash only.

Tante Zoe's at 1 Crow Street offers Cajun-Creole cuisine, with fish claws 'n' tails as a typical appetizer. Open for lunch and dinner six days, for dinner only on Sundays.

Good for a lunch or evening pizza is **Fat Freddie's** at 20 Temple Lane, off Dame Street. **Little Lisbon**, a Portuguese restaurant at the junction of Dame and Fownes streets, makes the most of Irish fish. You can bring your own wine—unusual for Dublin restaurants. Evenings only; closed Sundays. No credit cards.

Caesar's at 18 Dame Street and **Nico's** at 53 Dame Street are lively Italian restaurants, moderately priced and close to the Olympia Theatre, while the **Lord Edward** at 23 Christchurch Place, named after the Lord Edward Fitzgerald who led the United Irishmen in the abortive 1798 Rising, excels in fish. Lord Edward is quite expensive, but worth it for the service and attention to detail. At **Burdock's**, next door in 900-year-old Werburgh Street, people come from all over Dublin to wait in the rain for a special. Burdock's is a fish-and-chips take-away, one of the best in the city. It's cheap, but may or may not be closed on Tuesdays and Sundays or other days. Don't arrive before 5:00 P.M.

The **Old Dublin** at 90–91 Francis Street is right in the heart of Medieval Dublin, near Dubh Linn (the Black Pool), one of the city's first settlements. The Old Dublin excels in Russian and Scandinavian cuisine; fish is a forte. It's advisable to reserve; Tel: (01) 54-20-28 or 54-23-46. Closed Sundays.

South Great George's Street/Camden Street
The **Marks Brothers** on 7 South Great George's Street on the South Side has some of the best sandwiches in town, and great dishes for vegetarians. Lunch only. Farther south, at 31 Upper Camden Street, **Oisín's Irish Restaurant** serves what one critic describes as "indigenous food": Irish stew, bacon and cabbage, spiced beef, and the infamous Dublin coddle, a mixture of potatoes and other vegetables, sausage, bacon, and additional ingredients, depending on where you eat it. Expect a throat-scorching sup of *poitín,* that devilish Irish firewater, when you arrive. Reservations necessary; Tel: (01) 75-34-33. Closed Sunday and Monday nights.

Grafton Street/Nassau Street
There are plenty of interesting little tributaries off Grafton Street itself. Grafton is a main shopping street and is in effect a southern extension of O'Connell and Westmoreland streets. Starting with Andrew Street, at the Trinity College end, there's the intimate and friendly **Trocadero**, with realistic prices. The "Troc," as it is fondly known among theatergoers and others who like it for its night-owl hours, has an atmosphere described as "stagey"; its walls are festooned with photos of familiar faces from the acting profession. Booking is strongly advised; Tel: 01-77-55-45. Opposite the Trocadero is the **Cedar Tree**, a Lebanese restaurant with a large fountain,

popular with those many Irish who have worked in the Middle East.

The **Old Stand** in Exchequer Street and the **Stag's Head** in Dame Court are two of many pubs in the area known for a good lunch, while the pricey **Radjoot Tandoori** at 26–28 Clarendon Street—near the Westbury Centre—is one of Dublin's finest Indian restaurants. There are plenty of dining spots within and around the Powerscourt Townhouse Centre in South William Street. Try the excellent **Periwinkle** seafood bar tucked away on the ground floor of the Centre, with its sumptuous chowder, for lunch. In Johnston's Court, linking the Clarendon Street entrance to Grafton Street, the **Wildebeest** (formerly known as the Colony) is very "in," serving everything from pasta to steak to fish à la carte at student prices, and with live music at night; open for lunch and dinner Monday through Saturday. The **Cornucopia**, at 19 Wicklow Street, has been awarded the title of best vegetarian restaurant in the country, with a breakfast menu from 8:00 A.M. (Saturdays 9:00 A.M.) that offers vegetarian sausages and scrambled free-range eggs. For those eating on the premises, seating is on cramped stools. Open till 9:00 P.M. six days, closed Sundays.

In Grafton Street itself, there's the refurbished **Bewley's Oriental Café** for breakfast or lunch seven days a week, with a waitress-service mezzanine level overlooking the street and still lots of the favorite sticky buns. **Captain America's**, also in Grafton, was the first of its type to hit Dublin: inexpensive hamburgers, Tex-Mex, and barbeque, with loud music and a fully licensed bar.

Such is the Irish climate that street cafés appear only during warm summer weather, between showers. For a street-side version of Café Costes on the Place des Innocents in Paris, try the **Buttery Brasserie** on the Royal Hibernian Way, which links Dawson Street to Grafton Street via Duke Lane. Full bar, coffee, tea, and lunchtime salads—and it becomes a trendy pub at night.

In Nassau Street along the southern side of Trinity College, the **Kilkenny Kitchen** within the Kilkenny Shop—itself very interesting for regional crafts—is always bustling, daytime only, while the nearby **Coffee Bean** at lunch becomes **Caper's** in the evening, one of the city's finest health food and vegetarian restaurants, specializing in salads, quiches, and lasagne; reasonably priced with a good view of the playing fields in Trinity. Closed Sundays; no credit cards.

St. Stephen's Green Area

It's very difficult to get seats in **Shay Beano** at 37 Stephen Street, between the south end of S. Great George's and William Street, but the restaurant's inexpensive French cuisine is well worth the wait. Close by on Lower Stephen Street is **Fuji**, the newer of Dublin's two Japanese restaurants, which is open seven days. **White's on The Green** (number 119) is a sophisticated "business-lunch" venue with a menu for the adventurous; try the nettle soup, if it's still on. Starched and polished, White's gives elegant attention to detail and is priced accordingly—some will tell you it is one of Dublin's best restaurants. Reservations advisable; Tel: (01) 75-19-75 or 75-11-81. Count Dracula's creator, Bram Stoker, gives his name to the basement establishment at 16 Harcourt Street, off St. Stephen's Green—for the author spent some time in the building. **Stoker's**, open for lunch and dinner Monday through Friday and for dinner only on Saturday and Sunday, is in the moderate price range. **Mitchell's**, in the cellar of its own wine shop in Kildare Street, is an expensive lunch venue for the captains of industry—and of politics, Mitchell's being within spitting distance of the Irish parliament.

Merrion Row/Baggot Street/Merrion Square

The **Grey Door** at 23 Upper Pembroke Street off Baggot Street is a cozy, exquisite dining room within the former drawing room of a Georgian house. It specializes in Russian and Scandinavian cuisine and is quite expensive. Closed Sundays. The new **Lane Gallery Restaurant** at 55 Pembroke Lane, off Pembroke Street, has a creative menu in the French tradition. It's slightly pretentious and pricey, but the food is good for all that. Open Monday through Friday for lunch, Tuesday through Saturday for *dégustation* in the evenings (Tel: 01-61-18-29).

The **Unicorn** at 12 Merrion Court off Merrion Row is a favorite of the aspiring and actual intelligentsia, who also frequent Doheny and Nesbitt's pub nearby. One of Dublin's established Italian restaurants, with a lovely seafood pizza, Unicorn is particularly lively during Saturday lunch hours. Closed Sundays.

Turn down into Merrion Square and to the restaurant within the **National Gallery**; run by Fitzer's of Camden Street, it is excellent for lunch, and also is open until 8:00 P.M. on Thursdays. Closed Mondays.

You may need a map to locate 46 St. James's Place and **Patrick Guilbaud** (first locate St. James's Street, off Lower

Baggot Street). Serving superb French cuisine in a spacious room with natural lighting, the place has received accolades for "supreme excellence." It's pretentious, pricey, and popular with gossip columnists. Closed Sundays. Booking advised (Tel: 01-76-41-92).

Off the Beaten Track

You probably have enough restaurant choices in the city itself to keep you from starving, but a few out-of-the-way spots are worth mentioning if you happen to be in the vicinity.

North Side. Out in the fishing port of Howth at the head of the East Pier, the **King Sitric**, named after the first king of Dublin, has a reputation for seafood, with prices on the high side. It's situated in a Georgian house that was once the home of Howth's harbormaster, and serves such delights as Howth crab and lobster, squid, John Dory, and black sole. The **Abbey Tavern** in the village itself is an Old World tavern with stone walls, flagged floors, Irish music, and sirloin steak for the tourists. It's quite expensive, and reservations are advised; tel: (01) 39-03-07.

South Side. A good Sunday brunch venue is at the **Royal Hospital**, Kilmainham, to the southwest of the city center. The price covers food, music, and a guided tour of the current exhibitions.

In Ballsbridge, if you tire of **Jury's Coffee Dock** (open 23 hours a day in Jury's Hotel, with a standard menu for both meals and snacks and efficient service night and day) there's the elegant and expensive **Kite's** at 15–17 Ballsbridge Terrace, serving Cantonese food. **Le Coq Hardi**, in a Georgian town house at 35 Pembroke Road, is constantly winning awards for its nouvelle cuisine. It combines the best of French and Irish cooking with such dishes as cabbage with quail and chicken and bacon baked in Irish whiskey. Expensive. Tel: (01) 68-41-30.

On the Grand Canal at Portobello near the suburb of Rathmines, **Locks** at 1 Windsor Terrace has made a name for itself as a provincial French restaurant; expensive and highly recommended. Closed Sundays; Tel: (01) 54-33-91. Closer to the bridge linking the suburb of Rathmines to the city, a new and expensive restaurant called **Shannons** has opened in the upwardly mobile area of Portobello Harbour. Shannon's decor was described by the *Irish Times*'s food critic as possessing "glamour without glitz." The same critic found the food to be "unremarkable." Tel: (01) 53-83-52.

Blackrock, a suburb on the South Side coast, can boast the luxury Japanese restaurant **Ayumi-Ya** in Newtownpark Avenue, and the much-praised and imaginative **Park**, serving cosmopolitan fare at a new address on The Mews, 40 Main Street. **Restaurant na Mara** in Dún Laoghaire farther along the coast resides in what was in the 19th century the Kingstown railway terminal building. It's formal and quite expensive, but good for fish. Tel: (01) 280-6767 or 280-0509.

The **Beaufield Mews** in Woodlands Avenue, Stillorgan (off the Dublin–Wicklow road), is ten minutes south of the city. This 18th-century restaurant claims to be Dublin's oldest, and the original cobbled courtyard is sheltered by long-standing trees. Family-owned, Beaufield Mews also has an antiques shop in the loft. It's medium-priced with a European menu. Open Tuesdays to Saturdays, 3:00 to 9:00 P.M. Also in Stillorgan at 4 Lower Kilmacud Road is **Chinese Sichuan**. The only restaurant sponsored by the Chinese government in all of Britain and Ireland, it offers fantastic food, excellent service, and incredible value. Booking advised (Tel: 01-288-4817 or 288-9560); closed Sundays. Next to Chinese Sichuan is **Mr. Hung**, a Thai restaurant opened in 1991 by a Hong Kong restaurateur. It's relatively inexpensive and is open seven days a week. Booking is advisable on weekends; Tel: (01) 288-8727. All three of these restaurants are a taxi ride from the city center.

Really in Wicklow territory, but within driving distance of Dublin—and worth the journey if your credit is good—are **Tinakilly House** in Rathnew (the former home of Captain Robert Halpin, commander of the *Great Eastern,* who laid the first transatlantic cable), with an extensive wine cellar to accompany an imaginative menu; **Hunter's Hotel** in Rathnew, one of Ireland's oldest coaching inns, boasting the best of Irish meat, fish, and vegetables; and, on the way back to town, the Greek-Cypriot **Tree of Idleness** on the seafront in Bray (closed Mondays) for what one critic has described as a "glorious indulgence."

—Lorna Siggins

BARS AND NIGHTLIFE

When Bob Hawke, the Australian prime minister, visited Dublin in 1987, he did not spend every one of his few nights at glittering banquets or shows. This had nothing to do with security. Rather, he gave the security forces a large headache, and lots of overtime pay, when he decided to embark on a tour of Dublin pubs. This, Mr. Hawke recognized, was what the capital was all about.

Despite the stereotype of the drunken redheaded Irishman (with its roots in bigotry), you may spend days in Dublin before encountering an example. In fact, statistics show that Ireland is not a nation of drunkards; it is a nation of pub drinkers.

We are not recommending that you try to take in all 700 or so of Dublin's pubs. The following list is highly selective, and must be, for pubs are a very personal thing. (An earlier section of this chapter provides an overview and highlights of the Dublin pub scene.) By the same "logic" that ignores millions spent on new technology and insists that pulling a pint is *still* an art form, it is often held that the plusher the surroundings the poorer is the porter (a.k.a. Guinness). As for the trend toward pub grub at lunchtime, this is anathema to any midday imbiber, who knows that the barman must not be distracted.

You can usually judge a good premises by the crowd that is in it, rather than by its cleanliness or comfortable decor. Pubs get lively from 9:00 P.M. on, and, under new legislation, "drinking-up" time is now extended to midnight, Mondays through Saturdays between April and October (Sundays, all year, closing is at 11:00 P.M.) and 11:30 P.M. in winter. It also permits full liquor licenses to restaurants. Most people have their "local," where you are expected to join in the chat; you're excused if there's music in session, in which case you may be invited to shake a leg.

You might like to begin on the quays with the oldest pub in Dublin, the **Brazen Head**, at 20 Lower Bridge Street. The site dates as an inn from 1198; the present building is 17th century (15 of the United Irishmen were arrested here in 1798). On a Friday night you may have to struggle to reach the bar, where old copper kettles and bellows hang beside posters for Wills Anchor Navy Cut cigarettes at 5½ old pennies, but there's often good Irish music, an open fire in winter, and that much abused descriptive noun "crack"—untranslatable, with the nearest English word being "fun."

Over on the other side of Bridge Street, past Christ Church Cathedral, is the **Merchant**, where you can watch set dancing, which is undergoing a great revival. Set dancing is not the conventional Irish or *ceili* dancing, but was introduced by the Normans and patronized by the landed gentry. The sets, which vary from county to county, derive from the quadrille, or square dance, with much foreign influence. Adapted to the quicker tempo of Irish reels, jigs, hornpipes, and polkas, set dancing spread—with the help of foreign regiments—throughout 19th-century Ireland. A Tipperary man, Connie Ryan, is credited with its revival. For dates and other venues, check the listings sections in publications like the fortnightly *In Dublin* magazine.

A brisk walk west to **Ryan's** in Parkgate Street, near Heuston Station (but on the North Side) is worth it for the great character and conversation that can be enjoyed here, even if you have to take a taxi back. Note the mahogany and brass fittings, the Victorian design, and the little pigeonholes and tea drawers behind the counter, a legacy from the days when Ryan's was also a grocery. There is now a restaurant here as well. Sadly, the two front snugs—little cubbyholes where women drank in the days when men preferred to have the bar to themselves—have been removed by the owner to make space for more imbibers.

Back in the center of Dublin, on the South Side off Westmoreland Street, the **Palace Bar** at the Bewley's Café end of Fleet Street, and **Bowe's** at the other, are worth their pints. Both there and in the newer **Doyle's** in nearby College Street you might be drinking elbow to elbow with journalists from *The Irish Times*. (It should be noted that Doyle's, which lacks atmosphere, used to be called the Oscar Wilde, but sadly all reference to the Irish writer has been carefully removed by the new proprietor.)

Scribes from *The Irish Press* tend to frequent **Mulligan's** in Poolbeg Street, between Trinity College and the river, not exactly handsome with its strip lighting, but James Joyce was a patron, and Mulligan's, which has changed little since Joyce's death, has maintained a mixed bag of regulars since it first opened—in 1782.

O'Neill's in Suffolk Street off College Green and the **Stag's Head** in Dame Court south off Dame Street nearby are haunts of students from Trinity College, and of academics who can bear the company of their students. Founded in 1770, the latter's stained-glass skylights, wrought-iron chandeliers, and leather upholstery give it much of its character. The **Old Stand** in Exchequer Street, the **International Bar** in Wicklow Street—good for music—and the **Long Hall** in Great St. George's Street are also recommended.

The **Bailey** and **Davy Byrne's**, immortalized by Bloom's patronage in *Ulysses,* are very "in," both on Duke Street off Grafton. Both have a cosmopolitan singles-bar atmosphere; no spitting on the wood and sawdust floor here, thank you. **Kehoe's** on South Anne Street (parallel to Duke) serves what experts say is one of the best pints in town. **Neary's** in Chatham Street off Grafton is a theater pub, close to the Gaiety, and **McDaid's** on Harry Street just to the north is yet another, where playwright Brendan Behan sunk his black (pints). **O'Donoghue's**, where the Dubliners launched their career in folk music, is still a favorite music pub on Merrion Row just east of St. Stephen's Green North, as is **Toner's**, which is believed to be the only public house in Dublin that Yeats ever visited— and he didn't stay long! Up the road farther east in Baggot Street is **Doheny and Nesbitt's**, fashionably known as Nesbitt's, where civil servants, well-known journalists and campaigners, and musicians gather, and where its own "Doheny and Nesbitt School" of economists agonize over the ills of the country.

Back down by the Liffey, in the South Side dockland area of Sir John Rogerson's Quay, the unassuming **Dockers'** pub is a haunt for those seeking a glimpse of the rock band U2 or newer, "rising" bands recording in the nearby Windmill Lane studio. It's about a 15-minute walk from O'Connell Bridge along the south bank of the river toward the estuary and Dublin Bay.

But that is not to say that all the decent pubs are south of the Liffey. Apart from Ryan's, there is also **Kavanagh's** in Aughrim Street, just east of St. Brendan's Hospital, an Old World Dublin pub with plenty of character on the North Side; the **Meeting Place** in Dorset Street, a well-known Irish folk and traditional music venue; and a different **Kavanagh's** in Glasnevin, affectionately known as the "Gravedigger's," at the back gate to Glasnevin Cemetery near the Botanic Gardens. But you have to leave something to the Dubliner. . . .

Dublin is the home of U2, the Hothouse Flowers, Sinéad O'Connor, the Chieftains, and the Dubliners, so the music scene is always fairly lively in the capital. For cabaret there's **Jury's** and the **Burlington** for the unabashed tourist. Many of the jazz, folk, and rock gigs are in pubs or late-night venues like **Mother Redcap's Tavern** on Back Lane, opposite Tailor's Guild Hall, near Christ Church Cathedral, and **Bad Bob's Backstage Bar**, beside the Project Arts Centre in East Essex Street, between Dame Street and Wellington Quay. For dates and details, refer to *In Dublin,* or to *Hot Press,* the fortnightly music paper. The former also carries theater and cinema listings. A particularly noteworthy theater among the many in the city is the new **Tivoli** in the Liberties on Francis Street. The new **Andrew's Lane Theater,** off College Green/Dame Street, is also worth checking out.

And what is there after pub closing time? If nightclubs are your scene, try the big hotels and the **Leeson Street** strip for late-night disco music and wine that can cost an arm, if not a leg. **Suesey Street**, 25 Lower Leeson, and the **Pink Elephant**, South Frederick Street, are among the trendy spots. For many, the Pink Elephant is the place to try to spot U2—music people and people-who-wish-they-were-or-like-to-be-seen-with-music-people are among its clientele. On the Leeson Street strip, nightclubs with ever-changing names are generally located in basements, guarded by big doormen who don't look for a cover charge. The sting is the wine—usually plonky and very pricey from at least £15 a bottle—and the fact that after all that you have to take a taxi home.

For post-nightclub recovery, try **Jury's Coffee Dock,** which is open 23 hours a day, in Jury's Hotel and Towers, Ballsbridge.

—*Lorna Siggins*

SHOPS AND SHOPPING
Aran and tweeds, linen and lace, a bit of Waterford crystal—it is a commonly held belief that that is all visitors are interested in when it comes to buying Irish. We know that this isn't true, or at least that it doesn't have to be. The Irish clothing industry, for example, has undergone a revolution in recent years, and no longer are chunky Aran sweaters and tweed caps for the North American tourist the standard fare. Sweater shops in Wicklow Street, Powerscourt Townhouse Centre, Nassau Street, and beyond have plenty of big, bright, colorful machine-made and hand-knit articles designed with an eye to fashion. Dublin is a walking city—although it won't be for much longer if motorway-mad Dublin city councillors have their way. Though it no longer has its weaver streets and tallow-chandler streets and barber streets (the Guild system finally broke up in 1840, after about 600 years), such is its geographical layout that shopping here becomes an adventure.

Remember that open hours are usually 9:00 A.M. to 5:30 P.M. Monday through Saturday, and until 8:00 P.M. on Thursdays; some shops—apart from weekend markets—are now open on Sundays. For details of VAT (value-added tax) refunds, and a guide to sizes, weights, and measures, ask for a Bord Failte shopping brochure, which also lists shopping venues by item.

Grafton Street Area

Grafton Street, Dublin's version of Bond Street, and named after an 18th-century viceroy, is closed to automobiles. It is famous for its century-old department stores **Switzers** and **Brown Thomas**, both of which are good for tweeds. **Weir's Jewellers** (expensive) was founded by a Glasgow goldsmith in 1869. Principles, Benetton, and Laura Ashley are among the international outlets that have opened here in recent years. The refurbished Bewley's Oriental Café on Grafton, dating from 1927, is famous for its sticky buns and Jersey milk; many cups of its coffee have been sipped by Dublin's cognoscenti.

Off Grafton, Wicklow Street, characterized by leather, sheepskin, and shoe shops, winds on up to South Great George's Street, where there is another branch of Bewley's. You can get your ears pierced, have keys made, or buy antique clothing in the beanbag-, pets-, and book-filled **South City Markets** arcade, just off South Great George's Street. Wend your way back down Wicklow Street to South William Street and take the front entrance into the **Powerscourt Townhouse Centre**, built in 1774 for Lord Powerscourt and now sensitively refurbished for commerce. Here you can buy handmade shoes (men's) at Tutty's, or a Persian carpet, or jewelry to match a dress from the major Irish clothing designers. Or eat or drink.

Back on Grafton Street, via Johnson's Court, amble down Duke Street and South Anne Street, havens for antiques and curio hunters. **Cathach Books** at 10 Duke Street has antiquarian printed matter. The **Royal Hibernian Way** links Dawson Street to Grafton Street, via Duke Lane. This sophisticated shopping mall was formerly the site of the much-mourned Royal Hibernian Hotel, demolished in 1984.

The **Westbury Mall**, off Harry Street, adjoins the luxurious Westbury Hotel. Not the place to go looking for your pair of Wellington boots for bog trotting, but there's the **Best of Irish** shop for knitwear, crystal, china, Belleek porcelain, and jewelry. Yet another new shopping mall, the **St. Stephen's Green Centre**, has transformed the more genteel face of the Green, on the corner of St. Stephen's Green West and South King Street.

Walk down Dawson Street, bustling with designer boutiques, passing **Waterstone's** and **Hodges Figgis** (with its excellent Irish section) bookshops on the way. **Fred Hanna's**, another good bookstore around the corner in Nassau Street, also deals in secondhand volumes. Farther along on Nassau you'll find good tweeds, linens, and woollens at **Blarney Woollen Mills** and the **Kilkenny Design Centre**, formerly a state-sponsored outlet for the best of Irish design and workmanship.

If you continue straight east along Nassau Street, with the grounds of Trinity College on your left, you will come to tiny Clare Street and the inimitable **Green's** bookshop, which has two floors full of secondhand books spilling out onto trays in the street, and a post office downstairs to boot.

Also near this area—within walking distance of the National Gallery of Ireland on Merrion Square West—are commercial art galleries, but call ahead to check open hours. The **Gorry Gallery** at 20 Molesworth Street stocks mainly Irish artists of the 18th, 19th, and 20th centuries (Tel: 01-679-5319).

Central Bank Area

Known as Dublin's Left Bank—or Marais for those who know what Paris is like now—the Central Bank area is neither. A warren of streets here lead down to the Liffey on the South Side near the bank, where jewelry, lace, secondhand linen, fireplace surrounds, Victorian dressers, music, and science-fiction books can be rooted out around Crown Alley, Merchant's Arch, Temple Bar, and East Essex Street. In **Rory's Fishing Tackle**, 17A Temple Bar, there's everything from fly rods to flasher rigs, and lots of maggots.

As you walk up College Green toward the Central Bank, look for **Books Upstairs** (opposite Trinity College and the Bank of Ireland) at number 36, open late in the evenings and also Sunday afternoons. Farther up at 56 Dame Street is the **Alchemist's Head** bookstore, for science fiction and the occult.

The **Temple Bar Gallery** and studios at 4–8 Temple Bar welcomes visitors who wish to view some of the city artists' work from 11:00 A.M. to 5:30 P.M. weekdays and from noon to 4:00 P.M. on Saturdays (Tel: 01-71-00-73). Farther up, across Parliament Street, **Cathair Books** at 1 Essex Gate claims to be the city's oldest bookshop—and bookselling here does date as far back as the 1690s. Their stock includes antiquarian and contemporary books, prints, newspapers, and postcards. Walk down Parliament Street away from the Liffey and toward the City Hall and you'll see the **Riverrun Gallery and Restaurant** on your left. The spacious, well-lit restored premises exhibit a good representation of contemporary Irish art. Open from 10:30 A.M. to 5:30 P.M. Monday to Saturday (Tel: 01-679-86-06).

Henry Street District

On the South Side of the Liffey, look for the **Gallery of Photography** at 37 Wellington Quay, which houses exhibitions of international and Irish photography and sells a selection of posters, postcards, prints, and books (Tel: 01-71-46-54). **Robert's Bargain Books**, stocking offbeat Irish and international titles, is a new additon to Crampton Quay alongside **George Webb**'s bookshop—the latter a renowned secondhand dealer, now owned by Hanna's of Nassau Street. North across the Liffey by the Ha'penny Bridge, linking Crampton Quay to Bachelors Walk, antiques shops predominate along the quays. You'll also see **Dublin Woollen Mills**, good for chunky knits, while the **Winding Stair** bookshop beside it, at 40 Lower Ormond Quay, is a heavenly retreat from the city bustle. Named after a poem by W. B. Yeats, it occupies two floors and has a fine selection of rare and secondhand titles in addition to contemporary publications, with poetry a specialty. Very lively, with coffee and homemade cakes for browsers.

Crossed by the north–south Liffey Street, the pedestrianized **Henry Street** is the more concentrated shopping area of the city, where the *real* Dubliners can be found. There are plenty of department stores here, such as Arnott's, Marks and Spencer, Roches stores, and Penneys, as well as boutiques. The ILAC (Irish Life Assurance Company) Centre is a lively shopping mall, but it has detracted from Moore Street, running north of Henry, which was once a bustling market area. Up in O'Connell Street itself, awash with discount stores and fast-food shops and described as a "honky-tonk freeway," the saving graces are **Clery's** department store, where you can buy linen, crystal, and Belleek, and **Eason's** bookshop, both dating from the 19th century and both ravaged by the 1916 Rising hostilities around the nearby General Post Office. **McDowell's Jewellers**, also destroyed in

1916, recently has been elegantly refurbished and has antique silver, Waterford crystal, and Claddagh rings.

Off the Beaten Track
Irish craft and design is well represented in the city center, but if you have the time it is worth venturing a little farther afield. The **Tower Design Centre** is in the IDA Enterprise Centre, Pearse Street. To reach it on foot take the College Street turn off Westmoreland Street (down the other side of Trinity College) and keep walking down Pearse Street until you come to a canal bridge. Buses 1, 2, and 3 from Clery's department store in O'Connell Street will also take you there. If you're travelling by DART train, get off at the Pearse Street station and walk toward Ringsend. The tower building, constructed in 1862, has housed a sugar refinery, a distillery, and an iron foundry; in 1978 the Industrial Development Authority (IDA) purchased and restored it. More than 14 craftworkers are based here, and you can buy pewter, silver and gold jewelry, Irish bog oak artifacts, hand-crafted wooden toys, knitwear, hand-painted silks, pottery, and wood carvings. There is also a restaurant/coffee shop. Open 10:00 A.M. to 4:00 P.M. weekdays; Tel: (01) 77-56-55.

The **Marlay Craft Centre** (Tel: 01-94-20-83) in Rathfarnham is a 25-minute drive from the city center south toward the Dublin foothills. In the courtyard you can buy pottery, glass, weavings, and assorted crafts, and there is also a small coffee shop. Open 10:00 A.M. to 5:00 P.M. weekdays, 11:00 A.M. to 5:30 P.M. weekends. After shopping you might take a walk in nearby Rathfarnham Park, one of the city's most magnificent parks.

Irish Food Specialties
Ireland boasts its own cheese, homemade chocolates, and other delicacies, which can be bought in the city center. For smoked salmon, **Caviston's** of 59 Glasthule Road, Sandycove, **Molloy's** of 47 Donnybrook Road, and **Peter Dunn's** of 6 Upper Baggot Street are recommended, while Howth Harbour has **Peter Forman's** on the west pier. Most fish shops are closed on Sundays and Mondays. Ask whether it is wild or farmed fish before purchasing, and don't wait till you get to Dublin Airport, where it is grossly overpriced. Remember that there is a significant difference between "smoked Irish" and "Irish smoked"—the latter may have been imported.

—Lorna Siggins

DUBLIN ENVIRONS
THE PALE AND BEYOND

By Bernard Share

You will not hear the word "Pale" used in Ireland now, except in the context of mockery or political point-scoring; but it is a useful enough term to define the area surrounding and contiguous to Dublin, particularly as it has always been rather more a state of mind than a precise geographical definition. First attested historically in 1446, the Pale was that area considered by the Anglo-Norman invaders and their successors, if not by the resident Irish, to be under their occupational control and influence. As the fortunes of the insurgents waxed and waned there were times when it virtually ceased to exist.

In its greatest extent the Pale embraced the present-day counties of Louth (north of Dublin), Meath (to the north and northwest), Dublin, and Kildare (southwest)—the area, in effect, surrounding the capital on all but the southern side to a distance of some 30 miles. Wicklow to the south, mountainous and inaccessible, in marked contrast to the flat plains or gentle hills of the other counties, continued to resist English attempts to include it within their scheme of things. The O'Tooles and the O'Byrnes, from their rocky, boggy fastnesses in Wicklow, continued to harass and provoke the settled citizens of Dublin until modern warfare finally caught up with them. A drive through their territories, even to this day, will quickly reveal what the forces of law and order were up against. On a quiet weekday the countryside is much as the

106

O'Tooles and the O'Byrnes left it: a starkly beautiful, virtually uninhabited natural wilderness, and all within an hour's drive of the center of a capital city.

The people of the Pale reflect both its geography and its complex and at times convoluted history. In Wicklow they are "mountainy men," small farmers fighting a running battle with nature, their domain increasingly eroded at the edges by suburban sprawl and the value system that it implies. On the other sides of the city (the east, of course, is all water) the suburbs straggle out perhaps even less entrancingly, but you can still be clear of them in half an hour. The north Kildare people love horses— and look it. Meath is rich pasture and prosperous farms. Louth, boasting the Boyne Valley, is otherwise a little down on its luck. But closeness to the capital means that there is a wide range of amenities developed for percipient city dwellers, and which visitors will also appreciate.

MAJOR INTEREST

The Boyne Valley (stone monuments older than the Pyramids of Egypt)

The Hill of Tara and the other two Celtic royal hills

The Wicklow Glens (rural solitude within a stone's throw of the city center)

Great houses (some of Ireland's finest 18th-century mansions)

Glendalough (early Christian Ireland at its most evocative)

Well-run restaurants in appealing locations

Good pubs

Fishing

Horse racing

The Bog of Allen (peatlands rich in botanical interest and potential)

Before the Pale

Irish history did not, of course, begin with the arrival of the Anglo-Normans in A.D. 1169. Antedating this admittedly pivotal event were centuries of Celtic and pre-Celtic civilization, all amply exemplified in the larger surroundings of Dublin. The great prehistoric chambered tomb at Newgrange in the Boyne Valley dates most probably from 3000 B.C. There is evidence of Bronze Age cultivation (1750 to

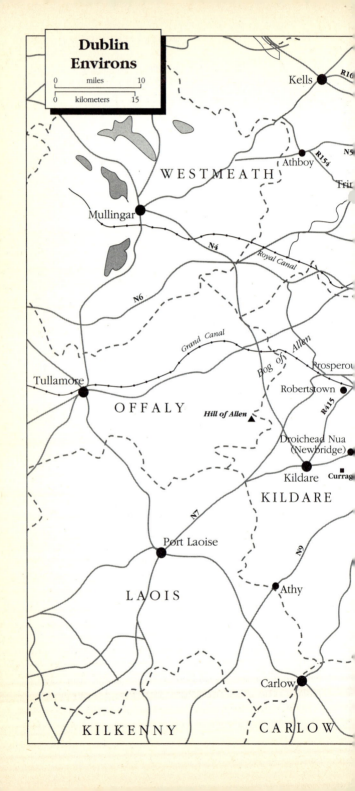

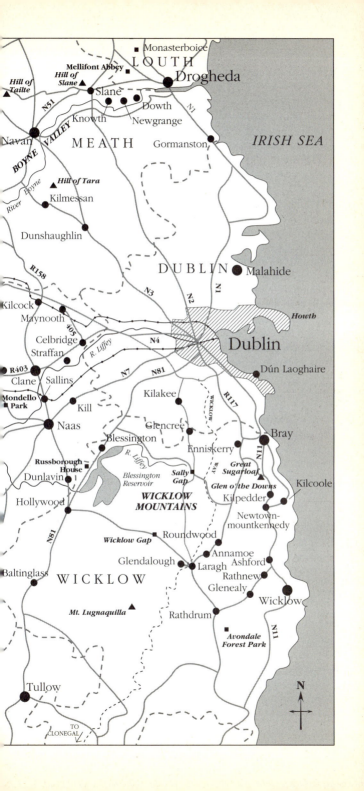

500 B.C.) on the slopes of the Wicklow Mountains. The date
of the arrival of the Celts themselves is still the subject of
learned controversy, as is their provenance, but a date of
1500 B.C. meets with general support. At the great Celtic
sites—the Hill of Tara, seat of the high kings, and the Hill
of Allen, associated with the legendary Finn mac Cumhail
(MacCool) and his band of warriors known as the Fianna
(hence the modern term Fenian)—little or no visible
evidence remains of the glory of the Celts. The informed
imagination must do the work, reclothing these unremarkable eminences with the panoply of a culture that flourished when the rest of Europe was immersed in darkness,
producing exquisite gold artifacts and, in the leanest period of the Christian era, illuminated manuscripts associated with long-established centers of learning such as
Ceanannas Mór (Kells) and Cill Dara (Kildare). The original Celtic place-names, many rendered unlovely by insensi-
tive anglicizing (Kill, County Kildare is an example; the
original is *Cill*—a church), can provide an insight into a
world long gone. Those with a linguistic bent will find
further-reading suggestions in the Bibliography.

King and Castle

Territory wrested from the inhabitants by force of arms
must be constantly defended. The fortified castle, a form
of architectural expression unknown to the native Irish,
thus became the Anglo-Norman trademark, and 500 years
of castle building has left the Pale rich in examples,
ranging from the almost perfectly preserved specimen to
the shattered single bastion marooned in a boggy
meadow. Most may be visited quite informally; others are
in the care of a local custodian, who will provide a key.
    The Norman legacy is more than a sermon in stone.
The great Norman names—the Fitzgeralds, earls of Kildare, for example—have resounded down the centuries,
having, in the course of time, become "more Irish than
the Irish." But many strands are woven into the past and
present culture of the Pale, as the literary associations
attest: Jonathan Swift (Celbridge and Laracor, County
Meath); the poet Francis Ledwidge (Slane); and, more
recently, the fragmented but revealing glimpses of the
Wicklow landscape in the work of Samuel Beckett. Other
talents thrive: The colorful race meetings at the Curragh,
Punchestown, Naas, Laytown, and Fairyhouse proclaim
the kingdom of the horse; breeding, training, racing, and

selling constitute a major business, mirrored in the pub talk of counties Kildare and Meath.

At Mondello, close to Naas, is Ireland's only motor-racing circuit. Quieter pleasures may be pursued on the banks of the Grand and Royal canals running west out of Dublin, where good fishing abounds, or in cruising their waters. In all, the Pale is a countryside of contrast, from the mountain summits of Wicklow, where the deer, if not the antelope, play, to the civilized pleasure of a good dinner in a 12th-century castle keep (Barberstown, between Celbridge and Clane, County Kildare). All are only an hour from Dublin.

COUNTIES
LOUTH AND MEATH:
THE BANKS OF THE BOYNE

Take the N 1 northward from Dublin to Drogheda (follow the signs for Belfast); at Gormanston, some 11 km (7 miles) before Drogheda, you will pass—or stop at, as you feel inclined—**The Cock**, reputedly the oldest pub in Ireland, with origins in the 14th century, the property of one family for most of its recorded history. A beer garden here is an added attraction on sunny days. **Drogheda**—*Droichead átha,* "the bridge of the ford"—was established by invading Vikings under Thorgestr, alias Turgesius, in A.D. 911. There were already separate native settlements on each side of the River Boyne, early indications of a rivalry that was to persist. Then the Normans under Hugh de Lacy built a castle at Millmount, which has all but vanished, but the military barracks that succeeded it (left at the traffic light immediately after the railway bridge, then right at the top of the hill) have been transformed very imaginatively into the **Millmount Craft and Cultural Centre**, incorporating an excellent town museum. A good, moderately priced wine bar and restaurant here, **The Buttergate**, offers dramatic views over the town, and the **Sennhof Gourmet Restaurant** in the Boyne Valley Hotel features Swiss specialties.

In 1649 Cromwell, the lord protector of England, breached Drogheda's walls, the town having declared for the Royalists, and in a crime against humanity spectacular even by modern standards butchered, on his own admis-

sion, 2,000 people and deported the remaining citizens to
Barbados. The "curse of Cromwell" is still a vivid folk
memory; there are few names more universally execrated
in Ireland.

Visible relics of a turbulent past include the head of
Saint Oliver Plunkett in St. Peter's Church (West Street),
who was hanged, drawn, and quartered in London in
1681; and, in the other, Protestant St. Peter's (Magdalene
Street) the graves of Isaac Goldsmith, uncle of Oliver
(whose country lies westward of our area in Longford/
Westmeath) and Bartholomew Van Homrigh, father of
Swift's Vanessa (see below, Celbridge). St. Laurence's
Gate barbican is all that is left of the town walls.

The most prominent architectural feature in Drogheda,
and one that adds a certain aerial dimension to a low-lying
town, is the high railway viaduct carrying the Dublin–
Belfast railroad, viewable from The Mall, where **Greene's**
extensive antiques galleries will detain the lover of period
furniture (closed Wednesdays). Three good places to
pause before heading north, still on the N 1, to
Monasterboice: **Gleeson's Pub**, with its fine oak ceiling,
opposite the Tourist Information Office in West Street
(free parking adjacent); **Weaver's**, another pub in West
Street; and **Mrs. Carbery's** on the Quays. Drogheda's seaside resort, Bettystown, has a six-mile beach on which a
colorful horse-race festival is held each August. Its
Coastguard Inn restaurant has a good reputation.

Monasterboice

Take a left 8 km (5 miles) north of Drogheda to Monasterboice. An ancient monastic settlement, Monasterboice
is remarkable for its tenth-century **Muirdeach's Cross**,
which features excellently preserved biblical scenes in
sculptured panels on its east and west faces. The adjacent
ninth-century round tower may be entered (get the key at
the house at the gate).

Visit Monasterboice as a side excursion from
Drogheda; there is too much in the Boyne Valley proper
to include it in a one-day trip. About 5 km (3 miles) west
from Drogheda on the N 51 is the site of the **Battle of the
Boyne**, fought on July 12, 1690, between a Catholic Scot
and a Dutch Protestant for the throne of England, an
event that has left an indelible mark on Irish history. A
right-hand turn from the battle site (it's signposted) leads
to **Mellifont Abbey**, the first (1142) Cistercian house in

Ireland, founded on the site of a seventh-century convent. Of particular interest are the massive gatehouse, the chapter house, and the octagonal lavabo, of which five walls still stand. The setting, on the banks of the little River Mattock, makes an attractive picnic spot. The Boyne waterway, fallen into disuse, is being restored, and it offers good fishing (some species restricted; inquire at tourist offices in Dublin). The energetic may consider walking all or part of the riverside path from Drogheda to Navan (about 30 km/20 miles one way along the north bank of the river).

Newgrange

At the precise moment of the winter solstice the sun shines down the long, low passage of the huge prehistoric tomb at Newgrange and strikes a rock face in the cruciform, corbeled inner chamber. Who planned it, all of 4,500 years ago? Was it, in fact, the world's first astronomical observatory? What hands fashioned this fearful asymmetry? Whoever they were, these proto-Irish, they have departed leaving little or nothing but their inscrutable burial monuments. Visit Newgrange—and its companion graves of **Knowth** and **Dowth**—at an off-peak time if you can: A certain solitude is of assistance in adjusting to the time scale and its implications. The construction of Newgrange required, it is estimated, some 180,000 tons of stone. (The façade is a modern restoration.) There is an excellent and unobtrusive information center at the entrance, and a 700-acre National Archaeological Park is being created on a site centered on these remarkable monuments. As in the case of the Australian aboriginal culture, the Neolithic art found at Newgrange in the form of rock carvings is too remote in time to make a large impact on present-day consciousness, though it continues to inspire Irish artists working in a variety of media. The site remained important into Celtic times: The Irish name is *Brugh na Bóinne,* "the palace of the Boyne." Newgrange is south of the N 51, 18 km (11 miles) west of Drogheda, and is well signposted.

Close by the tumulus is **Newgrange Farm**, where the Redhouse family invites you to sample the flavor of contemporary rural life through guided tours of a functioning farm. Open weekdays from April through September 10:00 A.M. to 6:00 P.M. and Sundays 2:00 to 6:00 P.M. There are picnic areas and a coffee shop.

Slane

You can reach Slane by returning to the N 51 from Newgrange and continuing west, but two other possibilities are to approach it from Dublin via the Derry road, N 2 (straightened, according to popular rumor, to permit King George IV of England rapid access to his paramour Lady Conyngham in Slane Castle), or by the picturesque route that skirts the south bank of the Boyne from Drogheda. Slane is a good example of an 18th-century landlord village built around a central octagon (inevitably known locally as the Square) with a good eye for symmetry and decorum. **Slane Castle**, in the possession of the Conyngham family since 1641, is presently the residence of the earl of Mount Charles (the title borne by the eldest son). Mount Charles's atmospheric restaurant and nightclub, within the castle itself, is a well-patronized attraction. Tours of the castle are conducted on Sunday evenings. The restaurant is open Wednesday through Sunday, the nightclub on Saturday. For something simpler, try the **Conyngham Arms** in the village, with a buffet that's open all day.

Just north of the village on the Derry road is the **Hill of Slane**, upon which Saint Patrick, in the year 433, lit the Paschal fire as a direct challenge to that kindled for older ceremonial purposes by King Laeghaire at his court on the Hill of Tara. The confrontation of the spiritual and the temporal, as Muirchu, Patrick's biographer, tells it in an account written some 200 years after the event, resolved into a competition in prestidigitation, with Laeghaire's wizards gloomily predicting an unfavorable—for the Irish—outcome. Ercc, the first convert, became the first bishop of Slane and is commemorated in the ruins of a Gothic church in the castle Demesne.

Kells

Turn right at Slane Castle to Kells (or Ceanannas; you will see both on signposts), or continue from Slane via Navan (or start from Dublin on the N 3) to investigate the atmosphere, if little else, of the **Hill of Tara**, 9.5 km (6 miles) northwest of Dunshaughlin. *Teamhair na Ríogh* (Tara of the Kings) was an important settlement in the Bronze Age and not finally abandoned until A.D. 1022. Tara's halls are now discernible only as earthen ditches and ramparts, but a major excavation is in progress. The modern statue of Saint Patrick is best ignored.

Beyond Navan on the Kells road toward the northwest lies the third of the royal hills, the **Hill of Tailte**, where the Irish version of the Olympic Games, *Aonach Tailteann*, was held from the prehistoric era until A.D. 1168—and revived briefly in the first flush of regained independence in the 1920s. **Kells**, where Saint Colmcille founded a monastery in the sixth century, gave its name to the magnificent gospel manuscript now in Trinity College, Dublin, and recently reproduced in full authenticity by Swiss master craftsmen. An eighth-century building known as **St. Columba's House** (Columba is an anglicization of Colmcille) in Kells is in the style of St. Kevin's Church in Glendalough (see below); there is a 100-foot round tower, unusual in that it boasts five windows, each facing an ancient entrance to the town. Close by is the finest of the High Crosses of Kells, rich in sculptured ornament. There are three others; the example in the marketplace was employed as a gallows during the Rising of 1798.

Head from Kells via Athboy to Trim, passing the Meath Gaeltacht (Irish-speaking area) of Rathcarn.

Trim

"Whoever stands in King John's city sees/The tide of life for ever ebbing back," wrote the poet Donald Davie of the antiquities of Trim, southwest of Navan, where, to his eye, "Great walls lie beached on fields like bladder wrack." True, certainly, of the remains, imposing even in dereliction, of **Trim Castle**, the largest Anglo-Norman fortress in Ireland, founded in 1173. The five surviving towers and one of the two gate towers date from 1220. The river that skirts it is the Boyne. The castle, under extensive restoration, is open to the public. Trim has two other fortresses: Nangle's Castle, and Talbot's Castle (1415) off High Street. Transformed into a school, Talbot's provided the early education of the duke of Wellington, Arthur Wesley, or Wellesley, who lived in Dublingate Street (now Patrick Street), where a monument commemorates this somewhat reluctant Irishman. The school had been owned earlier by Swift's Stella (Esther Johnson), who sold it to the dean—at a profit.

If you are able to share other people's nostalgia, **The Station House** restaurant and hotel in Kilmessan is particularly appealing. (From Trim on the Navan road make a right past Bective Abbey, founded 1146, the present ruins dating from the 12th and 13th centuries.) The Station House occupies the site and some of the buildings of the junction of two long-vanished railroads, and has been most attractively reconstituted by Thelma and Christopher Slattery. The gardens, cuisine, and ambience can be commended.

NORTH COUNTY KILDARE

The sector west and southwest of Dublin bounded roughly by the Dublin–Galway (N 6) and Dublin–Tullow (N 81) roads, though flat and visually undramatic, contains much of interest. **Maynooth**, the former seat of the Fitzgeralds, 32 km (20 miles) from Dublin on the N 4, may also be reached by outer suburban rail from Dublin's Connolly Station or by number 66 or 67A bus. **Carton House**, in Maynooth, is only rarely open to the public (Tel: 01-628-62-50 or 628-62-93 for information), but if you strike it lucky there is some good stucco work by the Francini brothers to be seen in it. Maynooth is a university town, the establishment having grown out of the ecclesiastical (Catholic) seminary founded in 1795 by the British administration to stem the dangerous (to them) practice of priests going for training to the Continent in the wake of the French Revolution. Still the seedbed of the Church in Ireland, it has been an open university since the mid-1960s. The faculty of physics plays a significant role in the European Space Program. Eamon de Valera, the New York–born former president of Ireland, lectured here in mathematics. The **Russell Library** houses an important collection of early Irish manuscripts. A new library was opened in 1984 and memorializes the visit of Pope John Paul II in 1979. There is, intermittently, good music to be heard in the chapel.

The **castle** at the college entrance was probably built around 1176 by Maurice Fitzgerald, an associate of Strongbow, and after a checkered history was dismantled in 1647 by Owen Roe O'Neill. There remain a massive keep, some towers, and fragmentary outworks. (There are ambitious plans for its restoration as a major tourist center.) The pub on the nearest corner, **Cassidy's Roost**, is a remarkable exercise in classical kitsch, with tables out on the sidewalk in summer for drinks and pub snacks.

More elaborate fare is available at **Moyglare Manor Hotel** (the Galway side of the town; follow the signs), a finely situated Georgian country-house hotel and restaurant for local gourmets and expense-account diners; no lunch on Saturdays. Moyglare offers luxurious bedrooms, garden suites with noble views, fine antique furniture, and, as the season dictates, log fires and candlelight. The wine list features some remarkable and almost-vanished years of the great names (prices to match) to set against a distinguished cuisine.

From Maynooth the road south to Celbridge crosses the railway and the **Royal Canal**, which was opened as far as Kilcock in 1796, to the Shannon in 1817, and closed to all traffic in 1961. This section has now been reopened for pleasure boating as far as Mullingar.

Celbridge

As you enter Celbridge's main street the gates at the left are those of **Castletown House**, one of the finest Georgian mansions in Ireland and headquarters of the Irish Georgian Society. Castletown was built from 1722 to 1732 for William Conolly, speaker of the Irish Parliament. It remained in the family until 1965. The Long Gallery is the most impressive of the 100 or so rooms. In the dining room a cracked oval mirror is said to commemorate an unexpected visit by the Devil who, in the guise of a dinner guest, insinuated himself into the company of the then owner, "Tom" Conolly, in the early 1800s. The visitor having refused to leave, the parish priest was summoned, who threw a missal at him. It struck him a glancing blow on the head and hit the mirror, whereupon Satan decided to call it a day and vanished through the hearthstone—also cracked—in the conventional puff of smoke. Castletown is open to the public, and there is a restaurant in the basement kitchen that offers good value in unusual surroundings. Reservations are essential; Tel: (01) 628-82-52. Castletown also hosts cultural events that include Music in Great Irish Houses, an annual series of summer concerts featuring leading international artists. Booking is normally heavy, so it is best to call; Tel: (01) 628-82-52. (Other venues—varying with each series—include Slane Castle and Russborough House, County Wicklow; see below.)

Celbridge is the birthplace of Arthur Guinness, gener-

ally referred to by Irishmen in terms of respectful grati-
tude as "Uncle Arthur," and has close associations with
Jonathan Swift, dean of St. Patrick's, Dublin: pamphleteer,
patriot (of his own kind), and lover—if that is not too
unambiguous a word to apply to his relationship with two
women, Esther Johnson (Stella) and Esther Van Homrigh
(Vanessa). Vanessa's home, **Celbridge Abbey**, was built by
her wealthy Dutch father, and it is now the property of the
St. John of God Brothers, who welcome interested visitors. It is said that Vanessa constructed a bower by the
Liffey side for the entertainment of Swift on his rare rides
out from Dublin to see her and "drink her coffee"—a
locution interpreted by some as a euphemism. The Ro-
mantics, led by Sir Walter Scott, who visited Celbridge,
believed that Vanessa died of a broken heart—a verdict
the dean chose neither to confirm nor deny. Celbridge
now hosts an annual Swift Seminar; for details, Tel: (01)
628-81-61/2/3.

Bog Lore

The road from Celbridge to Clane to the southwest, a part
of one of the straightest roads in Ireland but otherwise
unremarkable, passes (left) a turn to Straffan, where there
is a butterfly farm (specimens available for purchase) and
the luxurious and very expensive K Club (golf course and
hotel) in the former home of "French Tom" Barton,
founder of the wine firm of Barton et Guestier, Bordeaux,
in the 18th century. James Joyce was educated at
Clongowes Wood College, near Clane (not open to the
public), and the opening of *Portrait of the Artist as a
Young Man* is set there. Onward from Clane the Prosperous road skirts the great **Bog of Allen**, a vast area of
peatland. Much of it is utilized for fuel by Bord na Mona,
the state peat authority, which has pioneered the relevant
technology and advises on peat production as far away as
Burundi, Central Africa. The vast yellow peat-harvesting
machines are themselves worth watching in action, even
from a distance, as they creep like lazy mastodons across
the golden-brown surface of the bog. The historic and
ecological significance of the bog is only now fully coming to be realized as most European deposits become cut
out. The Dutch, having destroyed their own, have
launched a campaign to save a number of Irish bogs in
their original condition, when they act as host to flora and
fauna of considerable interest. Historically, the boglands

played an important role in the struggle of the Irish against a succession of invaders, because only those with local knowledge were able to move freely in the treacherous terrain over tracks invisible to the inexperienced eye.

The town of **Prosperous** is a popular center for fishing (rudd, tench, bream) on the adjacent **Grand Canal**, opened from Dublin to Sallins for passenger traffic in 1780 and completed to the Shannon by 1803. Trade boats ceased to ply in 1960, and the canal now carries cruising traffic. **Lowtown Cruisers**, based a mile west of Robertstown, offer luxury craft for hire; Tel: (045) 604-27; Fax: (045) 603-72. Though amenities are relatively undeveloped along the canal, there are pleasant waterside pubs at Sallins and at Robertstown, a "canal village" that preserves one of the original hotels built for the 18th-century passenger business. The canal offers much to interest the industrial archaeologist, in particular the **Leinster Aqueduct** (2.5 km/1.5 miles west from Sallins by water; or follow the towpath), built to carry the waterway across the River Liffey. The French traveller De Latocnaye described it in 1796 as of "really prodigious length and height." A series of brochures mapping canal bank walks in this area is available from County Kildare Sports Advisory Committee, Naas (Tel: 045-970-71) or from local libraries.

Off the Prosperous–Kildare road is the **Hill of Allen**, a modest eminence magnified by its dominance of the surrounding bogland, and which was the legendary headquarters of the equally legendary Finn mac Cumhail and his warriors, important figures in pre-Christian Irish epics.

The Curragh

Naas (*Nás na Ríogh,* which means "the meeting place of the kings") and Kildare (*Cill Dara,* "the church of the oak") are on the main (N 7) Dublin–Cork road. **Kildare** owes its existence to a religious foundation by Saint Brigid in the fifth century, and St. Brigid's Cathedral (now Protestant) is a 12th-century structure currently undergoing major restoration. There is a fine specimen of a round tower here. **Naas**, the county town, has an attractive streetscape with several interesting shops, including one offering handmade shoes (**Tutty**, at the Dublin end of the main street). The **Manor Inn**, focus for the race-going fraternity and almost impenetrable during Punchestown

Races week (May), serves an excellent homemade steak-and-kidney pie and a very adequate house wine.

Between Naas and Kildare is the former (British) garrison town of Newbridge, on the edge of the Curragh, an extensive plain that is the center of Irish horse breeding and training and the home of the National Stud (at Tully, 1.5 km/1 mile from Kildare town). The National Stud incorporates a Japanese garden of considerable charm. A race meeting at the Curragh is recommended, if only for the atmosphere. The **Irish Derby**, run in May or June, is the most important event on the calendar and currently the richest race in Europe. Frank Fallon's **Red House Inn**, on the main road between Naas and Newbridge, grows its own vegetables and features a patio bar.

An attractive alternative route to the Wicklow Mountains (see below) follows the Kilcullen road (N 9) out of Naas as far as the turn left for Dunlavin, where a diversion right will bring you (3 km/2 miles, posted) to **Rathsallagh House**, described by its genial giant of an owner, Corkman Joe O'Flynn, as "not a hotel." It is that, however, and much more: 500 acres of farmland, golf range, gardens, hunting country, plus a gourmet restaurant offering Kay O'Flynn's country-house cooking. Very special. Resume the route from Dunlavin to Hollywood to reach the mountains.

COUNTY WICKLOW

"A road still carriageable climbs over the high moorland. It cuts across vast turfbogs, a thousand feet above sea level, two thousand if you prefer. It leads to nothing any more. A few ruined forts, a few ruined dwellings. The sea is not far, just visible beyond the valleys dipping eastward, pale plinth as pale as the pale wall of sky. Tarns lie hidden in the folds of the moor, invisible from the road, reached by faint paths, under high over-hanging crags."

The writer is Samuel Beckett, recalling, in the novel *Mercier and Camier,* the Wicklow of his youth. The road to which he refers is the **Military Road**, built by the British in response to the 1798 Rising, and which traverses the mountain system from Kilakee, in the south Dublin suburbs, up to the Sally Gap, a crossroads in the middle of nowhere, and onward to Laragh and Glendalough. A similar route runs from the Dublin–Tullow road, N 81, near Blessington via the Sally Gap to the Dublin–Glendalough road north of Roundwood (the highest village in Ireland).

A third begins at the little village of Hollywood, south of Blessington, and crosses the **Wicklow Gap** to Laragh. This last road is perhaps the most impressive introduction to the pleasures of Wicklow. Lined with state forests (entrance only on foot in most cases; there are picnic tables), the road rises through the valley of the Kings River to the gap (a parking place and lookout with fine views eastward to the sea). At the junction in Laragh turn right for Glendalough, which may also be reached from Dublin via the Bray road (N 11). A private bus service, St. Kevin's, operates to Glendalough from St. Stephen's Green, and there are regular tours from Busaras, the central bus station in Dublin's Store Street.

Glendalough

This sixth-century foundation encapsulates early Christian Ireland, and should not be missed. The setting, in a steep-sided valley (*Gleann Dá Locha,* "the valley of the two lakes") chosen by Saint Kevin for its remoteness, still preserves something of that quality in spite of its popularity as a tourist attraction. (Avoid weekends if possible. The light late in the evening is particularly evocative.) Saint Kevin (d. 619?) established a monastic center of learning here that endured until the 16th century. Something of a misogynist, the saint, as legend has it, was pursued by a determined female across the upper lake to a cave where he had taken refuge. (Boats are available for hire to visit the cave.) The settlement was plundered by the Danes in the 11th century and by the English of Dublin in the 14th, but the remains are more than sufficient to convey a vivid impression of the flowering of Irish monasticism. The building known as **St. Kevin's Kitchen** is in fact a two-storied oratory in the Celtic manner, with a steeply pitched stone roof. The cathedral dates from the ninth century. St. Mary's Church marks the supposed site of Saint Kevin's grave. The round tower is the fourth highest in the country (after Kilmacduagh, Galway, and Kildare), the conical cap having been reconstructed using the original stones. **Glendalough Craft Centre** specializes in weaving and jewelry. A new and comprehensively equipped visitor center forms the nucleus of a major national park that is being developed in the area.

The Wicklow Way

This is ideal walking country, whether you are a dedicated hiker or have just a day, or half a day, to devote to a short ramble. A long-distance path, named the Wicklow Way for one of the ancient roads of Ireland, *Slí Cualann*, runs from the south Dublin suburbs at Marley Park (buses 74, 48A, and 48B) to Clonegal in County Carlow, a total distance of some 78 miles. It offers a rich variety of scenery and terrain, from barren mountains to lush farmland, with glimpses of wildlife—including red and sika deer, hare, fox, squirrel, and the occasional badger. You will also be exploring the area that provided the background for several of John M. Synge's plays, including *In the Shadow of the Glen*. Short sections of the Way are perfectly feasible for the inexperienced or for those with limited time. For the more ambitious, bed-and-breakfast accommodations are available at points along or somewhat off the route at places such as Glencree, Roundwood, and Laragh. (To arrange accommodations contact the Wicklow Tourist Information Office; Tel: 0404-691-17 or 691-18.) A good deal of the Way is, however, at some remove from even the basics of civilization, and all normal precautions associated with hill walking should be taken, particularly in regard to advance planning, suitable clothing and footwear, and information to third parties as to your intentions. Full-scale maps and descriptive details on the Way are available from tourist offices and bookstores. Alternatively, you could joint a six-day guided walking tour. For details, contact **Countryside Study Tours**, Knockrath, Rathdrum, County Wicklow; Tel: (0404) 464-65.

Blessington and Russborough

Blessington, a one-street town with a 17th-century church 31 km (19 miles) from Dublin on N 81, is a good starting point for a circular tour of Blessington Lake, which is in fact a man-made reservoir set in attractive countryside in the foothills of the Wicklow Mountains. The reservoir is fed by the circumambient Liffey, which rises near the Sally Gap a bare 12 miles from Dublin but requires nearly eight times that distance to reach the sea. Go 5 km (3 miles) south from Blessington on N 81 to reach **Russborough House** (to the right; signposted), a fine

Palladian mansion built in 1741 by Richard Cassels, or Castle, the German architect also responsible for Castletown and Carton. Russborough, owned by the Alfred Beit Foundation, is open to the public; inquire locally for times. Guided tours reveal such treasures as works by Vermeer, Goya, Gainsborough, Rubens, Hals, and Reynolds; Baroque plasterwork by the Francini brothers; and an abundance of Caribbean mahogany.

On leaving Russborough turn right on the main road for Poulaphouca (*Poll a' Phúca,* "the Pool of the Pooka," a malignant spirit that takes the form of a black dog). Here, where the Liffey is dammed for hydroelectrical purposes, a sign points left to **Tulfarris Hotel and Country Club**, a late Georgian country house hotel and leisure center beautifully situated on the far shore of the lake. It may take a little finding, but it is worth the trouble, with golf, tennis, fishing, sailing, windsurfing, a choice of bars and restaurants, and elegant public rooms. From here you may continue the lake circuit back to Blessington or divert right into the mountains via Valleymount and the Wicklow Gap.

Other Routes through Wicklow

A glance at the map of Wicklow will suggest several round-trip routes from Dublin, some of which, via the Military Road, have already been mentioned. One possibility is to travel out via **Enniskerry**, a pretty dormitory village at the foot of Glencree, through which a scenic road rises to the upland area known as the Featherbed. At the head of Glencree is a cemetery holding the remains of German victims of the Second World War, some of whom crash-landed in Ireland and others whose bodies were washed ashore.

Up the hill beyond Enniskerry toward Glendalough is **Powerscourt Demesne**; the gardens here, open to the public, provide a fine view of the two Sugarloaf Mountains. The house (1731–1741) was destroyed by fire in 1974, together with its valuable contents. Powerscourt Waterfall, which impressed William Thackeray (*Irish Sketch Book,* 1843), is one of the highest waterfalls in Ireland. It's just a few miles from the house. The Glendalough road climbs up to the Calary Bog and through Roundwood (site of the highest pub in Ireland) and Annamoe to Laragh. If you are not visiting Glendalough turn left here to Rathdrum, but take the right fork up a steep hill, where a beautiful route crosses the hills to Glenmalure, a dead-end valley at the foot of Lugnaquilla (3,039 feet), Wicklow's highest mountain and a challenging, though not difficult, climb. On the outskirts of Rathdrum (also accessible by rail and bus service from Dublin) is **Avondale Forest Park**, centered upon the former home of Charles Stuart Parnell, the charismatic 19th-century political leader. The house is now a museum, and the park contains stands of noble and unusual trees.

From Rathdrum the return to Dublin by road is via Glenealy and Rathnew, where a right turn (Wicklow road) will bring you to the entrance (left, 2 km/1 mile) to **Knockrobin Country House**, an 1830s mansion restored in Victorian amplitude by Alison Andrews. The restaurant (Victorian specialties) is open Tuesday through Saturday for dinner, and Sundays for lunch. Reservations are essential; Tel: (0404) 694-21. The hotel overlooks Broadlough bird sanctuary, whose resident fauna include peacocks and some fine wolfhounds.

Back in the direction of Dublin turn left at Ashford to the **Devil's Glen**, "which forms," wrote Thackeray, "a delightful wild walk, and where a Methuselah of a landscape painter might find studies for all his life long. All sorts of foliage and colour, all sorts of delightful caprices of light and shadow—the river tumbling and frothing amidst the boulders. . . ."

On a less dramatic scale, but equally impressive, are the lovely gardens of **Mount Usher** (right, just before Ashford, on the main road). A turn right at the village (posted) suggests an alternative route to Dublin via the coastal route passing **Hunter's Hotel**, one of Ireland's oldest coaching inns and now in the fifth generation of the same family. The fine gardens are bordered by the River Vartry. Golf, tennis, riding, and sea fishing are available. Alternatively, continue on the N 11 via Newtownmountkennedy, the village with the longest name in Ireland, and through the picturesque Glen o' the Downs, after which, on your left, is the Great Sugarloaf: an extinct volcano, as its form suggests. No immediate eruptions are predicted by *Old Moore's Almanack*.

GETTING AROUND
A glance at the map will reveal that the lines of communication in the area run radially from Dublin, and since the distances are not great and the roads generally adequate

most visitors will probably opt to explore on a daily basis from the city, setting off along one of the main arteries—N 1, N 2, etc.—numbered counterclockwise around Dublin. Two important exceptions should be made: The Boyne Valley requires more time—perhaps a circular tour with a night spent in a country hotel—as does the Wicklow region, which would be a pity to dismiss in a day.

Because, it is said, the Irish never really took to living in organized communities until it was forced upon them, these counties constitute a maze of little roads, many of them apparently designed to bring you back to the point from which you set out. This phenomenon is in no way mitigated by the amiable local habit of turning signposts to point to somewhere else altogether. So if you are proposing to travel, for example, from Trim to Kildare Town (a perfectly feasible trajectory), keep a firm hand on the map should your confidence, or your orientation, desert you.

On account of the road pattern and the location of many places of interest well away from main arteries, public transport is by and large not the best method of exploring the environs of Dublin. Exceptions and alternatives are noted. Specialized bus tours do, however, operate to the most popular locations from Busaras (the central bus station) in Dublin; details are available from Bus Atha Cliath (Dublin Bus) or tourist offices.

ACCOMMODATIONS REFERENCE

The telephone country code for the Dublin environs is 353. When dialing telephone numbers in the Republic from outside the country, drop the 0 in the area code. The rate ranges given below are projections *for 1992; for up-to-the-minute rate information it is always wise to telephone before booking. Unless otherwise indicated, rates are per person sharing and do not include meals or service.*

▶ **Hunter's Hotel. Rathnew**, County Wicklow. Tel: (0404) 401-06. £35 year-round.

▶ **Knockrobin Country House. Rathnew**, County Wicklow. Tel: (0404) 694-21 or 673-44; Fax: (0404) 694-20. £40 year-round.

▶ **Moyglare Manor Hotel. Maynooth**, County Kildare. Tel: (01) 628-63-51; Fax: (01) 628-54-05; in U.S., (800) 223-6510. £55 year-round.

▶ **Rathsallagh House. Dunlavin,** County Wicklow. Tel: (045) 531-12; Fax: (045) 533-43. Low-season rates vary; high season, £54.

▶ **Station House. Kilmessan,** County Meath. Tel: (046) 252-39; Fax: (046) 255-88. £25, breakfast and service included.

▶ **Tulfarris Hotel and Country Club. Blessington,** County Wicklow. Tel: (045) 645-74; Fax: (045) 644-23. £37.50–£47.50.

THE SOUTHEAST
WEXFORD, KILKENNY, TIPPERARY, WATERFORD

By Lorcan Roche

Lorcan Roche is a freelance writer as well as a drama critic for the Irish Independent, *Ireland's largest-selling daily newspaper. He was formerly associate editor of* Travel-Holiday *magazine in the United States. He is a direct descendant of a Norman family that first arrived in Wexford in 1167.*

There is a certain irony inherent in this chapter being written by a "Jackeen," a born-and-bred Dubliner. Tradition in this part of the world would have it that a Jackeen is utterly incapable of assessing Life Beyond The Pale, because for him it simply does not exist. It is rather like asking that quintessential Manhattanite Woody Allen to discourse on the probability of a new form of Renaissance thinking emerging in Peoria, Illinois. To most Jackeens, Dublin is the center of the universe, and it is highly improbable, if not altogether impossible, that anything interesting in terms of accommodations, cuisine, and amenities might be stirring beyond the confines of the capital.

A week-long journey or so will scotch such foolish misconceptions and introduce you to the finest hotels, food, scenery, and people this island can muster up—and it can be done in such a way as to inflict minimum damage on your wallet.

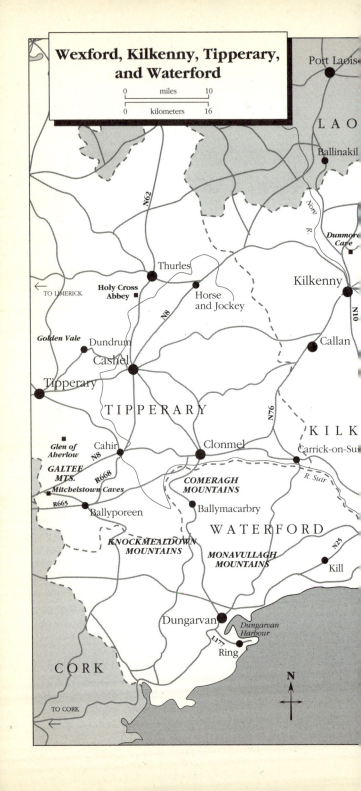

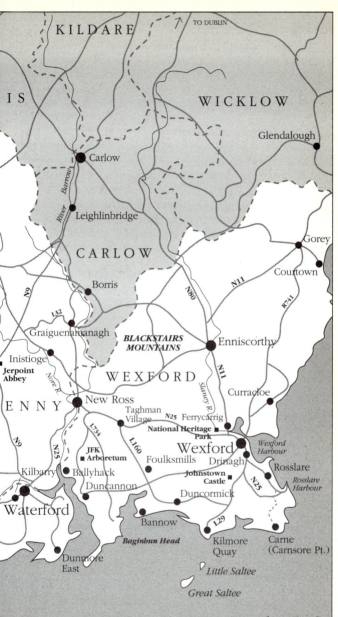

The Southeast has several distinct natural advantages: The Wexford/Waterford coastline is warmed by the Gulf Stream, and its waters are an immensely rich source of seafood. Its rivers are clean and provide excellent fishing; its beaches are unsurpassed on the island. And finally, the entire region—Wexford county in particular—records more hours of sunshine than any other in Ireland. Because of this climatic asset the county is Ireland's chief producer of soft fruits.

Situated as it is, so close to Britain and the Continent, the Southeast was one of the first parts of Ireland to experience invasion. The clement weather, fertile soil, and bountiful seas saw to it that the "visitors" invariably chose to stay, and they have left a lasting impression on their point of entry. The Southeast can, in fact, be regarded as the beachhead of Ireland where, in terms of history and the development of culture, some of the first tentative and not so tentative steps were taken.

MAJOR INTEREST

Wexford
Selskar Abbey
Wexford Festival of Opera
National Heritage Park
Enniscorthy Castle
Johnstown, 19th-century Gothic castle
Beaches in Wexford
Saltee Islands bird sanctuary

Kilkenny
Kilkenny Castle
The Black Abbey
St. Canice's Cathedral
Jerpoint Abbey, 12th-century Cistercian ruin
Kilkenny Arts Week
Arts and crafts

Tipperary
Cahir Castle
Rock of Cashel
Holy Cross Abbey
GPA-Bolton Library
Ormonde House, Anne Boleyn's birthplace

Waterford
Reginald's Viking Tower
The French Church Medieval ruins

Waterford Glass Factory
Deep-sea fishing at Dungarvan
Nire Valley scenic drive

COUNTY WEXFORD

The "Model County," south along the coast below Dublin and Wicklow, is a favorite destination for visitors, and not just because the beaches at Courtown, Curracloe, Rosslare, and Duncannon are the best in the south of Ireland. In many respects, in fact, Wexford fails to live up to the scenic standards set by the majestic, rolling countryside of, say, Tipperary. And its mostly ruined, scattered castles (nearly 140 were built here between the 12th and 16th centuries, as Norman knights were rewarded with tracts of land) cannot hope to instill in the visitor the same instant respect as Medieval Kilkenny. In Wexford, more than anywhere else in the Southeast, it is the people who matter most.

A stoic breed with an appealing sardonic wit, they are fiercely proud of their well-ordered county and of its noble history. Their collective folk memory of the 1798 Rising, which was spurred more by outrage at English injustice than by any French-inspired desire for liberty, equality, and fraternity, remains strong.

Those superb seamen, the Vikings (a.k.a. Norsemen), first made their presence felt in Wexford in A.D. 819, when they raided a monastic settlement on Begerin. Like the Belgic Celts who had sailed into Wexford around 500 B.C. in search of the Wicklow gold mines, the Vikings, with their austere Scandinavian background, probably felt they had tumbled across Valhalla on earth. The Irish monks, whose sacred objects of gold and silver were snatched by the marauding sea rovers, described the Vikings as being "vomited up" by the waves.

The Vikings formed a settlement at the mouth of the River Slaney, on a bay (Wexford Harbour) right at the southeast corner of Ireland, and called their new home Weissfjord, after the mate of their one-eyed warrior god, Odin. Weissfjord developed into one of their most lucrative strongholds, and like its nearby Viking twin, Waterford (Vadrefjord), it retains a dominant Viking influence in its haphazard design and in the profusion of steep lanes and slips leading from the harbor to the town center.

The first Norman incursions at Bannow and Wexford in 1169 and at Baginbun in 1170 were largely freelance family affairs provoked by the banished king of Leinster, Dermot MacMurrough, who promised the Welsh-Norman mercenaries land, easy living, and the hand of his handsome daughter, Aoife, in return for a secure throne. Whereas the Vikings left only a strong seafaring tradition, a few surnames (Doyle, Larkin, Cosgrave), and a few placenames (Selskar, Tuskar, Saltees), the Normans bequeathed a new way of life. And there were positive attributes: Organized farming replaced the wandering herds of the Irish, and Wexford was swept into a new agricultural era from which it derives its current "Model County" standards.

Wexford Town

Wexford Town is a delightful introduction to the general area, and is well served by hotels, restaurants, and bed-and-breakfasts. Both the **Talbot** and **White's** are reputable and moderately priced hotels and dining spots. The **Pike Room** of the Talbot and **Captain White's** seafood restaurant in White's Hotel are long-standing, traditional eateries for locals on special occasions. The **Guillemot** dining room in the Talbot serves excellent seafood—try the lobster or pink trout—and has a very good wine list. In all, the Talbot, being the more modern of the two, probably has the edge in terms of cuisine, and without argument in terms of leisure facilities; it has a swimming pool, gym, squash courts, saunas, and a solarium. If you're looking for bed-and-breakfast accommodation in town, check out the spacious, comfortable, and reasonably-priced **Faythe House**, at the top of the town, once the site of an old fishing suburb.

There is no public transport in Wexford, which is essentially a series of narrow lanes and alleyways crisscrossing the snaking Main Street. The very active **Wexford Historical Society**, beyond ensuring that the town's monuments are well documented, organizes excellent walking tours of the town. The society is located at 12 Ard Carman.

On Crescent Quay at the harbor you will find a statue of Commodore John Barry, born in nearby Ballysampson in 1745, who was the first commissioned officer to capture a ship under the authority of the U.S. Navy during the American War of Independence, and who is in fact credited with the founding of that navy. The mudflats, or slobs, of Wexford Harbour are now home to the impressive **Wildfowl Reserve**, where 50 percent of the world's white-fronted geese winter.

In the **Bull Ring**, the ancient marketplace where the horrible practice of bullbaiting was introduced in Norman times, stands the statue of a pikeman, a tribute to the people who took part in the 1798 Rising. This small historic square, near the north end of Main Street, was also the site of a Cromwellian massacre in 1649, when many of the townspeople were butchered. The house on the northeast corner of the Bull Ring was where Jane Francesca Elgee, a.k.a. Speranza, the writer and mother of Oscar Wilde, was born. And across the road above the cozy **Thomas Moore Pub**, Anastasia Codd, mother of Thomas Moore of *Irish Melodies* fame, who was as well-known as Byron in his time, first saw the light of day.

At the **Bohemian Girl**, on North Main Street, Kay and Seamus McMenamin serve excellent bar food during the day, and after 8:00 P.M. they open a small but distinguished restaurant above. Their attractive establishment has won several noteworthy National Bar and Catering awards. **Tim's Tavern**, at the south end of Main Street, is another reliable house of cheer, serving decent food in a homey atmosphere. **The Granary Restaurant**, at Westgate, serves good food in an informal atmosphere at reasonable prices. Another favorite is the **Crown Bar**, down little Monck Street. A late-19th-century coach inn, the Crown may on first impression appear to be a museum—it has an unusual collection of weaponry, including Michael Collins's revolver and pikes from the Vinegar Hill battle of 1798—but it is in fact a pleasurable drinking spot. Con Macken runs another unusual establishment, **Cape of Good Hope**, a grocer's-cum-pub-cum-undertaker's on North Main Street. And the newly opened **Centenary Stores** on Charlotte Street is another very interesting watering hole, serving delicious sandwiches in a relaxed atmosphere.

Near **Westgate Tower**, the only one of the five fortified gateways to the town's walls that still stands, are the ruins of **Selskar Abbey**. It is commonly held that Henry II of England did penance here in 1172 for the murder of Thomas à Becket. A notice on the main gate will tell you how and where to procure the entrance key.

Initiated in 1951, the **Wexford Festival of Opera** has earned an international reputation by staging rarely performed operas. During the festival—the last 11 days of October—the town adopts a Mardi Gras atmosphere, and accommodations are always heavily booked. You could not, however, hope to arrive at a better time for a visit.

Around Wexford Town

In 1987 the very important **National Heritage Park** opened in Ferrycarrig, just 5 km (3 miles) north of Wexford Town on the main road. Intelligently designed, wonderfully executed, and ideally situated on the Slaney estuary, the Heritage Park brings the major eras of Irish history to life. The excellent **Ferrycarrig Hotel** at Ferrycarrig Bridge is only a stone's throw from the park. All of the guest rooms have views of the Slaney, and the hotel's **Conservatory** restaurant serves truly exquisite food. It has earned itself a reputation, under the watchful eye of manager Matt Britton, as a gourmet's delight. The wine list is excellent—the specialty of the house is a very interesting Cahors wine from France—and one of the best dinners in Ireland can be had here for just £20 per person. No trip to Wexford is complete without a visit to the Ferrycarrig Hotel. If, on the other hand, you feel the need for a light meal or snack, a good choice in this area would be the recently refurbished—and now more popular than ever—**Oak Tavern**, a seafood restaurant at Ferrycarrig Bridge on the lovely Slaney. Grilled salmon steak and Dover sole are recommended.

If you head northwest from Wexford Town on the N 11, after about 25 km (15.5 miles) you'll reach Enniscorthy and **Enniscorthy Castle**. The castle's well-preserved square-towered keep, built in 1568, houses a folk museum. A good place to stay in the area is **Marlfield House**, a fine Regency-period home standing in its own woodland at Gorey, about another 25 km (15.5 miles) on the N 11. A 1990 Relais & Château Worldwide Breakfast award winner, the hotel is owned and managed by Ray and Mary Bowe, who are discreet, attentive hosts. The food at Marlfield is mouth-wateringly good, and the atmosphere perfect for unwinding.

Horetown House in Foulksmills, west of Wexford Town, is officially a bed-and-breakfast establishment, but in reality this grand 18th-century manor is a home away from home where the proprietress, Vera Young, has made an art out of making people feel relaxed and comfortable. Horetown House boasts one of the finest equestrian centers in the Southeast, and Mrs. Young's son David is happy to arrange outings for novice, intermediate, and experienced riders. The adjoining **Cellar Restaurant**, run by another son, Ivor, offers exceptional value and delicious food. If you want something out of the ordinary at unbelievably low prices visit Horetown House; you won't want to leave. To get there take N 25 west from Wexford Town and turn left after 10.5 km (6.5 miles) at Taghmon Village. Continue south on L 160 for 6.5 km (4 miles) to Foulksmills.

If you continue west on N 25, 24 km (15 miles) west of Wexford Town you'll come to the **John F. Kennedy Arboretum** on Slieve Coillte, a hill near the birthplace of the late president's great-grandfather. The arboretum boasts 3,000 varieties of trees and shrubs. Still farther west, at **New Ross**, 35 km (22 miles) west of Wexford Town, you can take one of the **New Ross Galley Cruises** on the River Barrow and enjoy lunch, afternoon tea, or dinner while plying the calm waters of the winding tidal river, which is banked by wooded slopes and pretty vistas. The boats leave from the quay below New Ross bridge. South of New Ross, on the estuary, is the little ferry port of **Ballyhack**, where you'll find the excellent **Neptune** restaurant.

For those on a restricted budget, **Whitford House**, just southwest of Wexford Town off the N 25, is one of the finest modern guesthouses in the area, being more of a small hotel than a bed-and-breakfast. Its swimming pool is open in the summer. Also off the N 25 southwest of Wexford Town is **Johnstown Castle**, a 19th-century Gothic Revival structure with magnificent gardens and an agricultural museum of farming implements and the like.

Rosslare Harbour, with its busy ferry terminal, and **Rosslare Strand** just a couple of kilometers (about a mile) away, with its fine sandy beaches, are 18 km (11 miles) south along the coast from Wexford Town via the N 25. Both are bustling places, and well served by restaurants and hotels. In particular, the traditional **Kelly's Strand Hotel** and the modern **Hotel Rosslare** are good choices, if somewhat expensive. Kelly's has a swimming pool, tennis, and golf; the Rosslare has a squash court and sauna. **Le Gourmet**, a small, local restaurant, serves consistently superior cuisine at affordable prices. **Casey's Cedars Hotel** is another Rosslare establishment with a growing reputation for fine food at reasonable prices. It's a relaxing place; sometimes other hotels in the area can be noisy, and Casey's is a little bit off the beaten track and very enjoyable for overnight stays.

An 8-km (5-mile) drive south of Rosslare Harbour through bumpy territory will bring you to **Carne** (Carnsore Point on most road maps) and **The Lobster Pot Bar and Restaurant** (Tel: 053-311-10), where you can enjoy delicious homemade soups, salads, and sandwiches in a maritime setting. In the evening, sing-alongs are commonplace. The Lobster Pot is worth making the effort to reach, particularly now that a new dining room serving the freshest and finest of seafood is open from 6:30 P.M. The Lobster Pot was awarded a National Catering Award in 1990.

Similarly, the fishing village of **Kilmore Quay**, on the south coast about 30 km (20 miles) southwest of Wexford Town, merits a visit. You can enjoy the freshest of prawns in the transformed deckhouse of a wrecked sailing ship at the attractive **Wooden House** here. Kilmore, mentioned in ballad-writer P. J. McCall's "Wexford Fishing Song" (which you should request if you happen on a late-night sing-along), is also the stepping-off point for the **Saltee Islands**. Local raconteurs and fishermen Willie Bates, Jack Devereux, and Devereux's son John will take you out to the islands for a small fee. (Contact them through the Wooden House.) The Saltees, a 45-minute boat trip from the mainland, are Ireland's largest bird sanctuary; during spring and summer the Great Saltee and Little Saltee are home to more than three million birds. The islands are also a source of rich lore, having been the haunt of Neolithic man, Medieval monks, and 17th-century pirates and smugglers.

Wexford Crafts

Pottery, leatherwork, weaving, woodworking, and silversmithing are the major crafts in County Wexford. Sources are **Wexford Pottery** in Duncormick; **Albert Kendrick Leather and Suede Work** and **Carley's Bridge Pottery**, both in Enniscorthy; and **Pat Dolan Silversmith**, in Glenmore, New Ross. The **Kiltrea Bridge Pottery** in Enniscorthy is notable for its beautiful plant pots and terracotta kitchen accessories. The shop is located in a tranquil setting overlooking the River Urrin, near the Blackstairs Mountains.

COUNTY KILKENNY
Kilkenny Town

Kilkenny Town, about 75 km (46.5 miles) northwest of Wexford Town and 50 km (31 miles) north of Waterford, is Ireland's finest Medieval city (there are 28 in all), and stands as an eloquent monument to aesthetic value and architectural grace long since departed. The breadth of vision with which its original Norman planners were gifted has not been lost on the latter-day citizens, who have maintained and developed the city as an unrivaled, atmospherically rich attraction. The Keep Kilkenny Beautiful (KKB) campaign, initiated in the early 1980s, has ensured that streets are spic and span and that shop fronts are suitably Old World. The campaign has paid large dividends: **Kilkenny Castle** is now the single most visited historic building in Ireland, although few visitors will disagree that it is the city itself that has the real drawing power.

After the death of Dermot MacMurrough, king of Leinster, at Ferns in 1171, his son-in-law, Richard, earl of Pembroke, better known as Strongbow, laid claim to his vast territories, which included Ossory (County Kilkenny). William le Mareschal, Strongbow's son-in-law, constructed the first stone castle here between 1207 and 1213. Numerous prosperous Norman families were attracted to the area, and a vital, affluent city literally sprang up. During the 13th and 14th centuries Kilkenny was second in importance only to Dublin.

Parliament convened regularly in Kilkenny Castle. It was here, in 1366, that rigorous apartheid laws were enacted. These Statutes of Kilkenny prohibited, among other things, intermarriage between Anglo-Norman and Gaelic families, as well as the adoption of Irish surnames, dress, language, music, and legal code by the colonists, who were rapidly becoming more Irish than the Irish themselves. These laws led to bitter acrimony in Kilkenny, as elsewhere, and set the stage here for the turbulent rise to power of the Butler family (earls of Ormonde). Their role in the history of Kilkenny, and indeed Tipperary, cannot be overemphasized. The Butlers' wealth and political stability ensured that the city remained a focal point of power and prestige. In 1641, when the Great Rebellion of Ulster broke out, a roughly hewn but ambitious parliament, the Confederation of Kilkenny, convened in the city in an attempt to restore the civil and religious rights of the old Irish families and the "old [English] foreigners."

The Confederation brought unprecedented glamour and excitement to the city for eight years, but the English Civil War disrupted the fragile arrangement, and when the wretched Cromwell arrived in 1650 he found Kilkenny disillusioned and unwilling to put up even token resistance. There followed the ritual statue-breaking and window-smashing in the still-glorious St. Canice's Cathedral (where Cromwell stabled his horses), but the city (which derives its name from the Irish *Cill Channaigh,* "Canice's Church") escaped relatively unmolested. Its citizenry, however, was offered that infamous Hobson's Choice: "To Hell or Connacht," Connacht being a province in the west. In reality many of the dispossessed became victims of Cromwell's lesser-known policy of "Barbadosing"—sending Irish to work sugar mills and plantations in the West Indies.

Around in Kilkenny Town

Start your tour of Kilkenny with the *City Scope,* a 20-minute computerized *son et lumière* show at the Tudor **Shee's Alms House**, on Rose Inn Street, where the tourist office is located. The film, which can be seen any day but Sunday, is based on a meticulously crafted model of the city at its zenith in 1641 and will provide you with excellent information on the city's interesting sights, such as Kilkenny Castle, Black Abbey, and St. Canice's Cathedral. Kilkenny City is sited on an "S" bend in the River Nore. The castle, high on a northern slope, is redolent of the magnificent robber-baron castles along the Rhine, with the graceful Nore acting as a natural moat. Streets in the city are broad and elegantly laid out and at times make Kilkenny appear larger than it is.

Tynan Walking Tours provide an intelligent, relaxing way to explore Kilkenny. Tours depart Mondays through Saturdays from outside Shee's Alms House (10:30 A.M., 12:15 P.M., 3:00 P.M., and 4:30 P.M.) and on Sundays at the same times from outside the gates of the magnificently restored **Kilkenny Castle**, at the southeastern end of the city (while there be sure to see the tapestries and great hall). **Rothe House**, an archaeological museum on Parliament Street, has a nice collection of Medieval costumes and musical instruments. **Smithwicks Brewery**, just across from Rothe House, offers tours at 3:00 P.M., Monday through Friday.

The **Black Abbey**, on Abbey Street, was built in 1225 by William le Mareschal, earl of Pembroke, for the Dominicans, or Black Friars, as they were known, and survives today as an active Dominican priory. In 1543 the property was confiscated by Henry VIII, and the church became a courthouse, leaving the friars homeless. The friars returned during the Confederation, but Cromwell's troops defaced and vandalized the abbey. It was partially restored in the 19th century and more recently in the late 1970s. Among the items of interest are a 1264 figure of the Blessed Trinity and the 500-square-foot east window, which depicts the 15 mysteries of the Holy Rosary.

Built in the 13th century on the site of an early Irish monastery, **St. Canice's Cathedral** is the second-largest Medieval cathedral in Ireland. It is noted for its stained-glass windows and 16th- and 17th-century tomb sculptures. St. Canice's Library, to the northwest of the cathedral, has 3,000 volumes from the 16th and 17th centuries. The cathedral is reached via St. Canice's Steps (1614), which are linked to St. Canice Place by Velvet Lane.

Jerpoint Abbey, founded in 1158 by Donal MacGiollapatrick, king of Ossory, has a colorful, though troubled, history. In 1387 the abbot of Jerpoint was fined heavily for accepting Irish monks into his community, a direct transgression of the infamous Statutes of Kilkenny. The abbey was tremendously important to the Cistercians; its surviving architecture testifies to this. Here in this peaceful riverside setting you can see a Hiberno-Romanesque chancel and transepts, 15th-century cloisters and monuments, and effigies from several centuries. The powerful Butler and Walsh families are entombed here, and there is a fascinating array of carvings in the main cloister. There is also a pleasant, tidy café opposite the abbey where you can enjoy a snack or refreshment.

The **Marble City Bar** is an excellent wateringhole, but **Edward Langton's Pub**, an Edwardian-style establishment, is even harder to pass by once you've viewed the inside. Langton's is continuously garnering National Catering Awards, and with its recently expanded French-style tearoom, it's definitely not to be missed. The genial proprietor, Eamonn Langton, provides a discreet but attentive personal touch, and the food is excellent. Tell him the man from Berlitz sent you. Or, if you prefer the genuine article in terms of Old World decor, visit **Tynan's**, established 1861, where the young barman Michael is a fund of local information and gossip.

If you like to mix history with your drink, visit **Kyteler's Inn** on Kieran Street, which has recently been refurbished with great care and attention. In the early 14th century this building was the home of Dame Alice Kyteler, a beautiful and powerful woman accused of witchcraft and condemned to death by the Lord Justice of Ireland (four of her husbands had died mysteriously, leaving her considerable wealth on each occasion). Dame Alice's friends managed to smuggle her out of the country, but her handmaiden, Petronella, was burnt at the stake in her place. Kyteler's Inn serves bar snacks and is a congenial meeting place for locals and visitors alike. Directly opposite Kyteler's is another popular spot, **The Pantry**, an affordable, extremely well run coffee and cake shop. (Readers with a sweet tooth should visit **White's**, the oldest sweet shop in town, boasting a magnificent shop front.)

The **Kilkenny Arts Week**, now in its second decade, is without question the most important and best-attended arts festival in the Republic. During the last nine days of August, Kilkenny's many fine buildings become venues for classical music by orchestras, chamber-music ensembles, instrumentalists, and singers, and for readings by poets, novelists, and filmmakers. Jazz and traditional music are also on the agenda, and the city fairly hops for these nine days.

The **Dunmore Cave**, 11 km (7 miles) north of Kilkenny on the Castlecomer road, is an outstanding example of a natural limestone cavern. Now a national monument, the cave features a massive 20-foot stalagmite called Market Cross, and is open June to October; guides are available.

If you are a racing fan you will be pleased to know that 14.5 km (9 miles) east of Kilkenny on N 10 is the recently refurbished **Gowran Park**, one of the finest racetracks in the Southeast. Kilkenny folk like to have a flutter on the horses, and there is always good fun to be had here.

Kilkenny Crafts

Kilkenny is sometimes called the Marble City because of a highly attractive black marble produced in its local quarries. Many local artists work in this medium. The **Kilkenny**

Design Workshops, located opposite Kilkenny Castle in its beautifully restored stables and coach houses, are renowned for their locally crafted silver jewelry, ceramics, fashionable clothes and knitwear, leather, and even pots and pans. However, some of the items made here seem to be unnecessarily expensive, and many locals will tell you the center is, of late, a "tourist trap." Elsewhere in County Kilkenny, **C. and E. Chesneau Leather Goods** in Bennettsbridge, south of Kilkenny town on the Wexford road, is a very worthwhile shop, and **Callan Crystal** sells beautiful hand-cut lead crystal at its works in Callan, 16 km (10 miles) south of Kilkenny Town on the N 76. In Graiguenamanagh, 35 km (22 miles) southeast of Kilkenny Town on the L 32, **Duiske Glass** has an excellent range of hand-cut, decorated giftware, and **Cushendale Woollen Mills** has an interesting range of rugs and shawls in mohair and wool.

Staying and Dining
in the Kilkenny Area

Most hotels in the Kilkenny city center lack parking facilities and are not on a par with the modern, comfortable, and expensive **Newpark Hotel**, just north of the city on Castlecomer Road. It is situated in 50 acres of parkland and has tennis courts, a swimming pool, children's playground, sauna, and a gym. The hotel's Damask Dining Room provides satisfying fare, and its recently added suites are most attractive. The **Hotel Kilkenny**, in a restored 19th-century mansion off the city's Ring Road, is comfortable but not as luxurious as the Newpark, and is more of a local drinking and dancing spot, so it can get noisy at night. It does have a swimming pool and a gym, however.

Farther afield in Borris, just over the Carlow-Kilkenny border to the east of Kilkenny Town, Breda Coady provides elegant cuisine and surroundings at **Step House**, a late-Georgian-period residence with five inexpensive guest rooms, all tastefully appointed (Room One has a four-poster). Breda does most of the cooking and handles local game, especially pheasant, expertly. (The restaurant is, accordingly, moderately expensive.) Step House is not to be missed.

Similarly, the **Lord Bagenal Inn**, in Leighlinbridge, is more than worth the short drive over the Carlow border, just 25 km (16 miles) northeast of Kilkenny on the way to

Carlow Town. Chef Derek Hughes provides exciting food; his beef Wellington stuffed with chicken liver pâté is especially impressive. The Lord Bagenal's fixed-price dinner menu from Wednesday through Sunday is an excellent value at £10.50.

In Kilkenny, Eugene McSweeney runs **Lacken House**, a restaurant with inexpensive rooms. McSweeney serves superb though expensive cuisine, and like many of the other establishments mentioned here makes the most of local game and fish. McSweeney is in a class of his own, however: He is 13 times a national Gold Medal champion chef who has demonstrated his considerable skills on television in the United States. Breda McSweeney was recently elected to the prestigious Guild of Sommeliers and provides valuable assistance with their extensive wine list.

The Maltings, owned and run by the O'Neill family, is a beautifully situated restaurant along the banks of the Nore in the gentle village of **Inistioge**, 16 km (10 miles) south of Kilkenny. The Nore salmon served here is mouth-watering, and the minted lamb is also highly recommended; prices are moderate. If you fall in love with Inistioge, as is highly probable, stay here a day or two with Patricia Cantlon, proprietress of **Cullentrae House**. A colorful character even by Irish standards, Patricia is a superb cook, and her "bring your own wine" idea is very popular with her many diners. Bed-and-breakfast rates apply, and dinner is also available.

COUNTY TIPPERARY

Tipperary, west of Kilkenny, is Ireland's largest inland county (although Lough Derg in the county's northwest can create the illusion of vast coastline). It offers unmatched scenery, with rolling green flatlands (The Golden Vale) and the gently rising Galtee Mountains, which afford lovely views of the county from Mitchelstown to Cahir. "Tipp" is a prosperous county with a distinguished sporting tradition; its stud farms and greyhound-breeding skills have won it international acclaim.

Inland Tipperary, north of County Waterford, was spared most of the ravages of the Viking era, and its early Christian (eighth- and ninth-century) illuminated manuscripts and sacred vessels reside in abundance in Dublin's National Museum. In the late 12th century King

John arrived to grant lands to, among others, the illustrious Butler family (mentioned in the Kilkenny section). The Butlers are so called because they held the exclusive right to pass the first goblet of wine to the newly crowned king of England—a right that they continued to exercise down to the coronation of George IV. Until 1811 the Butler family was also entitled to one-tenth of the cargo of any wine-laden vessel landing in Ireland. As was the case in Kilkenny, the stability of the Butler's played a dramatic role in the preservation of County Tipperary, which escaped many colonization attempts, except those of Cromwell. (As an acknowledgment of their influence, the Butler family crest was incorporated into the county coat of arms.)

Tipperary is famed also for its role in the birth of the "Whiteboy" movement. In the late-18th century, bands of tenant farmers wearing white smocks over their clothing exacted cruel reprisals on landlords and their livestock. At a later period, Tipperary was disparagingly referred to as "Turbulent Tipp" because of the Market Day fights that occurred regularly between rival clans. Tipperary suffered terribly in the famine of the 1840s, principally because the dispossessed had moved neither to Hell nor to Connacht, but to marginal upland areas where the potato had become their staple diet. From 1841 to 1861 the population withered from 435,000 to 239,000 as a result of emigration and starvation. In fact, the county's population was in steady decline until the late 1960s, when its newfound pride and its now-thriving dairy farming began to attract people back to the land.

Cahir

Cahir is a peaceful, prosperous market town on the River Suir at the east end of the Galtee Mountains. It has a beautiful wooded park and a lovely church (St. Paul's, designed by Nash in 1820), and is the starting point for the spectacular scenic drive known as the Vee, which takes in views of the Galtee, Comeragh, and Monavullagh mountains.

James the Foreigner, ancestor of the Butlers, had constructed for himself in the early 15th century the largest castle of its time at Cahir (*cathair,* meaning "stone fort"). The highly defensible **Cahir Castle** managed to escape Cromwell intact, and it has recently been skillfully restored. The castle has been used as a set piece for various period movies, including *Barry Lyndon* and *Excalibur*. A 20-minute audio-visual presentation shown in a cottage on the castle grounds will orient you before you go to see the county's sights and monuments.

Southwest of Cahir, off the N 8, are the **Mitchelstown Caves**, where the staggering limestone formations have been christened House of Commons, House of Lords, the Cathedral, and the Organ. A kilometer or two (about a mile) south of the caves on R 665 is an eyeblink of a village called Ballyporeen, which achieved some small fame when it was learned that Michael Regan, great-grandfather of Ronald Reagan, was baptized in the church here in 1829. (Reagan shed a tear at the family burial place in Templetenny Cemetery during a much-ballyhooed visit several years back.)

Kilcoran Lodge Hotel, a former hunting lodge 10 km (6 miles) south of Cahir on the sheltered slope of the Galtee Mountains, is a delightful place to stay in the area. Guests can fish for salmon and trout, shooting, horseback riding, and golf can also be arranged. Both the restaurant and lounge bar open onto spectacular views of the Galtees, and food and service are excellent.

Cashel

Most visitors to Cashel, 18 km (11 miles) north of Cahir, come to see the **Rock of Cashel**, often referred to as "the Acropolis of Ireland," which rises dramatically from the flat surrounding terrain just north of town. The Rock is crowned by a jumble of structures from several periods of history, including a 12th-century round tower, the 13th-century Cormac's Chapel, and the 15th-century Hall of the Vicars Choral, but this detracts nothing from its imposing power. Floodlit at night, it looks like a still from a Gothic horror movie. The Rock was the seat of the kings of Munster for 700 years, and it was here that Saint Patrick said one of his first masses in Ireland. The great saint is reported to have explained the concept of a three-in-one divinity with the aid of a shamrock, thereby unwittingly giving Ireland its emblem.

In Cashel you should also visit the restored 17th-century artisan's cottage **Bothan Scoir** and the impressive **GPA-Bolton Library**, which displays manuscripts from the 12th century and books and bindings from the earliest years of printing, as well as early editions of Machiavelli, Erasmus, Luther, Calvin, Dante, Cervantes, and others.

Cashel should be your base in Tipperary. The structure now housing the **Cashel Palace Hotel**, built in 1730 by Bishop Bolton, served as a bishop's palace for 230 years, and is perhaps the only building in town that manages to stand up to the domineering Rock; in fact, the hotel has its own walkway up to the Rock. The walkway, however, is the least important attraction of this opulent, very expensive hotel. The food at its **Bishop's Buttery** is expertly prepared and served; the Irish stew of the young chef, James Mc Donnell, is renowned. The bedrooms, all recently refurbished, will also delight, in particular the sumptuous Bishop's Suite. Formal and informal dining is available. Cashel Palace is a treat, if you can afford it.

Also near the Rock in Cashel is **Chez Hans**, an expensive restaurant where the German chef-proprietor makes excellent use of fresh local game, organically grown vegetables, and freshly caught brill, salmon, sole, trout, and plaice. His desserts are delicious.

Cashel has several decent pubs along Main Street, among them **Daveren's**, **Reilly's**, and **Paky Leahy's**. The **Pepper-Steak House** on Main Street is also to be recommended for casual, enjoyable, and moderately priced dining, but it is open only in summer.

Elsewhere in Tipperary

The fully restored **Holy Cross Abbey**, 20 km (12 miles) north of Cashel on the N 62, on the west bank of the Suir, is an architectural gem. Of particular interest are the stone-mullioned windows in the nave and chancel. The groined ceiling and the abbey's elaborate stonework are of beautiful carved black marble. Founded in 1168 for the Benedictines, it was transferred to the Cistercians in 1182 and is now a parish church, where two relics of the Holy Cross are enshrined. Its gardens, identical to those of the Vatican, are a perfect picnic spot.

Dundrum House Hotel, built in the same year as Cashel Palace, is a splendid country manor home in Dundrum, about 12 km (7.5 miles) northwest of Cashel via the R 505. Austin and Mary Crowe are the hosts, and the tranquillity here is beyond description. Good food and good trout fishing (from a series of islands linked by catwalks on a nearby lake) are among the many plusses of Dundrum House. **Rectory House Hotel** is another reliable establishment in Dundrum. Intimate, charming, and family-run, it serves good food at reasonable prices. Farmhouse holidays are popular in Tipperary, and **Rahard Lodge** is a fine choice in this category.

In the busy market town of **Tipperary**, 12 km (7.5 miles) southwest of Dundrum via R 661 or 20 km (12.5 miles) west of Cashel, the hearty helpings at the inexpensive **Brown Trout Restaurant** on Abbey Street will satisfy even the largest of appetites. The **Glen of Aherlow**, between Cahir and Tipperary Town, is the site for, quite simply, one of the most stunning views of the Galtee Mountains in Ireland. Your itinerary should also include **Carrick-on-Suir**, east of Cahir and just northwest of Waterford City; it was the birthplace of Anne Boleyn (at **Ormonde House**, which has been reopened after a major refurbishment and is well worth a visit), the Clancy Brothers, and cyclist Sean Kelly.

If you find yourself in **Clonmel**, about 15 km (9 miles) east of Cahir—and you should—lunch at **La Scala** on Market Street, where Tom Cryan serves very good food, from beef fondue to crêpes de mer, at reasonable prices in a nice atmosphere. The **Clonmel Arms Hotel** in Clonmel is a moderately expensive hotel with 34 rooms and a pleasant atmosphere. It's been refurbished recently under the watchful eye of owner/manager Brendan Pettit, whose family has run the hotel for three generations. The food is fair and the bar is lively; Thursday night is jazz night.

COUNTY WATERFORD

Waterford City on Ireland's south coast is similar in layout to the smaller Wexford Town, with narrow streets and lanes leading to the town center from the long quayside. Waterford Harbour, with its 700-foot-long bridge, is a beautiful sight; at the harbor mouth three peaceful rivers—the Nore, Barrow, and Suir—merge as they meet the sea.

Reginald's Tower, built in 1013, takes its name from the Viking warrior Ragnvald, son of Sitric, founder of the city. Located at the west end of the quay (next to the Tower Hotel), it provides the key to unlocking the history of Waterford and should be your first destination. Strongbow and Aoife MacMurrough held their wedding reception here in 1170; the marriage consolidated Strongbow's legal title to the lordship of Leinster, thus setting the seal on the future of the nation. The tower played host to a succession of invited and uninvited guests throughout the centuries. Robert Fitzstephen, one of the first Normans to land in Ireland, was imprisoned here by Henry II for failing to ask leave of his majesty to lead the Irish expedition.

Henry's son, the 18-year-old spoiled brat Prince John, cavorted here for eight months in 1185, much to the disgust of the Norman knights, who saw in him an obstacle to their dream of a country of their own, and of the Irish chieftains, who held him in contempt; Perkin Warbeck, pretender to the throne of Henry VII, attempted to stay here in the 15th century; and in 1650 Oliver Cromwell tried unsuccessfully to take the tower.

The oldest parts of Waterford are to be found around Reginald's Tower; only Derry Town in Northern Ireland has more of its original walls and wall towers intact. Several of the Norman towers are extant and in perfect condition, the most important located at Railway Square, Castle Street, Patrick Street, and Jenkins Lane.

The **French Church** of Greyfriars, in Barley's New Street, was founded by Sir Hugh Purcell for the Franciscans in 1240 and was splendidly endowed by Henry III. It became a place of worship for a colony of Huguenots, who fled religious persecution in France during the 17th century. You can visit the ruins by obtaining the entrance key from the house across the road.

For shopping, try **Michael Street**. At number 28 you will find the **Waterford Craft Center**; at number 9, the **Book Center**, which has a decent stock of Irish works; at number 16, **Handcrafts**, which specializes in made-to-order Aran knitwear; at number 30, **Joann's**, which has a good line in brass, silver, china, and crystal; and at number 11, **Woolcraft**, which has been selling lambswool sweaters since 1887. **Joseph Knox**, at 3 and 4 Barronstrand Street, has been one of Waterford's most-respected merchants for many years and stocks porcelain, fine bone china, and, naturally, Waterford crystal. (There aren't any savings in buying Waterford crystal near the source, however, and you might be better off waiting until you get to the airport duty-free shops.)

The **Waterford Glass Factory** in Kilbarry, 3 km (2 miles) southwest of the city on the Cork road (N 25), does not sell any crystal. But it does draw large numbers of visitors, and during the summer its very worthwhile half-hour tours are heavily booked, so call ahead (Tel: 051-733-11); the factory is closed weekends and during the first three weeks in August. Beyond what is mentioned here there is little else of major interest in Waterford City.

Teaser's is a pleasant coffee shop on the quays, and the **Reginald Lounge**, on the Mall next to the tower, is a fine place to slake your thirst and enjoy good pub food. Waterford has two very fine, if somewhat expensive, hotels: the Granville, on the quay, and Jury's. The family-run **Granville Hotel** possesses a relaxed, dignified charm; its recently added suites are tasteful and comfortable. The hotel bar is popular with locals and is a good spot for a chat. Meals at the Granville are hearty, enjoyable affairs, whether they be in the formal dining room or the informal grill room. **Jury's Hotel**, on a wooded hill overlooking the city on the northern bank of the Suir estuary, caters to business travellers and coach tours, and thus is not as luxurious as the Granville. Even so, the accommodations are quite pleasant. The hotel's leisure center contains a heated pool, a gym, and tennis courts.

For those who are not operating on a budget, or for those who want to treat themselves to a once-in-a-lifetime experience, **Waterford Castle** is a deluxe affair about 2 km (roughly a mile) below Waterford City on the Island at Ballinakill. The carved Elizabethan oak dining rooms, Portland stone walls, ornate fireplaces, and the superior cuisine combine to create the splendor of a bygone age—at very high prices. There is no bridge to the island, but the castle's private launch will bring guests across. There is also a ferry for cars.

However, if your budget is limited your best base for touring the area is the village of Dunmore East, 15 km (9 miles) southeast of Waterford City.

Dunmore East

A 19th-century chronicler described this fishing village southeast of Waterford City at the head of Waterford Harbour thus: "It is a fashionable, aristocratic neighborhood which verily looks down on all watering places along the southern coasts. All other places of resort bow their heads...."

Despite the hyperbole, Dunmore East, with its neat thatched cottages and its friendly, unassuming residents, *is* irresistible. There are no deluxe accommodations here, but at the small, family-run **Candlelight Inn** you will find enticing local specialties at very reasonable prices. Antoinette and Charlie Boland and their family will ensure that your every need is met. Accommodation here is simple, but the 11 rooms, which all have televisions, telephones, and showers or baths *en suite,* are clean and cozy. The nearby **Haven Hotel**, which opens only in summer, is a stylishly converted former mansion in six and a half acres of tiered lawns and woods overlooking the sea. Hosts John and Jean Kelly are attentive and considerate people; the hotel is inexpensive. The **Ocean Hotel**, nearer the harbor, is a popular gathering spot for locals. Run by Brendan and Noleen Gallagher and family, it has 14 rooms, mostly *en suite,* all with color television and telephones. A pleasant, informal atmosphere pervades.

Mrs. Klemm, a transplanted German and a gifted cook, runs a praiseworthy guesthouse, **Corballymore House**, another good base for forays into the countryside. (From Dunmore East, head for Waterford Airport; the house is clearly signposted from the easy-to-spot Murphy's Pub.)

Day Trips from Dunmore

From Dunmore you can journey southwest to the Gaeltacht (Irish-speaking) area around **Dungarvan**. Some of Europe's most rewarding deep-sea angling for blue shark, haddock, and cod takes place from Dungarvan Harbour, where boats are available for day trips. Around the south arm of the harbor at Ring (on the L 177), Laurann Casey and her brother Michael have restored and converted an old farm building into a thatch-roofed pub and restaurant worth investigating. It's called **The Seanachie**, Irish for "storyteller," and the food is first rate. **Cheekpoint**, a town to the east of Waterford City on the river, provides a lovely view of the area, and the **Suir Inn** and the **Jolly Sailor**, two friendly pubs here, are always worth a visit.

Situated almost midway on the Clonmel–Dungarvan road is the scenic **Nire Valley**, which snuggles in the foothills of the Comeragh Mountains; excellent trout fishing can be had along the River Nire. Pony-trekking along forest trails is a pleasant way to view this unspoiled beauty spot. **Paddy Melody's Pony-Trekking Centre** (Tel: 052-361-47), off the Clonmel road, has horses for both the novice and the experienced rider, as well as jaunting cars (horse buggies) for nonriders.

Larry and Eileen Ryan run a very reputable, modern dairy farmhouse in the middle of the valley at Ballymacarbry, north of Dungarvan (Tel: 052-361-41). The Ryan

Farm, or **Clonanav Farmhouse**, is just 300 yards off the Clonmel–Dungarvan road and is set in landscaped gardens with panoramic views of the Comeragh and Knockmealdown mountains. Good food is served, the vegetables and herbs picked from the Ryans' own kitchen garden.

GETTING AROUND

There is regular rail service from Dublin to Waterford, Wexford, Kilkenny, and Tipperary. Renting a car in Dublin or Shannon and driving from there is strongly suggested, however, as the towns in the Southeast are not well connected to one another and hiring a car in the country is more expensive. Each of the towns is walkable, but for travel beyond the city walls a car is necessary. Dooley Kenning Car Hire, with offices in Limerick, Dublin, and the Dublin Airport, provide a good service—and automatic-shift cars. Tel: in Dublin, (01) 77-27-23; at Dublin airport, (01) 37-11-56; in Limerick, (062) 531-03; in U.S., (908) 381-8948 or (800) 331-9301.

ACCOMMODATIONS REFERENCE

The telephone country code for the Southeast is 353. When dialing telephone numbers in the Republic from outside the country, drop the 0 in the area code. The rate ranges given below are projections *for the low and high seasons in 1992; for up-to-the-minute rate information it is always wise to telephone before booking. Unless otherwise indicated, rates are per person sharing and do not include meals or service.*

▶ **Candlelight Inn. Dunmore East**, County Waterford. Tel: (051) 832-15 or 832-39; Fax: (051) 832-89. Closed January. £25–£32, breakfast and service included.

▶ **Casey's Cedars Hotel**. Strand Road, **Rosslare**, County Wexford. Tel: (053) 321-24; Fax: (053) 322-43. £31–£38, breakfast and service included.

▶ **Cashel Palace Hotel**. Main Street, **Cashel**, County Tipperary. Tel: (062) 614-11; Fax: (062) 615-21; in U.S., (212) 832-2277 or (800) 223-6510. £58–£88.

▶ **Clonanav Farmhouse. Ballymacarbry**, County Waterford. Tel: (052) 361-41. Closed mid-November through January. £18, breakfast and service included.

▶ **Clonmel Arms Hotel**. Sarsfield Street, **Clonmel**, County Tipperary. Tel: (052) 212-33; Fax: (052) 215-26. £35–£45.

▶ **Corballymore House. Dunmore East**, County Waterford. Tel: (051) 831-43. £15, breakfast and service included.

▶ **Cullentrae House (Patricia Cantlon).** The Rower, **Inistioge,** County Kilkenny. Tel: (051) 236-14. £18, breakfast and service included.

▶ **Dundrum House Hotel. Cashel,** County Tipperary. Tel: (062) 711-16; Telex: 70255; Fax: (062) 713-66. £37– £39, breakfast included.

▶ **Faythe House Bed-and-Breakfast. Wexford,** County Wexford. Tel: (053) 222-49. £14–£15, breakfast and service included.

▶ **Ferrycarrig Hotel.** Ferrycarrig Bridge, **Wexford,** County Wexford. Tel: (053) 229-99; Fax: (053) 419-82. £35–£48, breakfast and service included.

▶ **Granville Hotel.** Meagher Quay, **Waterford,** County Waterford. Tel: (051) 551-11; Telex: 80188; Fax: (051) 703-07; in U.S., (602) 957-4200 or (800) 528-1234. £37–£65, breakfast and service included.

▶ **Haven Hotel. Dunmore East,** County Waterford. Tel: (051) 831-50. Closed November through February. £25– £35, breakfast and service included.

▶ **Horetown House. Foulksmills,** County Wexford. Tel: (051) 636-33 or 637-06; Fax: (051) 636-33. Closed January and February. £15, breakfast and service included.

▶ **Hotel Kilkenny.** College Road, **Kilkenny,** County Kilkenny. Tel: (056) 620-00; Fax: (056) 659-84. £34–£39, breakfast and service included.

▶ **Hotel Rosslare. Rosslare Harbour,** County Wexford. Tel: (053) 331-10; Fax: (053) 333-86; in U.S., (800) 223-9832; in Canada, (800) 531-6767. £27–£35, breakfast and service included.

▶ **Jury's Hotel. Waterford,** County Waterford. Tel: (051) 321-11; Telex: 80684; Fax: (051) 328-63; in U.S., (800) 843-6664; in Canada, (800) 268-1133; in London, (081) 569-5555 or (071) 937-8033; in U.K., (0345) 01-01-01. £39.

▶ **Kelly's Strand Hotel.** Strand Road, **Rosslare,** County Wexford. Tel: (053) 321-14; Fax: (053) 322-22. Closed mid-December through February. £34–£38, breakfast included.

▶ **Kilcoran Lodge Hotel. Cahir,** County Tipperary. Tel: (052) 412-88; Fax: (052) 419-94; in U.S., (305) 566-7111 or (800) 521-0643. £30–£35, breakfast included.

▶ **Lacken House.** Dublin Road, **Kilkenny,** County Kilkenny. Tel: (056) 610-85; Fax: (056) 624-35. £22–£25, breakfast included.

▶ **Marlfield House.** Courtown Road, **Gorey,** County

Wexford. Tel: (055) 211-24; Fax: (055) 215-72; in U.S., (212) 696-1323, (800) 372-1323, or (800) 223-6510. Closed early December through January. £60, breakfast included.

► **Newpark Hotel.** Castlecomer Road, **Kilkenny**, County Kilkenny. Tel: (056) 221-22; Fax: (056) 611-11. £30–£35.

► **Ocean Hotel. Dunmore East**, County Waterford. Tel: (051) 831-36; Fax: (051) 835-76. £20–£28, breakfast included.

► **Rahard Lodge (Mrs. M. Foley).** Kilkenny Road, **Cashel**, County Tipperary. Tel: (062) 610-52. Closed December through February. £13–£15, breakfast and service included.

► **Rectory House Hotel.** Dundrum, **Cashel**, County Tipperary. Tel: (062) 712-66; Fax: (062) 711-15. Closed December through February. £25–£30, breakfast and service included.

► **Step House. Borris**, County Carlow. Tel: (0503) 734-01. Open Easter to mid-December. £20, breakfast and service included.

► **Talbot Hotel.** Trinity Street, **Wexford**, County Wexford. Tel: (053) 225-66; Telex: 80658; Fax: (053) 233-77; in U.S., (212) 714-2323 or (800) 223-6764. £23.50–£28.

► **Waterford Castle.** The Island, **Ballinakill**, County Waterford. Tel: (051) 782-03; Telex: 80332; Fax: (051) 793-16. £68–£88, breakfast included.

► **Whitford House.** New Line Road, **Wexford**, County Wexford. Tel: (053) 438-45 or 434-44. Closed mid-December to mid-January. £24–£29, breakfast and service included.

► **White's Hotel.** George's Street, **Wexford**, County Wexford. Tel: (053) 223-11; Telex: 80630; Fax: (053) 450-00; in U.S., (602) 957-4200 or (800) 528-1234. £30–£38, breakfast and service included.

THE SOUTHWEST
CORK AND KERRY

By John O'Donoghue

John O'Donoghue worked as a freelance journalist for many years, mainly for The Irish Times, *where he specialized in writing about people and places. Since joining the Irish Broadcasting Service (RTE), where he is a senior staff reporter and commentator, he has covered a wide range of topics and events in Ireland. He has also written and presented documentaries for the BBC.*

The counties of Cork and Kerry, which together make up the southwest of Ireland, are like the palm of the hand, its fingers stretching into the Atlantic Ocean. The conflux of the land and sea provide this region with singular qualities.

Cork's sobriquet is the Rebel County, for reasons that are obvious enough in its many monuments and its place in the struggle for Irish independence. Kerry—no less mentioned for its part in that history—is also known as the Kingdom. This honorary title signifies the county's excellences, in the nonboastful opinion of its own people and also of the rest of Ireland and beyond.

Most travellers visit these two counties for majestic scenery of mountain and sea, usually discovered unexpectedly around an unpromising bend in the road; for a gourmet tour; for golf acknowledged by experts as some of the best in the world; for fishing (inquire at your hotel or the local angling club for a license); for mountaineering; for the cadences of both the English and Irish languages; and for the music, wild as the waves on the rocky shores. Visitors also come for the history going back to the earliest settlers from the Iberian Peninsula, but above all for the shrewd but friendly and curious people, whose sense of humor has made the turn of phrase a sport among themselves and a pleasurable (though not self-conscious) performance for the stranger—who will never feel like one in these parts.

MAJOR INTEREST IN CORK

Literary traditions
Irish music
Sea and river fishing

Cork City
English Market
South Chapel
Christ Church
Sullivan's Quay
Cork Public Museum
Crawford Municipal Art Gallery

Fota Island
Blarney Castle
Bantry Bay
Music in Ballyvourney and Coolea

MAJOR INTEREST IN KERRY

Kenmare
Sneem
Lakes of Killarney
Inisfallen
The Ring of Kerry
Dingle Peninsula

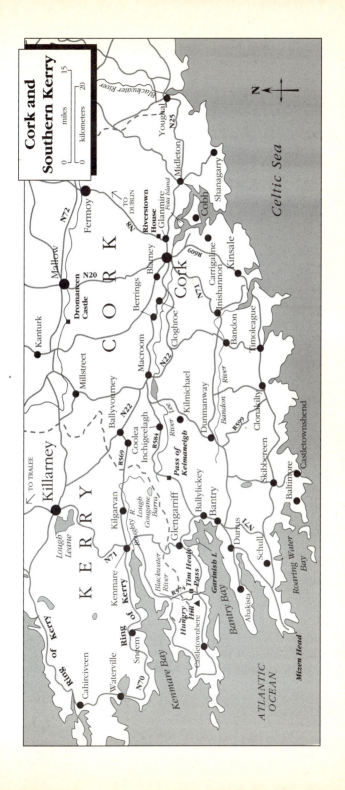

COUNTY CORK

CORK CITY

Cork City, after Dublin, is the largest city in the Republic of Ireland. Though its population of under 150,000 is not as busy as it used to be because of plant closings—including that of the local Ford assembly plant, a particularly poignant blow because Henry Ford's family originally came from County Cork—it is still an active commercial center. It is also a lively university town with a charm and openness that makes you feel comfortable chatting with anybody.

If the city of Cork—the center for touring the south and southwest of Ireland—was never called the Venice of Ireland, then it probably should have been; a walking tour of Cork City crosses innumerable bridges over the branches of the River Lee flowing into Cork Harbour. In the sixth century, when Cork, which means "marsh" in the Irish language, was founded by Saint Finbarr, these various courses of the Lee divided up areas of marshland and some dry land, on which the original city was founded.

As late as the 18th and early-19th centuries, many of the waterways were primary thoroughfares, bringing wine, butter, meat, wool, and leather to and from the houses of the city. Some of the waterways were later roofed over and then filled in to form some of the beautiful streets of the city today: the South Mall, for example, and Grand Parade and St. Patrick's Street, the main street of the city. A bollard on Grand Parade is a maritime reminder. Other signs of the early waterborne trade can be seen particularly along the **South Mall**, where a building's old main entrance door is today at the top of a flight of outside stairs; the huge doors at what is now street level once led to the boathouses of one of Cork's leading families, who called themselves the "Merchant Princes"—an example of Venetian pretensions. The dart (preserved in the Fitzgerald Museum) that the lord mayor of Cork threw into the sea annually to define the limits of his jurisdiction recalls the ring thrown into the sea to confirm Venice as its bride.

The center of Cork City is **St. Patrick's Street**, at the bottom of which is the statue of Father Mathew, the apostle of temperance. The central city area is very compact, and it is easier to walk than to use public or even private transportation. To the east is the main channel of the River Lee, leading out into Cork Harbour. To the northeast is the suburb of Montenotte, once regarded as an exclusive residential area and still retaining some of that character; to the north are the areas of Blackpool and Fairhill, where sizable numbers of blue-collar workers live; to the southeast are Douglas and Donnybrook, largely middle-class residential areas; and to the southwest, in Togher, are other densely populated areas. To the west along the Western Road are fine old Georgian houses and residences.

Dr. Sean Pettit of the Department of Education, University College, Cork (Tel: 021-27-68-71), will take you on a highly selective and colorful tour of the city, or you can easily explore on your own. Start with a part of old Cork, the **Paul Street** shopping area, which is currently enjoying a renaissance.

Begin your tour at the side entrance of the contemporary/Art Nouveau **Clouds Bar and Restaurant** of the modern and comfortable **Imperial Hotel** on the South Mall (where the fashionable of Cork assemble). Not all rooms at the Imperial are of the same standard of comfort or quietness, so be precise about your needs. The tearoom to the right of the foyer is a great place for morning and afternoon gossip, as is the Captain's bar to the left.

Turn left from the hotel onto Pembroke Street and head for Paul Street, where **Stephen Pearce** has renovated an old building with huge vertical windows that draw your eyes to his arts and crafts, pottery, wooden bowls, and glass. Beside Pearce's shop, equally attractively restored, is the **House of Donegal**, where you can pick up a length of tweed or arrange to have it sent to you. **Haggarty Designs**, a stylish clothing store, is in nearby French Church Street.

Cork's explosion of artistic activity—in the visual arts, crafts, fashion, and design—would have gladdened the hearts of the Huguenots who fled here at the end of the 17th century following the revocation of the Edict of Nantes. Though their church in French Church Street no longer exists, there is the **Huguenot** restaurant here, as well as many other bistros, coffeehouses, and bookshops

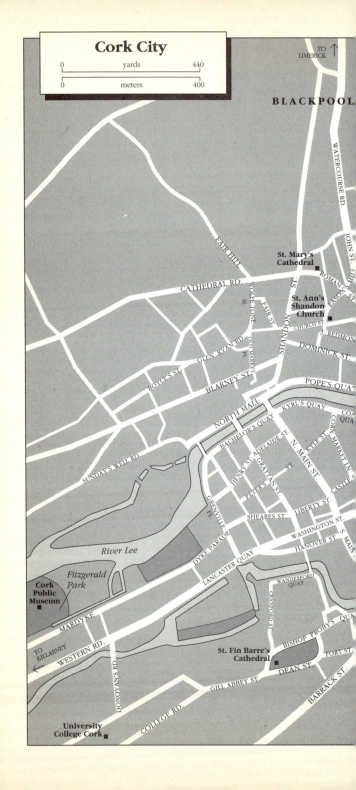

Cork City

| 0 | yards | 440 |
| 0 | meters | 400 |

TO LIMERICK ↑

BLACKPOOL

WATERCOURSE RD.

JOHN ST.

FAIR HILL

St. Mary's Cathedral

ROMAN ST.

EASON'S ST.

CATHEDRAL RD.

WOLFE TONE ST.

FAIR ST.

St. Ann's Shandon Church

SHANDON ST.

CHURCH ST.

REDMON

GLEN RYAN RD.

OLD MARKET PL.

DOMINICK ST.

BOYCE'S ST.

BLARNEY ST.

POPE'S QUA

NORTH MALL

KYRL'S QUAY

CO
QUA

BACHELOR'S QUAY

CORN MARKET N

SUNDAY'S WELL RD.

HENRY ST.

ADELAIDE ST.

GRATTAN ST.

N. MAIN ST.

KYLE ST.

CASTLE

PETER'S ST.

LIBERTY ST.

GRENVILLE PL.

SHEARES ST.

WASHINGTON ST.

River Lee

DYKE PARADE

HANOVER ST.

S. MAIN

Fitzgerald Park

LANCASTER QUAY

WANDESFORD QUAY

Cork Public Museum

MARDYKE

CRANFORD ST.

TO KILLARNEY

WESTERN RD.

DONOVAN'S RD.

BISHOP PROBY'S QUA

St. Fin Barre's Cathedral

FORT ST.

DEAN ST.

GILL ABBEY ST.

BARRACK ST.

University College Cork

COLLEGE RD.

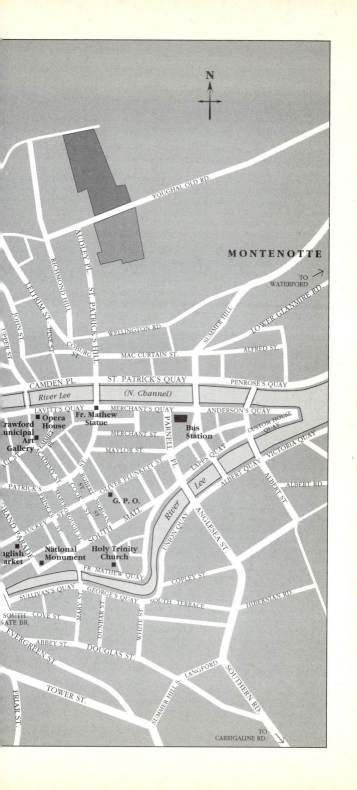

in which to savor an atmosphere that combines the best of contemporary Continental taste with the spirit of Cork.

Two other main shopping centers, not very far from this central maze of streets, are in the **Queen's Old Castle** on Grand Parade, and in the **Savoy Centre** on St. Patrick's Street. A new shopping area on Merchant's Quay is worth a visit as well. What's appealing about the young designers exhibiting and selling here is that they are not specifically "ethnic Irish" designers.

Though what might be called "updated" Irish fashion is available—and very good it is—designs here tend to belong to a new wave in Ireland, quite distinctive, not ironed-out cosmopolitan. Prominent young designers in Cork decidedly do not inhabit Hicksville—people such as Michael Mortell, with an international reputation for, particularly, suits and coats; Lainey Keogh, with her most innovative Irish knitwear; and Mariad Whisker, who designs for those under 25. The clothes of many of these up-and-coming designers can be found at **Rachel C.**, a shop in the Savoy Centre (mainly for women between 30 and 40). All of the Cork designers bear comparison with the best on the Continent.

Eating and Drinking in the Paul Street Area

To combine high fashion with quintessential Cork, walk down among the bistros and cafés in the pedestrian-only Paul Street area. You might want to cross into Oliver Plunkett Street to get stamps at the General Post Office or visit **Egan's Store**, right opposite, which has a fine display of china and Waterford glass. Almost next door is the **Hi-Bi**, a small upstairs bar with real personality. Hi-Bi is sometimes overrun by the restless young but by and large draws an intellectual crowd. Generally it is even quiet enough to bring in a book. The barman may ask for help with his upscale crossword, from which the background music—not Muzak, but classical—will not distract him or you; or he may be organizing an operatic quiz for the regulars. However, this is not at all a cliquish place.

An appetite for more than coffee can be satisfied at **The Vineyard**, a marble-topped-tables spot in Market Lane, or in Marlborough Street at the **Long Valley**, which serves homemade soup and prepares sandwiches with fresh meat cut off the joint as you watch. In St. Patrick's Street,

affectionately known to Corkonians as Pana, is **Le Château**, where pizzas, lasagne, and perhaps a word with the
chatelaine, Maura Reidy, may be enjoyed. Around the
corner in Emmet Place is **Glasseyallies Restaurant**, distinguishable by its clock under the gable—good airy ambience, but fairly pricey. Off St. Patrick's Street is the **Mut-
ton Lane Inn**, a small, intimate pub that specializes in
pints of Murphy's black stout and serves scampi and
salads. Many other eateries and drinkeries in this small
area are worth sampling.

Historical Cork

Along Grand Parade is the National Monument—a statue
of the Maid of Erin, honoring the Royal Munster Fusiliers
who died in the First World War—and the partially restored **English Market**, which, with its wonderful fountain
decorated with traditional Cork ironwork, has justly won
the European NOSTRA award for architectural restoration. On Grand Parade is a fine new amenity, a public
park that features not only the sculpted figure of an onion
seller of the market but also part of the old city walls.
Developed on a site donated to the city by the Church of
Ireland (Protestant), the park, with true Irish (and Cork)
irony, is named the Bishop Lucey Park, after a famous
Cork Roman Catholic bishop well known for zealously
maintaining his church's pre-ecumenical views.

That is not to say, though, that harmony has not existed
between the two major religious denominations in the
city, and indeed among all denominations. A few years
after the granting of Catholic Emancipation in 1829, the
opening and dedication of Cork's first really major Roman Catholic church—that of the Dominican order, on
Pope's Quay—was attended by a huge crowd of both
Catholics and Protestants.

A common cause for both traditions arose when the
Capuchin friar Father Mathew (whose statue—"the Stat-
cha"—in St. Patrick's Street is the traditional meeting
place for Corkonians) launched his crusade for temperance in the 19th century. The need for this campaign
and the social value of the friar's work was noted by
Thackeray—no lover of the Irish majority religion—on
his visit to the city in the middle of the last century. But
he also had some better things to say of Cork and
Corkonians. "The Market is but two minutes' walk out of
St. Patrick's Street where you come across a Grand

French emporium of dolls, walking sticks, carpetbags, and perfumery. The markets hard by have a cheerful look. . . . I think in walking the streets and looking at the ragged urchins crowded there, every Englishman must remark the superiority of intelligence is here and not with us. I never saw such a collection of bright-eyed, wild, clever, eager faces." He spoke as well of "the flash French and plated-goods shops." Little has changed in Cork since 1842 except the rags. For the flavor of times past, visit the open-air market at the Coal Quay on weekends.

A contrast to the classical façade of the Dominican church is a fine building called the **South Chapel**, which is tucked away in Dunbar Street, typical of the kind of out-of-the-way site chosen for Catholic churches as the penal laws relaxed. Traces of other history, especially of Medieval Cork, are nearby. **Christ Church**, an 18th-century Protestant parish church between Grand Parade and South Main Street, houses many of the surviving archives of old Cork, which could be of interest to those who would like to look up their ancestors. There is also a considerable likelihood that the English poet Edmund Spenser of *Epithalamion* and *The Faerie Queene,* who had estates from Elizabeth I in North Cork, was married in this very building. Next to Christ Church is the Queen's Old Castle (already suggested for shopping), more or less on the former site of a castle that guarded the old walled city's Watergate, through which ships entered up the various watercourses of the Lee.

For a good view of downtown Cork, pause just before you cross the bridge to **Sullivan's Quay**. This spot near the South Gate Bridge is a favorite of painters and photographers; upriver, you can see St. Fin Barre's Cathedral set against an evening sky, and downriver you look toward the magnificent white limestone confection of Holy Trinity Church. Nearby, as if ordained specifically for our friends of the easel and the camera, is the **Quay Co-Op**. Established in a converted pawnshop, it comprises a vegetarian restaurant, a bookshop with unusual selections, including travel and antiquarian books you may not find in more ordinary stores, and meeting rooms for self-help groups. The Quay is a fresh, clean, and inexpensive place to have a meal or a glass of wine, browse, or meet friends, and serves as redemption for the neighboring new government buildings, which many people consider obtrusive monstrosities. Before leaving Sullivan's Quay, step down the very old **Keyser's Lane** to the river. This is the original Viking area of Cork. (The same name crops up in many other places in Ireland and Europe, also indicating a Viking presence.)

Head west now past Barrack Street (known affectionately as "Barracka"), dropping in on the way at the **Gateway** pub (one of Ireland's oldest), where the duke of Wellington may have told stories from Waterloo. At the end of Bishop Street, **St. Fin Barre's Church of Ireland Cathedral**, designed by William Burges and completed in 1870, has many interesting and even amusing Gothic-style decorations on its exterior. The cathedral is on the site of the original round tower of St. Finbarr's monastic settlement of the seventh century, and it is not difficult to imagine the monks looking down on the lights of the first Viking encampment on the South Channel of the Lee, looking down, as it were, on their impending doom.

Down now to Lancaster Quay, on the banks of yet another of the channels of the Lee. By this time a new pub, across from Jury's Hotel, might be a welcome sight: **Reidy's** (of St. Patrick's Street's Le Château family) spirit and wine store. The building, renovated to an extremely high standard, makes good use of timber and prints to give it character; perhaps the fact that altar wines were blended here at one time will give a particular spark to your Port or Sherry, which you can have in the pub or take away. The aforementioned **Jury's Hotel** offers a high standard of luxury and service. In addition to the usual amenities—outdoor and indoor swimming pools, sauna, and exercise gym—it has a very interesting pub that achieves an authentic Cork ambience, with murals that show, in amusing juxtaposition, many of the city's personalities, past and present. Posters, old bottles, and documents from Cork's breweries complete the picture.

Michael and Deirdre Clifford, formerly of Dublin's exclusive White's on The Green, have moved their restaurant to 18 Dyke Parade on Cork City's Mardyke, famous in song and local folklore, parallel to the Western Road to the north. **Cliffords'** serves a table d'hôte of fine French food in what used to be the old Cork County Library—a Georgian house in which the Cliffords have preserved the beautiful old arches, stairways, and pillars, and restored the cornices. Open for lunch and dinner Tuesday through Friday and for dinner only Monday and Saturday (closed Sunday). Reservations are advised; Tel: (021) 27-53-33.

Two local breweries brew stout: Murphy's Brewery, and Beamish and Crawford. Their ownership has changed over the years, but the distinctive flavor of each of these brews is still appreciated in Cork, as is the whiskey known as Paddy, which is made by Irish Distillers. Launched in 1924, the liquor was so assiduously promoted by a sales-man of the time named Paddy Flaherty that retailers simply reordered "Paddy's" whiskey, hence the name.

The Western Approaches

Out a little farther west along the Western Road is the **Western Star** pub. Because it is near University College, Cork (UCC), it does have a student element, but, as always in Cork and Kerry, the clientele consists of many layers. On Monday, Wednesday, and Saturday evenings you will find a junction of city and country here. These are the nights for dog racing in the stadium on the Western Road, and the bookies, farmers, and city gents come here before and after they have had a flutter on the dogs. The Western Star is a bar where there are old mementos—jerseys and so on—of battles fought long ago in the rugby code of foot-ball; the back room even has a rock-music element, but it stays in the back room. But there is another layer yet. Staff from the UCC philosophy department might drop in for a meal or drink before an evening lecture. What amounts to informal seminars sometimes take place between staff and students; why bother moving into a formal lecture room when you can be edified in more relaxed surroundings?

Wherever you look in Cork or Kerry, you'll see stone and bronze monuments. Sculptor Seamus Murphy (1907–1975) was part of an important tradition in Irish stone carving, making statues and busts of historical figures, memorial headstones, and plaques. One amusing piece, a dog trough, is to be found on St. Patrick's Street with the Irish inscription *madraí*—dogs. (Even the dogs in Cork are presumed to be literate.) Murphy's work is omnipres-ent in Cork and Kerry. Of particular note is the beautiful and unique Gaelic style of lettering on his monuments.

At **University College, Cork**, two Murphy sculptures not to be missed are life-size bronze figures of the Cork writ-ers Sean O'Faolain and Frank O'Connor. A five-minute walk away, in Glasheen, an old Cork City locality, is St. Finbarr's Cemetery, where in Musicians' Corner you will find Murphy's headstones with carvings of musical instru-ments for Sir Arnold Bax and others. Between Mardyke

Walk and the river in the gardens of Fitzgerald Park is the **Cork Public Museum**; exhibits include Murphy's heroic-size bronze of Corkman General Michael Collins, first commander-in-chief of the Irish Free State, killed in the Civil War after Independence. Another Murphy piece in the park, described as the most important carving made in Ireland in this century, is a full-size polished limestone carving, *The Virgin of the Twilight.* Murphy also designed the Church of the Annunciation at Blackpool.

Shandon Street

Take a short walk from UCC north across the river to the **North Mall**, which is a continuation of Pope's Quay and leads on to Sunday's Well. Looking northeast from the North Mall, with its fine 18th-century doorways, you can see St. Ann's Tower of Shandon and its clock. **St. Ann's Church**, built in 1722, is the subject of Sylvester O'Mahony's "The Bells of Shandon"—a call back to Cork for every Corkonian. By arrangement it is possible to climb to the top of Shandon Tower and play a tune on the carillon; see the verger between 10:00 and 5:00 Monday through Saturday to set up a time. This is one of the oldest parts of Cork, where the original Viking settlement at Sullivan's Quay eventually moved. It was known until the Middle Ages as the Cantred of the Ostmen.

Near Shandon is the **Old Butter Market** and the building known as the **Firkin Crane**, restored with a new roof and windows, which exported Cork and Kerry butter through the 18th and 19th centuries, and where a great many cattle were once slaughtered and salted for export. This area was a great center for the collection of produce for victualing ships of the British navy, which came into Cobh (on the outer edge of Cork Harbour) and also into Bantry Bay before setting off on their worldwide voyages; it is now a center for many modern crafts shops.

Very near Shandon are two fine pubs: **The Chimes**, in Church Street, owned by the Quirke family and home of the Fair Hill Harriers (see Sports and Recreation in the Cork City Area, below) and St. Mary's Football Club, with darts, rings, and card games. The clientele is a mixture of visitors to the city, old-age pensioners, university students, and office workers. A hundred yards farther along, in the area known as St. Luke's, at the junction of Dillon's Cross and Wellington Road, is **Henchys**, one of the oldest pubs in Cork, dating from 1837. Home of a literary society, Henchys is where young poets recite their latest works; one of Ireland's best-known poets, John Montague, first tested the literary waters here. Mind you, you may have to wait for your pint as a price for this culture.

Thirty yards or so farther, in Montenotte, is the **Arbutus Lodge Hotel**, which has one of the very best tables in Ireland and which serves a Cork culinary specialty— *drisheen,* a relative of black pudding and the Scottish *haggis.* The Arbutus Lodge does not boast about the standard of its accommodations. Eat here but stay elsewhere, unless the table has been so lavish that early retirement is desirable. The **Montenotte District** has been said by Corkonians to be the epitome of upper-class self-consciousness, but this is no longer so. If some of Montenotte's glory may be faded, it still has its fine buildings with a magnificent view over the city.

Step into any of the very well-appointed bars in the **Metropole Hotel**, at Lower Glanmire Road and Mac Curtain Street, near the Kent Railway Station. The back bar and restaurant have a view over the River Lee and can be reached either from Mac Curtain Street or from the river—a great place for discreet encounters, or evasions! The Metropole is one of the principal venues of the **Cork Jazz Festival**, to which venerable and new practitioners of that art flock every year. The street was named after Thomas Mac Curtain, one of the two lord mayors of Cork who died in the War of Independence; his successor, Terence McSwiney, died on a hunger strike in Brixton Jail in London.

The Arts in Cork City

Our next stop brings us almost full circle from our start at the Paul Street shopping area, and not far away. Cross the bridge south from St. Luke's past the Father Mathew statue into St. Patrick's Street and turn right down to Emmet Place. You'll then come to the **Opera House**, a fine enough building that unfortunately turns an immense blank wall to the river. Most of the year a program of variety shows, as well as some straight drama, is offered. From time to time it presents a season of opera or individual performances by visiting operatic artists. Inquire whether the Cork Theatre Company, which produces plays by noted Irish dramatists, such as John Millington Synge, Brian Friel, Brian McMahon, and Samuel Beckett, is performing at the Opera House. The Everyman The-

atre, like the Cork Theatre Company, also lacks a permanent home. Though it usually performs only during the
winter months, it may be found most often now in Mac
Curtain Street in the **Everyman Palace**, formerly the Palace Cinema, which retains an elaborate, old-style interior
reminiscent of a music hall. Despite the fact that Cork
drama does not have a permanent base, it is alive and
well most of the year. The **Triskel Arts Centre**, in an old
back alley off Grand Parade near Singer's Corner (as in
sewing machine), is a center for all the arts: painting,
classical music, film, puppetry, and mime. It houses a
small, relatively inexpensive restaurant as well, where
food is available all day. The only mainstream cinema in
Cork is the Capitol Cineplex at Grand Parade opposite
Washington Street.

University College's Aula Maxima and the City Hall
Auditorium host symphony orchestras and larger events.
The large Gaelic Games venue sometimes hosts open-air
rock and Irish music concerts.

The Cork Film Festival takes place at the end of September and the beginning of October each year, and the Cork
Jazz Festival is at the end of October. The famed **Cork
International Choral and Folk Dance Festival** occurs every late April and May.

On Emmet Place, the **Crawford Municipal Art Gallery**
is a must-see. Its work by sculptor/stonemason Seamus
Murphy includes a plaster death mask of the wayward
but brilliant composer Sean O'Riada and a bronze bust
of Daniel Corkery, author of a book called *The Hidden
Ireland* and rightly credited with identifying some of
the movements in Irish culture not always fashionably
noticed.

But what might be called the glory of the gallery is the
Harry Clarke room. Enjoy his stained-glass, pencil, water-
color, and pen-and-ink work, with such marvelous titles
as *Ages Long Ago These Lovers Fled Away into the Storm*
and *Far o'er the Southern Moors I Have a Home for Thee.*
An excellent restaurant at the gallery serves lunch and
dinner among the pictures, more intimate and more
direct in their impact than those in the National Gallery in
Dublin, Corkonians claim. The executive chef here is
Myrtle Allen, whose internationally known cuisine (see
Cobh, below) is absolutely the best. It's a little expensive,
but worth it.

Not far away, the Cork Art Society's gallery at Lavitt's
Quay houses exhibitions by Irish artists.

James Scanlon, a modern stained-glass artist, has contributed six windows to the new apartments for the elderly (corner of Grattan and Sheares streets)—probably the best-known charitable cause in Cork City. The building is worth a visit for both the prize-winning architecture of Neil Hegarty and one ultramarine blue window in particular. The building and windows are specially flood-lit at night, and during the day the interior may be seen courtesy of the caretaker.

James Scanlon's private studios may be visited, by appointment; Tel: (021) 50-27-70. His public sculpture is on display in Sneem village (see below, in the County Kerry section).

Sports and Recreation in the
Cork City Area

There are two particular sporting activities for which Cork and its suburbs are famous. One is **bowl-playing**, or "bowlin," a far cry from the gentle French *boules* or the English bowling green. You'll find bowlers on Saturday afternoons, Sunday mornings, and midday on weekdays on quiet country roads on any side of the city. The game consists of bowling an iron ball at high speed along country roads, on a three-mile course and back again. The rules are a bit complicated and there is considerable betting, but great good humor; bowl-playing is best enjoyed as a spectator sport and for the camaraderie when the players and supporters return to the starting pub afterward. The crowds assemble at the **Black Man** pub out beyond Blackpool on the Dublin Pike, at **Healy's** of Cloghroe northwest of the city, or at **Blair's Inn** near Cloghroe.

Another great sport of the working man is **drag-hunting**. A piece of horse meat is drawn across a predetermined course in the countryside to lay down a scent, and the foot beagles (not foxhounds) assemble with their owners and supporters at various points around the area known as the Lough or up on Fair Hill. Groups called the North Harriers and the South Hunt have partisans every bit as fierce as the Blues and Greens of Byzantium. Drag-hunting is a test of the endurance of the various champion dogs. One of the greatest of them all, "The Armoured Car," is celebrated in a song of the same name by local folklore singer Jimmy Crowley. (History is never far away in Cork; this dog got his nickname from the armored car used extensively by the British forces in the War of Independence.) You can follow the hunt from stage to stage by car, but properly clad and on foot it's a great way to burn up calories.

Set dancing adds a flavor to Cork that is well worth seeking out. A form of country dancing with overtones of the hoedown, it's a very precise art, and some of its best proponents from the past are still spoken about with awe. The doyen of dancing masters of the present generation is Timmy the Brit—a butcher in the city. Apart from his legendary prowess in Irish dancing, he issues his instructions with a distinct English accent (more Cork irony). Look for exhibitions of Irish dancing at the South Parish Community Centre and various other venues and hotels all around Cork; any of the experts will be glad to teach you some basic steps. The most likely location in Cork City is one of the "spit and sawdust" pubs, a mecca for young and old for evening or weekend sessions. Currently the best folk pub is probably **An Spailpin Fanach** in South Main Street.

Gaelic hurling and football are two pastimes in Cork that engender enormous rivalry between the north and south sides of the city. Cork is accepted by the majority of Irish people as the home of the most consistent of the best practitioners of **hurling**, a fast and furious game that looks as if it must bring serious injury, if not death, to the participants, but its best players rarely do any harm to themselves or one another. Matches are played in various sites around the city throughout the year. If your visit happens to coincide with a county final or, better still, the Munster Final in Thurles or Limerick, it is worth getting a train ticket to see this spectacle. The main venue for **Gaelic football** is Pairc Ui Caoimh to the west of the city. (Gaelic football is explained at the end of the section Around Killarney, below.)

AROUND CORK CITY

From Cork City, a round-trip journey of about 40 to 50 km (25 to 30 miles) will take you to a number of interesting places. An important foray from the city is a drive out to Blarney to the northwest and to Blarney House, a beautiful residence of the Colthurst family (not open to visitors) on the grounds of **Blarney Castle**, famous of course for its Blarney Stone, the kissing of which is supposed to impart eloquence. The story goes that the resident MacCarthy chief of the time, on a visit to Elizabeth I, so pleased her with his flattery that she praised him for his eloquence, a virtue that then became attached to his castle—an early piece of Cork public relations. While here, look at the display at the Blarney Woollen Mills.

If too much of the good life has made you dyspeptic, a round of golf may be the answer. Courses are numerous in the area. Try the **Frankfield House** nine-hole golf course and golf range in Kinsale Road. Clubs may be hired at some courses, including **Bandon** and **Muskerry**; some of the courses, **Mahon Municipal Golf Course**, for example, cater especially to visitors. Mahon is busy, though. Make inquiries at **Maher's Sports Shop**, 6 King Terrace, Lower Glanmire Road, for equipment rental and friendly pointers. On Model Farm Road, off Deneheys Cross in the Wilton area of the city in the western suburbs, there is a new **tennis complex**, including a shop, bar, showers, and other facilities.

Out on the road to Dublin (N 8), in a wooded area in the attractive village of Glanmire, is **Riverstown House**, open to the public and containing some of the best plasterwork of the Italian *stuccodores* the Francini brothers. Then go back several kilometers (a couple of miles) to the roundabout and take the road to Midleton. Five hundred yards beyond, on the left-hand side, is **Dunkathel House**, an original country house, not fancified, open from May to September, noted for its collection of Irish furniture and for a permanent exhibition of the watercolors of Beatrice Gubbins.

Fota Island

Continue on and follow signposts to Fota Island, a wildlife park with an arboretum and a wonderful house that contains a collection of Irish landscape paintings from the mid-18th to the late-19th century, including some art masterpieces of national importance. The arboretum, built up by the Smith-Barry family, brings together in this magnificent setting trees and shrubs from all over the world. You can also reach Fota by train from the main station in Cork; in the days when the island was a private estate, the train stopped here on its way to Cobh and Youghal for the members of the family, but nobody else was allowed to leave or board, perhaps the only example of a private station on a public transport system in the world. Fota's spread of attractions within its extensive grounds is facing a challenge from developers that is being resisted by environmentalists.

Cobh

Farther on, southeast of Cork City at the transatlantic port of Cobh, is a memorial by the Irish sculptor Jerome O'Connor to the victims of the sinking of the *Lusitania* during the First World War (the wreck is off Kinsale). For countless thousands of Irish people, the view of Cobh was the last they saw of their native land as they emigrated to the New World. Chained in hulks offshore waiting to sail would be many other thousands, sentenced to the penal colonies in Australia and Tasmania. Tragically, it was also the final view of any land for those drowned in the *Titanic,* for which Cobh was the final port of call before the ship's fateful voyage. On a happier note, the *Sirius* sailed from here, the first steamship to cross the Atlantic.

Not far away is the townland (an ancient land division) of Shanagarry, headquarters of the Allen family and their many talents, the most famous of which is manifested in the food in the **Yeats Room** at **Ballymaloe House**, run by Myrtle Allen and her husband. In the Ballymaloe's dining room you'll enjoy a feast, not of Lucullan proportions but of the most delicate fresh and choice dishes, before you return to Cork City; or stay overnight in comfortable, though not sumptuous, surroundings.

North Cork

There are many delights in continuing farther east to the town of Youghal and up and along the Blackwater Valley on into North Cork. In the tiny village of Curraglass you can buy a side of smoked salmon at Raymond Carr's smokehouse. The **Blackwater Valley** has a specially signposted scenic drive. A beautiful pastoral area, it's home to one of the better-known fishing rivers in Ireland. Near the Blackwater's source between Mallow and Kanturk is **Longueville House**, an 18th-century period house and hotel looking across the river to the ruins of **Dromaneen Castle** (16th century), a national monument in a good state of preservation. The owners of Longueville House are the Callaghans of the clan who once owned Dromaneen Castle. Longueville's restaurant serves fresh sal-

mon in various delicate disguises with a warm, personal
touch.

North Cork has been home to many authors, including Elizabeth Bowen, who was born and lived in Bowen
Court (which no longer exists), near the village of
Kildorrery off the Fermoy-to-Mitchelstown road. One of
the bridges in the pretty village of Kanturk bears lines
about the poet Edmund Spenser, who had estates (Kil-
colman Castle) hereabouts granted to him by Elizabeth
I. There are underground caves at Mitchelstown. Northwest Cork also hosts the Millstreet Horse Show, in the
village of Millstreet at the end of July. But time constraints will probably make it more sensible to head
west from Cobh to the rest of County Cork and into
Kerry than to further explore North Cork.

Kinsale

A half hour's drive to the southwest of Cork City is the
seaside town of Kinsale, scene of the ultimately decisive
defeat for the forces of Gaelic Ireland and their Spanish
allies at the hands of the English at the beginning of the
17th century.

A walled town with a narrow entrance, Kinsale is
guarded by two magnificent forts, James Fort and Charles
Fort, both dating from the 17th century. You can take a
tour of **Charles Fort** or guide yourself through with a
leaflet. The 16th-century **Desmond Castle** is also known
as the French Prison because it was used to house prisoners during the Napoleonic Wars. Tours of Desmond Castle
are possible; follow the signposted tourist trail. Just north
of the town is the site of the Battle of Kinsale, where the
O'Neills and O'Donnells coming down from the north
tried to relieve a force of Spaniards who had come to
assist them; in a confused situation they lost the battle to
the Elizabethan forces under Mountjoy. The attempted
linkup with Spanish forces was only one of many examples over the centuries of Catholic Gaelic Ireland trying
to elicit assistance from Catholic Europe, particularly
Spain and France.

Kinsale is an interesting place to spend some time, and
it's small enough to cover on foot. It has a large yacht
marina that entices boats from France, Germany, Britain,
and much farther afield, creating a cosmopolitan atmosphere in this lovely little town. Many of Kinsale's build-

ings have been beautifully restored, and the town has won European and Irish architectural awards.

On a fine evening join the locals in an Irish *paseo,* where people walk up and down and look at and appraise each other. Because Kinsale is a trendy, upwardly mobile place the restaurants are quite good. One, **Man Friday**, is rather plush, with a bar where you can have drinks before your meal. The **Vintage Restaurant** and **Max's Wine Bar** are also worth a visit. Two places to stay around here are with the Griffin family at **Hillside House**, in Camphill, with good views of the countryside, or at the fashionable **Acton's Hotel** in town, where you will find comfort and the Continental flavor of Kinsale. Kinsale is the venue for a number of theme festivals throughout the year.

West to Kerry and Killarney

As you travel west out of Cork City, you are, in the local parlance, "making for" Killarney, the main tourist center of County Kerry, via Glengarriff and Kenmare (each at the head of a bay in the farthest southwest), a journey of about 130 km (80 miles)—or a little longer if you take certain routes and make small detours. On the assumption that your time has some limitation, only the more important stops will be mentioned (though there is plenty to be seen and noted) before getting to Killarney. Of the two basic ways to get to Killarney, the southern route is longer and runs closer to the sea. The other is more direct and more inland; we call it the alternate route.

THE SOUTHERN ROUTE TO KERRY

Douglas Street in Cork city center becomes Douglas Road and then Carrigaline Road as you head south out of the city (in Carrigaline visit the source of Carrigdhoun pottery). You might prefer to stay in Kinsale, discussed above, before starting westward, rather than beginning the journey right from Cork City. From Kinsale you can join the main Cork–Bandon road at Innishannon, or go straight to Innishannon from Cork City if you have already made the Kinsale visit. Innishannon and this stretch of the River Bandon are quite beautiful, especially in the autumn.

Bandon

All around the Bandon area are the signs—parklands, symmetrically planted trees, old, carefully sited houses— of the ordering influence of the English settlers who came here, particularly in the 16th and 17th centuries. But other people have lived here for thousands of years, and the skeletal remains of the past stick up through the landscape: stone alignments, hilltop forts, and, later in history, the tower houses and castle strongholds of the native Irish chiefs, the O'Mahonys, MacCarthys, and O'Driscolls. This area, once the center of Gaelic culture, politics, and the Brehon legal system (much more given to compensation than custodial resolution of crime), set-tled into decline after the Battle of Kinsale. Here too are the splendid ruins of pre-Reformation monastic founda-tions, such as the **Franciscan Friary** at Timoleague, due south of Bandon, so beautifully commemorated in an 18th-century Gaelic poem:

> Ivy sprouting in your arches
> Nettles on your cold, flagged floor.

The struggle between the old and the new—the planter and the old clan system, the old religion and the new— was long and bitter. Bandon Town was founded in 1608 by the great earl of Cork Richard Boyle (father of scientist Robert Boyle, of Boyle's Law). It was one of the first walled Protestant towns in Ireland, notable for its almost isolated resistance in Munster province to the Jacobite forces in the wars that extended to Ireland and finally established, after William of Orange, the Hanoverian succession. An amus-ing, though probably apocryphal, story told is that when the gates of Bandon were closed against the expected Jaco-bite forces somebody had written on the outside of the walls, "No papist may enter here," to which the reply was daubed, "Whoever wrote this wrote it well for the same is written on the gates of Hell"—all great rabble-rousing stuff that would probably land the protagonists in court today under the Prevention of Racism acts. As you drive through Bandon, and if you know your history and can distinguish a name of Gaelic origin from an English name, you can still distinguish papist from Protestant here.

The term "Horse Protestant" has an interesting prove-nance. Under 18th-century penal laws a Protestant could insist that a Catholic sell him his horse for £5—thus the centaur-like description. Today the Horse Protestants ride to hounds or compete in the many excellent horse shows in the area—Millstreet being the biggest—with their Catholic neighbors.

For highly regarded bittersweet evocations of Anglo-Irish culture, sample authors William Trevor (*Fools of Fortune*) and Molly Keane (*Good Behaviour*), both of whom have connections with this area.

Nowadays all the traditions, past and present, old and new, have been subsumed into one recognizable Irish, and even Cork, distinctiveness. Perhaps just in time, some of the English settlers' influence is being preserved. For example, the Kilbrogan Church (Church of Ireland) in Bandon has now been restored to house the West Cork Heritage Centre, which includes a collection of genealogical and other historical records for the area.

Around Clonakilty

The Presbyterian church in **Clonakilty** (southwest of Bandon on N 71) has been converted to a post office, overlooked by a statue of a pikeman from the other tradition. **Carbery Knitwear Ltd.**, in the town's former railway station, produces garments made only from natural fibers: wool, silk, cotton, and linen—56 shades in wool alone. A plain knit sweater costs between £50 and £80, and the top of the range is £100 to £130. Closed Saturdays.

The Irish country house is typified by **Drishane House** in the village of **Castletownshend**, farther west along the coast from Clonakilty, where Edith Somerville and Violet Martin, the authors of *Some Experiences of an Irish R.M.*, lived. The house is now a private residence.

Castletownshend is a remarkable spot, described by Peter Somerville-Large in *The Coast of West Cork* as a "mini Valley of the Kings." It's an oasis of Anglo-Irish history and people, with a Townshend still living in the castle and a genealogical tree of the family in St. Barrahane's Church. If you'd like to pause overnight here, you might try 17th-century **Bow Hall** in the village, run by Dick and Barbara Vickery. They serve up buttermilk pancakes with syrup and applesauce for breakfast, and freshly baked chocolate-chip cookies to send you on your way.

The improving efforts of people like Sir William Cox, lord chancellor of England under William III, who planted a colony of weavers and established the linen industry in this part of Cork, mainly around **Dunmanway**, has come to be acknowledged by the newer Ireland. Dunmanway itself, northwest of Clonakilty on R 599, has two triangular "squares"—a shape typical of an Irish planned town of the 17th century, the houses around the triangle forming a defense. The town won the national Tidy Towns competition in 1982, a sign of a change of the times very much for the better.

The New Invasion

Over the past 20 or 30 years many Continental Europeans and English, fleeing from the pressures of industrialized, competitive society, have settled in this part of West Cork. There's even a Japanese restaurant, the **Shiro Japanese Dinner House**, at Ahakista on the Durrus Peninsula, southwest of Bantry (Tel: 027-670-30). It's run by cosmopolitan German businessman Werner Pilz and his wife, Kei, whose beautifully dressed dolls and exquisite calligraphy decorate their tiny restaurant.

With their skills, mainly artistic, the new invaders have created a veritable series of colonies of gifted people who blend in wonderfully with their Irish neighbors, and in fact have given rise to the development of many new local skills and industries—not to speak of employment. Some of their work is in the **Cork Art Centre** on North Street, **Skibbereen**, west along the coast from Clonakilty. Many of these very welcome newcomers have exhibited another characteristic of all invaders of Ireland: They have become more Irish than the Irish themselves.

The older, native tradition in these parts is very well represented by the **Ceim Hill Museum**, 3 km (2 miles) southwest of Union Hall, east of Skibbereen (signposted). Ceim Hill is the ancestral home of Therese O'Mahony, the O'Mahonys being a historically dominant clan in this area. (Like other clans such as the O'Callaghans and the O'Keefes, they still hold their annual gathering at the ruins of a former family castle nearby. These events are attended by members of the clan from all over the world.) In the museum are prehistoric objects, instruments, and weapons as well as lace, farm implements, and, perhaps most interesting, examples of the West Cork cloak, so common up to a few years ago and now gone altogether from daily use. Therese is an herbalist who believes in picking her herbs from the wild and in sharing her many recipes and prescriptions. She will quote to

you from her mother's 1911 handwritten notebook for-
mulas for making starch, and methods for bleaching and
washing linen, washing lace and satin, and treating different fabrics using plants to keep the colors fast—a genuine piece of local continuity.

At **Baltimore**, southwest of Skibbereen, you can contact Dermot Kennedy (Tel: 028-201-41) about sailing
charters or rentals. You will enjoy beautiful scenery in
the safe and sheltered (and misnamed) Roaring Water
Bay, and afterward you can visit the pub with a Moor on
its sign—there is a tradition here that Baltimore was
sacked by Barbary pirates.

The Bantry Bay Area

The former oil terminal on Whiddy Island, just offshore
of **Bantry Town**, on the coast northwest of Skibbereen,
may not be one of the most picturesque sights in the
world, but the successful camouflage of the storage tanks
is an interesting attempt to reconcile industrial development with a scene of striking natural beauty. **Bantry
House** and gardens, a well-sited home of local gentry for
many generations and a museum as well, is open to the
public from Easter to the end of October. Bantry Bay is
best appreciated from the Bantry–Glengarriff road, with a
full unimpeded view that is at its best at sunset.

This tranquillity is not at all the scene that greeted a
French naval expedition at the end of the 18th century,
when, during an attempt to export the French Revolution
by assisting the Irish patriot Wolfe Tone and his United
Irishmen, it was scattered by a storm (echoes of the fate
of the Spanish Armada).

Glengarriff village, on the other side of the bay head
from Bantry, has now recovered somewhat from its former
tawdry reputation, and there are some excellent crafts
shops and good accommodations here. The old-fashioned
Blue Pool Hotel in the middle of the village is highly
regarded; there are no rooms *en suite,* but it's filled with
antique furniture and is a marvelous value. You will find
excellent cuisine and good value at **Casey's Hotel** next
door, renowned among trenchermen. The rooms are comfortable (lots of chintz), and a middle-class, middle-aged
atmosphere pervades. Impromptu sing-alongs have been
known to break out. Two other good choices are the
Bayview House, nestled in the hillside here and run by
Margaret Heffernan, and **St. Killian's** guesthouse, on the

road to Castletownbere on the north side of Bantry Bay. St. Killian's overlooks a mountain stream that flows into the sea, and it serves its own home-grown produce. The same friendly O'Sullivan family who run the guesthouse will either accompany you or provide a self-drive outboard motorboat to take you from Ellen's Rock, a few hundred yards away, to **Garinish Island**, which is less than ten minutes from the shore. You can cruise around the island and see gray seals basking on the rocks. Garinish Island was given to the nation by relatives of Annan Bryce, the man who turned what was a barren rocky island into spectacular gardens, helped by the subtropical climate that a benign Gulf Stream bestows on all of the coast of the Irish Southwest. Perhaps this is the place to mention that the waters and beaches of the Southwest are very welcoming to swimmers from the temperate zones of the globe, but are possibly too cold for others except during long, warm summers.

On a fine evening, walk back up the Bantry road from Glengarriff; about a mile up on the right-hand side is the site of the former Ma Roche's Hotel. On the grounds down toward the sea are the original monkey-puzzle trees (so named because their spiky leaves supposedly make them too difficult for even a monkey to climb). Imagine the sound of racquets on balls, midshipmen and local young ladies playing tennis in the 1920s and 1930s, when the hotel was one of the great social centers for the British navy, based at Berehaven at the mouth of the bay. This was one of the ports left in British government control at the time of Independence, and it was not reclaimed until the agreement between Neville Chamberlain and Eamon de Valera in 1938—just in time to preserve full Irish neutrality in the Second World War.

In this area the historic O'Sullivan Bere family granted leases to Spanish fishermen to fish in Bantry Bay for pilchards (if the Spanish could elude O'Driscoll pirates). After the defeats of Kinsale (the early 1600s) and later, the O'Sullivan Beres migrated northward hundreds of miles, an exodus comparable in its hardship to Mao Tse-tung's Long March in China, or the movements of the Voortrekkers in South Africa.

However, the romanticism associated with the ancient Irish chieftainships must be set against a background of brutality and primitive treatment within the clan system. The O'Sullivan chiefs, for instance, frequently maltreated their subordinate peoples; the hounds of the clan chiefs were fed better than the lowly members of the clan. If the dogs were not found in good condition when the chief came to hunt, the heads of his followers rolled.

The R 574 road, north from the middle of Bantry Bay's north shore a bit west of Glengarriff, crosses over the Caha Mountains through Tim Healy Pass—named for a former governor-general of Ireland—a journey that offers truly magnificent views over Bantry Bay and Kenmare Bay on the north (Kerry) side of this rugged spine of mountains.

Orienteering, mountaineering, or just rock climbing is excellent around here but can be dangerous because of the capriciousness of the Atlantic weather. This is wild, beautiful, rugged, but unyielding country, as indicated by the name of one of its bare peaks: Hungry Hill.

THE ALTERNATE ROUTE FROM CORK CITY TO KERRY

The main road out of Cork City west to **Macroom** (N 22) goes past the County Hall, a tall building beyond the Western Road with an amusing statue of two workmen looking up at it. The men seem to be not so much impressed as mockingly bewildered at the building's pretensions to grandeur, a good reminder of the essential personality of your average Corkonian. William Penn of Pennsylvania visited Macroom many times, and by all accounts was not very enamored of the people or their culture; but then the good William was an upright and somewhat straitlaced person, not a type very conspicuous in these parts.

Another route to Macroom, route 618, runs north of and parallel to the main road, along the valley of the River Lee through the pretty villages of **Dripsey** and **Coachford**. Additionally, if you haven't already visited **Blarney** on a foray out of Cork City, you can detour north to it and return again to the N 22.

As you approach Macroom on the main road you will have to decide which of two routes to Killarney in Kerry to follow. One, N 22, leads straight through Macroom and on to the Irish-speaking area of **Ballyvourney** and **Coolea**. These two Cork villages (together, population 300) boast an enormously rich and productive tradition of Irish music and literature—a quarter of this tiny population writes poetry in the Irish language. With the opening of radio and TV studios in the area, it is more likely that this material will be preserved, developed, and used as a treasure house, instead of being turned into pseudo-cultural productions. But above all the area was home to the composer and music teacher Sean O'Riada, who commuted regularly to University College, Cork, to teach his art and craft. He wrote Irish traditional music themes in the shapes and forms of classical music, and experimented with marrying those themes with Continental and other styles. His son Peadar and others of his family have maintained and developed the standards and inspiration of their father and mother. The choir from the area, which has won many plaudits, is based on an old Irish tradition of the exclusively male choir. There is nothing chauvinist about this; it simply goes back to an established monastic tradition that excluded women because they were considered a distraction—an insult and a compliment combined.

If you wish to spend the night nearby, you might try the **Dineen family** bed-and-breakfast, beyond Coolea toward Kilgarvan. It may suit your taste, as it has that of author Richard Condon. Set in what Condon calls the "beautiful, wild, gorgeous red sandstone mountains of County Kerry," it has "Irish linen, Irish china, Irish silverware, Gaelic spoken, and Irish bacon and cabbage, country style," plus a welcome drink and whiskey cake on arrival. After this stop, return to N 22 and continue through wild mountain country into Kerry and Killarney.

To follow a second, more southerly, route to Kerry, make a left just past Macroom and, going over the Shehy Mountains, join the R 584. A short detour via R 587 off R 584 will take you to the site of the 1920 IRA ambush of the British at **Kilmichael**, famed in song. This particular episode was followed shortly after by the British burning a considerable part of Cork City. Responsibility for this obvious reprisal was indicated in following days by Crown forces wearing burnt corks in their hats on the streets of Dublin.

Rejoining the R 584 again we soon come to the peaceful **Lough Gougane Barra**, where, the poem says, the Lough "Allua of swans flies forth as an arrow," and indeed the little oratory that commemorates where Saint Finbarr of Cork City began his monastic life still has swans on the nearby waters. On through the Pass of Keimaneigh, through the Shehy Mountains, the road comes out at

Ballylickey and goes on to Glengarriff and north to Kenmare and Killarney.

COUNTY KERRY

One of the clichés of travelling—"so much to see and so little time to see it"—is particularly true of Kerry. The long indentations and peninsulas of the county and the richness of its archaeological remains make it difficult to cover in a short time. It isn't really possible to do justice to the area of Killarney and also make a detailed tour of the Ring of Kerry (discussed in detail below), which takes in Cahirciveen, Waterville, Sneem, Kenmare, and back to Killarney—about four hours—*and,* without a very long stay, visit the Dingle Peninsula, too. Yet the latter is the richest source of archaeological sites, and at its tip are ancient Irish cultural artifacts with remarkable literary connotations. With limited time, then, see the Dingle Peninsula, and if you have a half day to spare take a bus tour (Dero's or another from Killarney, booked with the tourist office in the Town Hall) of the Ring. In bad weather, doing the Ring can be tricky in your own car. We begin our tour of Kerry in Kenmare—its name in Irish means "little nest"—which comes as an orderly surprise after the wild countryside leading to it.

Kenmare

Kenmare, laid out by the marquess of Lansdowne in 1775, was a model of a landlord's town: Two principal streets form an X, with a park at the bottom of the base. County Kerry in general is an impressive area of prehistoric monuments, and one of them is right here in the town— a circle of 15 stones with one boulder in the middle, an arrangement probably associated with human sacrifice.

The town was the scene of a different kind of human sacrifice in the middle of the last century, with the terrible suffering of the Great Hunger, followed by succeeding famines. With the terrible irony of changing times, the workhouse (now the district hospital), the scene of so much suffering during the famines, is only a short distance away from four of Kenmare's many excellent eating spots: **The Lime Tree**, which serves dinner in charming natural wood and stone surroundings from 6:00 to 9:30 P.M. Monday through Saturday, with prices ranging from £10 to £18 (Tel: 064-412-25); **The Purple Heather**, a daytime bistro; **An Leath Phingin**, on Main Street (Tel: 064-415-59), another bistro; and, the most renowned of them all, the **Park Hotel**, which won the Egon Ronay award for the best hotel in Ireland and the U.K. for 1988. The food at the Park is truly superb, at prices ranging from a bit higher than average to a good deal higher. But there is always a fire in the lounge, and the atmosphere is almost like that of an opulent but extremely friendly home. The dining-room window over-looks the Kenmare River, and the service here is of the kind that before you have actually realized you would like a second helping of vegetables, the waiter is there with them. In the same price bracket is the recently opened **Sheen Falls Lodge**, built around the former resi-dence of the Earls of Kerry and surrounded by 300 se-cluded acres of forest and lawns. Tall windows frame exquisite views of woodland, sea, and mountains.

For those with less demanding tastes there is the **Kenmare Bay Hotel** or, just back across the bridge, the very reasonable **Riversdale House Hotel**, which has a good dinner menu and is also beautifully situated by the river among ancient pines. Here you will be warmly received by Peter and Peggy O'Sullivan. As for shopping in Kenmare there is a branch of the **Quill's** chain of crafts stores in town.

Around Kenmare

If you must skip the Ring of Kerry, then before leaving Kenmare it's worth going out a little to see the beautiful and striking village of **Sneem**, the Irish word for "knot," in this case a figure eight. (Sneem is west of Kenmare on N 70, part of the Ring of Kerry.) For a wealth of local lore and tradition, consult T. E. Stoukeley's *The Knot on the Ring* or, if you're very lucky, Sneem's busy parish priest, Father Murphy, or schoolmaster Batt O'Shea.

This garden village boasts the biggest collection of outdoor sculpture in Ireland, including a remarkable series of international tributes to former president of Ireland Cearbhall O'Dalaigh, a distinguished Gaelic scholar and former chief justice of the Supreme Court.

The national memorial to the former president is the work of young Irish sculptor Vivien Roche. The flat stone—*leacht* in the Irish language—over the president's grave is by Seamus Murphy and takes the Irish traditional form of a simple cross and the name.

Here also stand James Scanlon's stone and glass constructions inspired by **Staigue Fort**, one of the best-preserved examples of the ancient forts that surrounded dwelling places. Staigue Fort is at Castlecove, about 11 km (7 miles) to the west.

Tamara Rikman, a prominent Israeli sculptor, has contributed a steel tree that combines some of the attributes of a cedar of Lebanon with Irish overtones. This was unveiled by the Israeli president Chaim Herzog, who was born and partly educated in Ireland, when his father was chief rabbi here.

In Sneem stay at quiet **Woodvale Guesthouse** overlooking Kenmare Bay, or at **Teahan's Farmhouse**; both are bed-and-breakfast accommodations. One of the **Quill's** crafts shops is here, too. A little farther on is the **Parknasilla Great Southern Hotel**, a very well appointed 19th-century mansion on extensive grounds with full facilities for indoor and outdoor sports and recreation: indoor heated saltwater pool, horseback riding, tennis, angling, sailing, water skiing, and free golf for guests (9 holes). The Parknasilla shares with Dromoland and Ashford castles the distinction of having been the venue for meetings of the European Community ministers and heads of state during Ireland's E.C. presidency in 1990.

From Kenmare, the N 71 takes you north to Killarney via Moll's Gap (visit **Cremin's** shop in Moll's Gap for woollens, rugs, and the like) and offers magnificent views of the Killarney lakes. Or you can go by the more eventful and equally rewarding Kilgarvan–Coolea–Ballyvourney route (for Coolea and Ballyvourney see The Alternate Route from Cork City to Kerry, above). In early August, **Kilgarvan** has a Rhymer's Festival, which carries on an oral-history tradition involving local and not-so-local events. In the past some of the recitations and their authors, now honored in the festival, were distinctly not in favor with the area's clergy because of their irreverence—another example of local thumbing the nose up, even at the religious establishment.

This area around the Cork/Kerry border seems to breed an atmosphere of individualism and revolt against the accepted wisdom. *In a Quiet Land,* by John O'Donoghue (no relation to this author), describes how at one level there was great piety, such as attendance at "patterns," religious exercises conducted around wells dedicated to ancient saints, and yet at the same time there was latent anticlericalism, in the not surprising form of objections to paying cash dues at appointed times of the year.

Because the people of Cork and Kerry were involved probably more than residents of other counties in both the War of Independence and the Civil War, many fell foul of the leaders of their majority church. Often they incurred excommunication and therefore exclusion from the comforts of their religion, a great deprivation considering the prospect of sudden death that awaited them. But they followed the advice of the 19th-century political leader Kerryman Daniel O'Connell that they should take their religion from Rome and keep their politics at home. They also received the consolations of their religion from monks who functioned outside the monolithic official structure of the Catholic Church, which was later grateful for the allegiance of former rebels who became national and international figures, such as Eamon de Valera.

THE KILLARNEY AREA

In the second half of the 19th century the lakes of Killarney were as famous as Sir Walter Scott's Gothic Highlands and Wordsworth's Lake District. On a more popular level, the town of Killarney, nestled in the mountains, and its surrounding lakes figured in the operetta "The Lily of Killarney" and Bing Crosby's "How Can You Buy Killarney." In any event, Killarney's beauty spots were either given to, or bought by, the state, and now constitute an extensive and beautiful national park.

Killarney used to be very commercialized but is no longer so pushy, and if you don't want souvenirs you don't have to buy them. The scenery fortunately has not been tampered with, though some who want only to row boats on the famous lakes don't like the idea of being crowded by the new covered water buses. But if it is raining, *chacun à son goût*. All the obvious tourist attractions are well advertised and signposted. The following suggestions concentrate on what doesn't always get deserved prominence.

Killarney Town

Killarney in the Irish language is *Cill Airne,* the "church of the sloe," in one interpretation. It's famous for the arbutus, a wild fruiting bush that grows nowhere else in Ireland. A full tour of the town takes two hours, but the following features can be seen in less time.

Behind the Town Hall is an ancient holy well where people "do the rounds," that is, walk around the well reciting certain prayers and then drinking the well water (not polluted). Just across the street is St. Mary's (Church of Ireland), which is notable only as a landmark. Also visit the Roman Catholic St. Mary's Cathedral (by Pugin), a fine example of Gothic Revival architecture.

The **Lewis Gallery** in Bridewell Lane includes the work of some 30 contemporary Kerry-based artists, the best known of whom is probably Pauline Bewick, whose delicate, languorous paintings have received wide acclaim. Also ask to see the weird and wonderfully fanciful paintings of an O'Donoghue chieftain's saga by a returned exile from America of the same clan (the legend is described in the discussion of Ross Castle, below). Director Frank Lewis is generous with his honest recommendations and insights.

Around the corner from St. Mary's Church is the starting point for journeys by horse-drawn jaunting car, a rather daunting mode of transport, but one on which most tourists feel it is worth having a trip. Be sure to pick a sturdy equipage: Hiring vintage horses, jarveys (drivers), and jaunting cars is ill-advised. Travellers in the past have paid the dubious compliment to the Killarney jarveys of including them in a triumvirate of people of whom international travellers must beware: the taxi drivers of Marrakech, the gondoliers of Venice, and these local tellers of tall tales, but the jaunting car can be good value if you negotiate the price.

There are a number of interesting pubs in Killarney. At **Jimmy O'Brien's**, near the friary, you will meet country people and hear traditional music; **The Laurels** specializes in ballads beloved of Irish-Americans; and in **Tattler Jack's** you will hear gossip and—among many other matters of great import—the latest state of play in Gaelic football.

Killarney offers an embarrassing proliferation of souve-

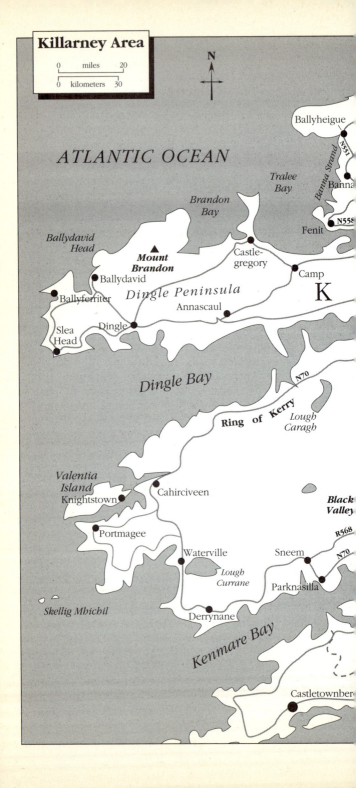

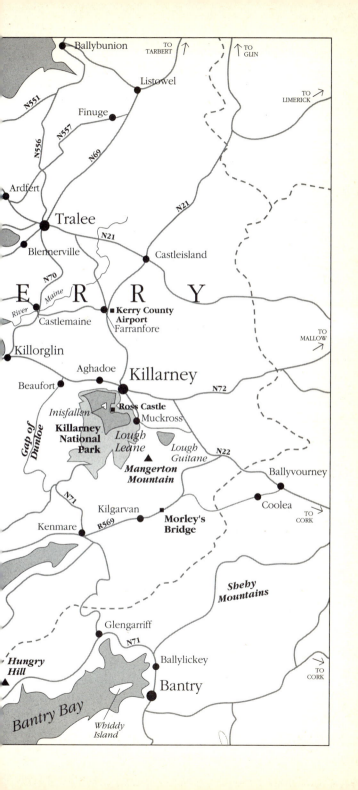

nir shops, almost all open from 9:00 A.M. to 6:00 P.M., many of them until 10:00 P.M. **Quill's**, with two shops in the main street, specializes in woollen goods, sweaters, tweeds, and jackets. Also in the main street is **Maybury's**, known for its Waterford glass, woollens, and tweeds. For crafts shopping, there's Muckross House (see below). In general, be cautious of prices in areas of high tourism.

In the Black Valley (follow the signpost to Sneem and the Youth Hostel at Moll's Gap), Flemish-born designer Lily Van Oost designs way-out wool knitwear with a look rather like craters on the moon. Though she doesn't have a shop as such, her work is on sale in the area, and she can be located by inquiring at the Black Valley Youth Hostel.

Every year in late spring Killarney is the site of a **Pan-Celtic Week**, a showplace for the work of artists and filmmakers from Ireland, Scotland, Wales, Cornwall, and Brittany. The first fixture on Killarney's well-sited **horse-racing course** is in early May each year; the second is toward the middle of July. The track is on the road to Ross Castle, 2 km (1 mile) out of town.

Just as Cork would be recommended by many people as a place to see the glories of the Irish sporting game of hurling, Kerry would certainly be equally advised as a place to see **Gaelic football** at its best. During the summer months matches are held at Fitzgerald Stadium on Anne's Road, beyond the junction of Anne's Road and Lewis Road. Gaelic football and hurling are becoming minor cult viewing on television as far away as Japan, and are spectacles not to be missed when played by skilled opponents on a fine day. Gaelic football, which involves both handling and kicking the ball, is more physical than soccer and less so than rugby. The team scores when the ball passes between goalposts set on a longer pitch than for soccer. The nearest comparison is to Australian Rules football, and competitions are played in Ireland and Australia according to an amalgam of the two codes.

Staying and Dining in the Killarney Area

The 168-room 19th-century **Great Southern Hotel**, set in spacious gardens right in Killarney, offers gracious comfort as well as easy access to all the major attractions.

Once one of the great hotels on the upper-class tourist routes of Europe, the Great Southern is equipped with an indoor swimming pool, a gym with a jacuzzi, tennis courts, and more. Also in town, beside the Town Hall (where the jarveys leave for their trips), is the reasonably priced **Three Lakes Hotel**. It has three types of rooms—standard, superior, and deluxe—all with private bath and shower and television. Choose your room carefully; most have views over the town but some at the back of the hotel have views over the national park (see below, in the Around Killarney section). The food is good but nothing special.

The **Lake Hotel**, about 2 km (1.5 miles) from Killarney Town out on the Muckross road, is set on lovely grounds and overlooks Lough Leane. Originally a private mansion, it was converted to a hotel in the 19th century; a new sun lounge looks out over the lake. Some newer bedrooms also overlook the lake; request one of these when picking your room. The spacious dining room has a lake view, although unfortunately the food is rather ordinary. Try the **Cahernane Hotel**, also on the Muckross road, for drinks on the lawn and reasonably priced snacks.

The 65-room **Castlerosse Hotel**, 2 km (1.5 miles) out on the Killorglin road—the Ring of Kerry road—has its own 36-hole golf course a half mile away on its extensive grounds, plus a restaurant that overlooks the lake. A pianist plays some nights, a guitarist plays other nights; the music is a mixture of old and new. The bedrooms are separate from the hotel, chalet/motel style, but the views from these rooms are spectacular.

The **Gleneagle Hotel**, on the road to Kenmare, is a very large sports/entertainment complex with indoor and outdoor tennis and other indoor sports. Water buses for lake tours can be booked from here. Though the place is rather rambling, busy with wedding parties and such, it's a good base for an active stay in Killarney.

At the village of Fossa on the shores of Lough Leane is the large (176 rooms) **Hotel Europe**, which, along with its excellent cuisine, offers what has been described as a James Bond–type gymnasium and exercise and relaxation facility: indoor swimming pool and tennis, horseback riding, and special rates on greens fees for certain golf courses.

Offering a stunning view from north of the town and down over the lakes is the large, modern **Aghadoe**

Heights Hotel, situated just opposite the ruins of a seventh-century church with the remains of a round tower; the restaurant provides a panoramic vista of Killarney as well as good food.

On the road northwest from town to Killorglin, past the Hotel Europe, is a modern church in a new Irish non-imitative tradition. Its shape, in black slate, suggests the mountains in which it is set; the startling interior, almost all in white, carries the eye up to the plate-glass window behind the altar, which frames the lakes and the mountains beyond in one massive, living landscape—reinforced by a line from the Psalms engraved on the wooden altar: "Praise the Lord all ye hills and mountains." Five hundred yards from the church is **Loch Lein House**, Kathleen Coffey's inexpensive bed and breakfast, which offers a lovely view of the lakes from a different perspective.

Carriglea Farmhouse, south of Killarney on the road to Muckross, provides the comforts of an old but well-restored farmhouse at similarly low rates, with dinner also available. The owner of **Linden House**, on New Road in Killarney Town, also serves as the chef. Also on New Road is **Gleanntan House**, a good value for bed and breakfast.

For more alternatives to staying in Killarney Town, consider one of the guesthouses located about halfway between Killarney and Tralee near Kerry County Airport at Farranfore in the valley of the River Maine. (The nearby village of Castlemaine is the birthplace of "The Wild Colonial Boy," one of Ireland's best-known ballads.) Among the best are the **Grange Grove Farm**, the **Oakhill Farmhouse**, the **Murphy Farmhouse**, the **Hilltop Farmhouse**, and **Tom and Eileen's Farmhouse**. All can be highly recommended. Also north of Killarney and near the airport is the **Walhalla Farm**, the site of several prehistoric archaeological remains worth seeing (Tel: 066-643-82 for information).

The best places for eating in Killarney are: **Foley's** (Denis and Carole Hartnett), serving dinner from 5:00 P.M. and providing excellent service and fresh orange juice; **Gaby's**, with a superb wine list; good but not so upmarket, the **Flesk Bar and Restaurant**, run by the "Klondyke" O'Learys, whose fine physiques obviously come from an ancestral gold rush survivor; and the **Malton Room** of the Great Southern Hotel, which retains much of the elegance and plushness of its 19th-century origins.

Around Killarney

Killarney is surrounded by the large **Killarney National Park**, which was originally individual estates. The park, which has a herd of indigenous native red deer, takes in all the lakes of Killarney. The estates of the earls of Kenmare—title and family now extinct—passed first into American and then state ownership. The estates form part of the national park and are open to the public, as is **Knockreer House**, with permanent exhibitions on the Browne family (earls of Kenmare) and the flora and fauna of the park. The entrance to Knockreer House is opposite St. Mary's Cathedral.

The Browne family, given in the 17th century the estates that formerly belonged to the O'Donoghues, was one of the very few among the newer settlers to maintain the practice of the Roman Catholic faith. Under the penal laws of the 18th century, every Catholic had to divide his property among his male heirs, which ensured a progressive reduction in the size and value of that property, as most Catholic families had quite a number of children. The interesting exception of the Brownes was that during that entire century each generation had only one male heir, and so this family managed to maintain both its religion and its estates intact. Their status lived on into the 1940s, when the local cinema still had specially upholstered and gilded seats for the lord and his lady.

In Muckross, south of Killarney on the east side of Lough Leane, is **Muckross House**, formerly owned by the Herbert family. Muckross House retains its period furnishings, and downstairs is a working folk museum, where a weaver, a potter, a bookbinder, and a blacksmith actually make their goods. A crafts shop sells their products here.

In modern contrast to the ancient religious history with which Kerry is so well endowed are the **Stations of the Cross** in the Catholic church near Muckross. These are by Imogen Stuart, daughter of the legendary Republican figure Maud Gonne MacBride and half-sister of the late Sean MacBride, international statesman and winner of the Nobel Peace Prize, the Lenin Peace Prize, and the highest United States decoration for efforts to further peace.

For almost 200 years Killarney has been an internationally known tourist resort, sometimes compared with the Lake District in England, but around Killarney the vegetation is especially lush. Wild rhododendrons make a great wash of pale purple along the lake shores in May and early June, and the waters, accessible everywhere to the public but dangerous for swimming and sailing, reflect the colors of heather, furze, and clouds.

In the **arboretum** close to Muckross House, plants that can't grow anywhere else in Ireland except in greenhouses flourish in the open. The so-called Kerry strawberry tree, the *Arbutus unido,* is remarkable in that its northern limit is otherwise the south of France. Two of the three most important natural oak woods in Ireland are in the area, one at Derrycunnihy Cascade and one at O'Sullivan's Cascade on the far side of **Lough Leane** (also known as the Lower Lake). You can hire a boat or have yourself rowed over from the Muckross Boat House; or you can drive your car through the park, despite what the horse jarveys say, to Muckross House and you'll find the boats a few yards away, through the gardens. Incidentally, the yew woods on Muckross Peninsula have been shown by pollen analysis to go back ten thousand years, to the Ice Age.

For mountain climbers and geologists the back of the **Lough Guitane** area, east of Muckross, has a remarkable rock formation formed by volcanic activity, quite similar to the formations at the Giant's Causeway in County Antrim in Northern Ireland. And for those who are seriously interested in strenuous activities, there are various orienteering courses at the resort of **Cappanalea**, 28 km (17 miles) west of Killarney on **Lough Caragh**, with canoeing and mountain climbing in the majestic **MacGillicuddy's Reeks**, home to eight peaks over 3,000 feet—but heed local advice about survival gear and weather. You can stay at Cappanalea in rather spartan surroundings, but it's not recommended. Try the 1913 red-sandstone **Ard na Sidhe**, a comfortable Victorian-style mansion complete with antique furniture, on Lough Caragh, or stay in Killorglin, 11 km (7 miles) away (see below).

Ross Castle, about 3 km (2 miles) from Killarney (going out of town, turn toward Kenmare, then turn right at Bowler's Garage), was once the fortification of an O'Donoghue chieftain whose spirit, according to legend, rises from the Lower Lake on a white horse every May 1. Ross was one of the last Gaelic strongholds to fall to the forces of Cromwell. There was a prophecy that the castle would remain impregnable unless attacked by water, and indeed the attackers did make their assault from the lake.

The island of **Inisfallen** across from Ross Castle in Lough Leane has the remains of the ancient monastery where Brian Boru, the first really effective high king of Ireland, is said to have received his early education, and where one of the most carefully compiled histories of ancient Ireland, the *Annals of Inisfallen,* was produced toward the end of the first millennium. An earl of Kenmare in the 19th century, seeing the possibility of tourist development, had part of the old ruins roofed in and held an international banquet here, attended by Leopold I, king of Belgium, Thomas Moore, the melody writer, and many other notables. Killarney has never looked back. There is no longer any visitor activity on the island, but you can land here if you hire or row a boat over from Ross Castle, and you can see the island, though you won't be given a chance to land on it, on the water-bus tour.

A trip through the **Gap of Dunloe**, a defile in the Kerry Mountains, west of Killarney on the other side of Lough Leane, is a must. One of Killarney's clichés, it is nonetheless beautiful. Visitors go by pony, or by pony and trap, through the gap (about seven miles) and down to the lake. They boat across, passing rapids, and join up again on the other side and return to Killarney. The combination of mountain, woodland, and lake vistas, and the simple array of scenery and perspectives—as well as the chat of the boatmen (not quite as mendacious as that of the jarveymen)—is worth a full day.

You can book the Gap of Dunloe tour through the Killarney Tourist Office. The bus leaves by 10:30 A.M. from the Town Hall and returns there at 5:15 P.M. (it's a good idea to get there 20 to 30 minutes early). All of the coach tour services are the same price, £21 for a full day, and in every other way similar. The pony ride begins 11 km (7 miles) from Killarney at Kate Kearney's Cottage, a historical cottage housing the Gap of Dunloe shop (no Kate Kearney still lives here). It is advisable to go by pony and trap—pony and spring cart—because some of the animals are temperamental, although the pony guides do walk along with the pony riders. Either way, you get to Gearameen, at Lord Brandon's Cottage (Lord Brandon is also long gone). You may bring your own lunch or you can buy tea, coffee, and snacks here. After lunch you walk a few yards down to the shore of the Upper Lake and take a large rowboat down to the Meeting of the Waters at Dinis Cottage and into the Lower Lake, and cross over to Ross Castle on its promontory.

The distinct advantage of booking a coach tour for this trip is that if you did it on your own, when you ended up at Ross Castle your car would be seven miles away. Of course you can drive up to Kate Kearney's Cottage and walk through the gap and simply take the views, but it's not quite the same thing as going on a pony trek.

THE REST OF KERRY
The Ring of Kerry

Even to use such a description as "the rest of Kerry" is an unfair remaindering of the rest of "the Kingdom." There is a choice of seeing the Ring of Kerry either by coach tour or by car. Any tour should take in the town of **Killorglin**, northwest of Killarney, which in August is the scene of Puck Fair, a traditional occasion for a gathering of Ireland's travelling people, presided over by a large billy goat, or Puck goat, ensconced on a monument in the center of the town. Long believed to be a symbol of fertility, the Puck quietly munching carrots is only one of many animals randomly chosen as a symbol for fairs around Ireland. But the idea of a pagan satyr symbol for an ancient fair lasting into present times—three days of madness—should not be lightly thrown over. **The Fishery**, at the bridge in Killorglin, serves smoked-salmon sandwiches for eating on the spot, and sells sides of smoked salmon, sealed in plastic, to take away. Stay at **Ashling House**, a family-run bed-and-breakfast here, or at the Ard na Sidhe nearby on Lough Caragh (discussed above).

The Ring of Kerry will take you near **Valentia Island** to the west, near Cahirciveen, and a quarry that provided slate for 14 miles of library shelving in the House of Commons at Westminster, as well as countless tops of snooker and billiard tables.

From this point (though not feasible at some times of the year) take a trip to the Skellig island named after Saint Michael: **Skellig Mhichil**. Here, in a most austere and isolated atmosphere, lived the hermits of the fifth and sixth centuries, followers of Saint Fionan. As Kenneth Clark said in his famous "Civilisation" TV series, " . . . for quite a long time—almost a hundred years—Western Christianity survived by clinging onto places like Skellig Michael, a pinnacle of rock eighteen miles off the Irish coast, rising seven hundred feet out of the sea." Here also is the second-largest gannetry in the world. To arrange a trip to Skellig Mhichil, also known as the Skellig Rock, ask for Des Lavelle or Dermot Walsh in Knightstown or Brendan Keefe in Portmagee (Tel: 0667-71-03), or ask around in Cahirciveen or Derrynane. A round trip takes all day and will cost about £15 per person. Bring lunch, a flask, and a guidebook, as there are no facilities at all on the island. Offshore, these waters provide the northernmost limit of tropical fish as well as the southernmost limit of Arctic fish. More ordinary fish may be caught from shore at **Culloo Rock**, 6 km (4 miles) west of Knightstown. Beware of the weather and the tides; the Atlantic Ocean can be treacherous.

Waterville, a small, simple town—just one long street—situated between Lough Currane and a rather nice beach, is a center for golf and fishing, with some good accommodations. The 27-room **Butler Arms Hotel** on the main street is an old family (the Huggards) hotel; the **Strand** and the **Villa Maria** are pretty average. For food look for the **Sheilin Seafood Restaurant**. The **Waterville Golf Links** (Tel: 0667-45-45) will arrange golf for visitors.

Sights of interest and accommodations in Sneem, to the east of Waterville on the Ring of Kerry, have been discussed earlier, at the beginning of the section on County Kerry (Around Kenmare).

The Dingle Peninsula

Whether or not you "do" the Ring of Kerry, be sure to make a tour of the Dingle peninsula, northwest of Killarney and west of Tralee. It features at its extreme tip, around Dingle and Ballyferriter, a most extraordinary survival of an ancient culture. Here is the main center for the Kerry Gaeltacht, where the Irish language is still spoken in an unbroken heritage going back thousands of years, where every refinement and subtlety of meaning has evolved over time.

An archaeological survey on this peninsula has identified more than 2,000 prehistoric sites, an even heavier prehistoric presence than in southeast England. On top of Brandon Mountain are the remains of an oratory where legend has it Saint Brendan prayed before his seven-year voyage, in the sixth century, which is believed to have included the discovery of America before Leif Ericsson or Columbus. There are 1,100 versions of Brendan's *Nava-*

gatio, a copy of which can be consulted in Kerry County Library in Tralee (discussed below). Brendan was born outside the town of Tralee, and is a very authentic historical person whose influence spread through various parts of the ancient province of Munster. His voyage was said to have been undertaken with 12 other monks—the image of Christ and his 12 apostles. A boat similar to that which would have been used by Brendan, made from animal skins, was used by Tim Severin in 1976 and 1977 to repeat the voyage in a strong form of partial validation. It is also wholly credible that the monks who lived in the isolation of the Skellig Rock and in other hermitages would have been hardy enough of body and mind to undertake a voyage of such length and hardship.

The contemporary mind boggles at the preoccupations of the person who prayed in **Gallarus Oratory**, a tiny stone structure, built in the first millennium, near **Ballydavid** in the northwestern part of the peninsula. The oratory, constructed of dry stone blocks gradually sloping in to form a ridged roof, hardly allowing room for an individual to stand upright, is an example of the rigorous isolation that early Irish monks endured. And that ancient holy person's mind would equally boggle at the **Round House**, the holiday home of a legal luminary, down the road in Ballydavid (tourist buses also stop here). The shape of the house was inspired by the ring and by the round forts that abound on this peninsula. The interior is not open to the public. Both sites are unique in Europe. If you would like to stay hereabouts, **Vincent and Sheila O'Gorman** provide pleasant bed-and-breakfast accommodations about 2 km (about a mile) west of Ballydavid.

For accommodations at the western end of the peninsula look for **Beiti Firtear** at **Slea Head**, which has two rooms *en suite* and fabulous views of Dingle Bay from all rooms. An American visitor, Bonnie Reina, who fell in love with the sea and sky here, has opened the **Slea Head House** guesthouse. It is fully modern and boasts a large collection of dolls and teddy bears. In **Dingle Town**, on Conor Pass Road, Pat and Anne Neligan will welcome you to a distinctive bed-and-breakfast, the **Duinan House**. **Benner's Hotel**, a charming 250-year-old establishment here, has been comfortably refurbished.

Doyle's Seafood Bar, on John Street in Dingle Town, run by Stella and John Doyle, has an old kitchen range, *sugán* (plaited straw) chairs, and an appealing stone-and-wood decor. Pick your own lobster from the tank in the bar (Tel: 066-511-74). On the same street is the **Half Door,** also excellent for local fish. (If you want to meet seafood socially, go down to Dingle Harbour; you may see the somewhat renowned dolphin named Fungie.) Ask about the Gregory Peck connection at **Ashe's** pub in town. Dingle also has a couple of good crafts shops: **Louis Mulcahy's,** especially fine for rugs and pottery, and **McKenna's. Café Liteartha** has a wide range of books both in English and in Irish. The **Singing Salmon** is open for lunch seven days.

On the way to or from Dingle and Ballyferriter, along the south shore of the peninsula, drop in at Annascul to **The South Pole Inn,** a pub started by one Tom Crean, who went to Antarctica with Scott and Shackleton. (There are more Crean memorabilia in the Dingle Library, and his relatives—the O'Brien sisters—can be contacted through Benner's Hotel in Tralee.) On the return journey to Tralee you will most certainly find somebody in the vicinity of either Castlegregory or the Dooks on the north shore to point out to you the habitat of the Natterjack toad, unique to this part of Ireland. You could also join an outing in search of the Kerry slug, likewise unique. Both animals either retreated here for the congenial climate or landed with the first inhabitants.

Tralee and the End of Kerry

Tralee, a prosperous and busy market town, is famous for its **Rose of Tralee International Festival** of not only beautiful but talented girls whose ancestors emigrated from Ireland in less than glamorous fashion; it is usually held in August or the first week of September.

The **Siamsa Tire Folklore Theatre** is based in a modern and attractive theater in Tralee and in a thatched building in Finuge, a small village to the north of Tralee and just southwest of Listowel. The group, which has toured the world with great success and acclaim, represents the traditional crafts and agricultural life of the area, and has attracted the admiration of the pope and an invitation from Australian prime minister Bob Hawke. This is a professional manifestation of a way of life that either has disappeared or is disappearing (performances here from early June to late September). Tralee is also known for good horse racing (toward the end of August each year).

For dining in town, try **Duffins,** a converted coach house with oak paneling and a gallery on Prince's Street, run by a friendly and informative duo, Pat Franklin and Rory Duffin; or the eponymous **Chez Jean-Marc**, which serves, as you might expect, mainly French cuisine. There are also the **Mount Brandon**, big, modern, a little impersonal, and **Benner's Hotel**, with a fire in the lobby and legal eagles at table during court sittings, which provides plain food at almost any time of the day and into the night. Accommodation at Benner's is spartan, though adequate, with toilets and showers in most rooms.

Another good place for dining in the area is a few miles from Tralee on the Killarney road, in **Ballyseede Castle**, amid attractive period furniture; the **Ballygarry House**, on the same side of Tralee, is also recommended. On your way to or from **Barrow Golf Course**, which is 11 km (7 miles) from Tralee on the Fenit road, enjoy fresh seafood or splendid steaks in the **Oyster Tavern** at the site of the old spa, one of the best-known eating places in Munster and beyond. Owner Jim McGrath provides wines that visiting French yachters can no longer find at home. Up the road is more good food in Jerry and Mary O'Sullivan's **The Tankard**.

There are plenty of good pubs in the Tralee vicinity. In town are the **Greyhound Bar**, for Gaelic football chat and local lore; **Bailey's Corner**, for the upwardly mobile of the area; the **Old Brogue Inn**, for the same, and an offhand atmosphere; on Castle Street, **Jess McCarthy's** has a good fire, local bachelors and bankers, and others of the middle-aged upscale crowd. About 16 km (10 miles) west of Tralee, at Camp, is **Ashe's**, a cottage-style pub; check the menu before making reservations; Tel: (066) 301-33.

On the way to Camp is **Fitzgerald's** pub on the right, with a bar footrail consisting of old rails from the long defunct narrow-gauge railway to Dingle. Also for railway buffs, there are old photos here, and, if you coincide with his daily visit, plenty of stories from Joe Dunne. From Ashe's inquire about a road passing under the magical Caherconree promontory fort and winding down to Dingle Bay. On the way to or from Camp visit the beautifully restored windmill, with its exhibitions, at Blennerville.

Another route from Tralee passes through Fenit and then heads north to beautiful **Banna Strand**, one of the four or five beaches in Ireland with the clearest water. The road then leads through another of the areas associated with Saint Brendan—**Ardfert** (stop at **Flaherty's** pub, which has pleasing wood furniture and good company)—and on to **Listowel** (National Festival of Irish Music in August and

Race Week in September), which is a staging point for an entry into Limerick to the east and Clare/Shannon to the north (via the car ferry at Tarbert, north of Listowel). This drive (via N 558 and then N 557 from Ardfert) also takes you through **Finuge**, one of the venues of the splendid entertainment group Siamsa Tíre, mentioned above. It is an excellent, although narrow and winding, alternative to the direct and dull N 69.

Ballybunion, on the coast to the northwest, has two world-rated golf courses right by the sea (Jack Nicklaus frequently flies in to play the courses) and the very comfortable **Marine Hotel**, run by Con and Bridget McCarthy, Joe O'Sullivan, and Dee. The hotel's restaurant has a reasonable menu and a view of the Atlantic—a view shared by *all* the well-appointed rooms. Try the hot seaweed baths nearby, and on a warm day run into the sea just yards away—bracing stuff!

GETTING AROUND
The principal access to this area is by air either to Cork City or Shannon Airport. Flying directly to Cork gives access to the routes and destinations mentioned in our text. Flight to Shannon and car rental at Shannon Airport brings you to the Tarbert car ferry into Kerry or via Limerick City along the shores of the Shannon River to Tarbert and a tour in reverse through Kerry and into Cork and out of Cork to Dublin. Aer Lingus has flights twice daily from Dublin into the expanding Kerry County Airport at Farranfore, midway between Killarney Town and Tralee. (For accommodations near the airport, see the Killarney section, above.)

There are also rail links to Cork City from Dublin and from Dublin to Killarney Town. The junction at Mallow is the one that goes to Killarney, but most trains go directly to Killarney and Tralee.

Alternative access routes include ferrying from Brittany to Cork and also from Britain and France to Rosslare, from which you can make a car trip to Cork.

ACCOMMODATIONS REFERENCE
The telephone country code for the Southwest is 353. When dialing telephone numbers in the Republic from outside the country, drop the 0 in the area code. The rate ranges given below are projections for the low and high seasons in 1992; for up-to-the-minute rate information it is always wise to telephone before booking. Unless other-

wise indicated, rates are per person sharing and do not include meals or service.

▶ **Acton's Hotel.** Pier Road, **Kinsale**, County Cork. Tel: (021) 77-21-35; Fax: (021) 77-22-31. £32–£44, breakfast and service included.

▶ **Aghadoe Heights Hotel.** Killarney, County Kerry. Tel: (064) 317-66; Telex: 73942; Fax: (064) 313-45; in U.S., (800) 44-UTELL. £48–£65, breakfast and service included.

▶ **Ard na Sidhe.** Near **Killorglin**, County Kerry. Tel: (066) 691-05; Fax: (066) 692-82. Closed October through April. £45–£57.50, breakfast and service included.

▶ **Ashling House (Mrs. M. Melia).** Sunhill, **Killorglin**, County Kerry. Tel: (066) 612-26. Closed October through April. £12, breakfast and service included.

▶ **Ballymaloe House. Shanagarry**, County Cork. Tel: (021) 65-25-31; Telex: 75208; Fax: (021) 65-20-21; in U.S., (800) 223-6510. £40–£44, breakfast included.

▶ **Bayview House (Mrs. Margaret Heffernan). Glengarriff**, County Cork. Tel: (027) 630-20. £12, breakfast and service included.

▶ **Beiti Firtear.** Suan Na Mara, Slea Head (Fahan), **Ventry**, County Kerry. Tel: (066) 590-78. Closed December through February. £12–£13, breakfast and service included.

▶ **Benner's Hotel.** Main Street, **Dingle**, County Kerry. Tel: (066) 516-38; Telex: 739-37; Fax: (066) 514-12. £30–£39, breakfast included.

▶ **Benner's Hotel.** Castle Street, **Tralee**, County Kerry. Tel: (066) 214-22; Fax: (066) 212-07. £20–£22, breakfast and service included.

▶ **Blue Pool Hotel. Glengarriff Village**, County Cork. Tel: (027) 630-54. Closed November through February. £15–£18, breakfast and service included.

▶ **Bow Hall (The Vickerys). Castletownshend**, County Cork. Tel: (028) 361-14. £26, breakfast and service included.

▶ **Butler Arms Hotel. Waterville**, County Kerry. Tel: (0667) 41-44; Fax: (0667) 45-20. Closed mid-October through mid-April. £35–£45, breakfast and service included.

▶ **Carriglea Farmhouse (Mr. and Mrs. M. Beazley).** Muckross Road, **Killarney**, County Kerry. Tel: (064) 311-16. Open Easter through October. £12.50–£14, breakfast and service included.

▶ **Casey's Hotel. Glengarriff Village**, County Cork. Tel: (027) 630-10. Open Easter through October. £19.50, breakfast and service included.

▶ **Castlerosse Hotel.** On T 67 near **Killarney**, County Kerry. Tel: (064) 311-44; Telex: 73910; Fax: (064) 310-31; in U.S., (602) 957-4200 or (800) 528-1234. Closed November through March. £41–£45, breakfast included.

▶ **Dineen family.** Near **Coolea**, County Cork. Tel: (064) 853-26. Closed October through March. £12.50, breakfast and service included.

▶ **Duinan House (Mrs. A. Neligan).** Duinan House, Conor Pass Road, **Dingle Town**, County Kerry. Tel: (066) 513-35. Closed November through February. £13, breakfast and service included.

▶ **Gleanntan House (Mrs. A. O'Brien).** New Road, **Killarney**, County Kerry. Tel: (064) 329-13. Closed December through February. £11, breakfast and service included.

▶ **Gleneagle Hotel and Country Club.** Muckross Road, **Killarney**, County Kerry. Tel: (064) 318-70; Fax: (064) 326-46. £24–£39, breakfast and service included.

▶ **Grange Grove Farm (Bourke family).** **Killarney**, County Kerry. Tel: (066) 643-72. Closed October through March. £13, breakfast and service included.

▶ **Great Southern Hotel. Killarney**, County Kerry. Tel: (064) 312-62; Telex: 73998; Fax: (064) 316-42; in U.S., (800) 44-UTELL. Closed January through mid-March. £42–£48.

▶ **Hillside House (Griffin family).** Camphill, **Kinsale**, County Cork. Tel: (021) 77-23-15. £12–£15, breakfast and service included.

▶ **Hilltop Farmhouse (Eileen Daly).** **Farranfore**, County Kerry. Tel: (066) 641-93. Open Easter through October. £12, breakfast and service included.

▶ **Hotel Europe.** On T 67 at Fossa near **Killarney**, County Kerry. Tel: (064) 319-00; Telex: 73913; Fax: (064) 321-18; in U.S., (212) 684-1820 or (800) 221-1074. Open April through October. £39–£57.50, breakfast and service included.

▶ **Imperial Hotel.** South Mall, **Cork City**, County Cork. Tel: (021) 27-40-40; Telex: 75126; in U.S., (800) 223-6510. £53–£58, breakfast and service included.

▶ **Jury's Hotel.** Western Road, **Cork City**, County Cork. Tel: (021) 27-66-22; Telex: 76073; Fax: (021) 27-44-77; in U.S., (800) 843-6664; in Canada, (800) 268-1133; in London, (081) 569-5555 or (071) 937-8033; in U.K., (0345) 01-01-01. £49.50.

▶ **Kenmare Bay Hotel. Kenmare**, County Kerry. Tel: (064) 413-00; Telex: 73880; Fax: (064) 415-41; in U.S., (602) 957-4200 or (800) 528-1234. £23.50–£26.50, breakfast and service included.

▶ **Lake Hotel**. Muckross Road, **Killarney**, County Kerry. Tel: (064) 310-35; Fax: (064) 319-02. Closed December through February. £25–£35, breakfast and service included.

▶ **Linden House**. New Road, **Killarney**, County Kerry. Tel: (064) 313-79. £14–£18, breakfast and service included.

▶ **Loch Lein House**. Golf Course Road, near **Killarney**, County Kerry. Tel: (064) 312-60. Closed mid-October through mid-March. £14–£18, breakfast and service included.

▶ **Longueville House. Mallow**, County Cork. Tel: (022) 471-56. £30–£70 (the highest rate gets you a deluxe room with views of the Blackwater River), breakfast included.

▶ **Marine Hotel**. Sandhill Road, **Ballybunion**, County Kerry. Tel: (068) 275-22 or 271-39; Fax: (068) 276-66. Closed November through mid-March. £23.50, breakfast included.

▶ **Murphy Farmhouse. Castlemaine**, County Kerry. Tel: (066) 673-37. £13, breakfast and service included.

▶ **Oakhill Farmhouse (Nellie and Batt Daly). Farranfore**, County Kerry. Tel: (066) 642-76. Closed October through April. £11.50, breakfast and service included.

▶ **Vincent and Sheila O'Gorman**. Glaise Bheag, Baile Na nGall, **Ballydavid**, County Kerry. Tel: (066) 551-62. £12, breakfast and service included.

▶ **Park Hotel. Kenmare**, County Kerry. Tel: (064) 412-00; Telex: 73905; Fax: (064) 414-02; in U.S., (800) 223-6764. Closed mid-November through mid-March. £95–£175, breakfast and service included.

▶ **Parknasilla Great Southern Hotel. Parknasilla**, County Kerry. Tel: (064) 451-22; Telex: 73899; Fax: (064) 453-23; in U.S., (800) 44-UTELL. Closed January through mid-March. £48–£59.

▶ **Riversdale House Hotel**. Muxnaw, **Kenmare**, County Kerry. Tel: (064) 412-99; Fax: (064) 410-75. Open Easter through December. £23–£30.

▶ **St. Killian's (Mary and Eamon O'Sullivan). Glengariff**, County Cork. Tel: (027) 633-76. Open June through August. £10, breakfast and service included.

▶ **Sheen Falls Lodge. Kenmare**, County Kerry. Tel: (064)

416-00; Fax: (064) 413-86. Closed mid-January through mid-March. £95–£100, breakfast and service included.

▶ **Slea Head House (Bonnie Reina).** Coumeenole, **Ventry,** Tralee, County Kerry. Tel: (066) 562-34. £11, breakfast and service included.

▶ **Strand. Waterville,** County Kerry. Tel: (0667) 44-36. Open June through September. £16, breakfast and service included.

▶ **Teahan's Farmhouse (Mary Teahan). Sneem,** County Kerry. Tel: (064) 451-93. Closed mid-November through February. £12–£14, breakfast and service included.

▶ **Three Lakes Hotel.** Kenmare Place, **Killarney,** County Kerry. Tel: (064) 314-79; Fax: (064) 332-17. £30–£38, breakfast and service included.

▶ **Tom and Eileen's Farmhouse. Castlemaine,** County Kerry. Tel: (066) 673-73. Open Easter through October. £11–£12, breakfast and service included.

▶ **Villa Maria.** Main Street, **Waterville,** County Kerry. Tel: (0667) 42-48. £15, breakfast and service included.

▶ **Woodvale Guesthouse (Alice O'Sullivan). Sneem,** County Kerry. Tel: (064) 451-81. £13, breakfast and service included.

THE WEST
CLARE AND CONNEMARA

By William Maxwell

William Maxwell, a resident of Dublin and a literary critic for the Irish Independent, *is also the press-division manager at Aer Lingus, Ireland's national airline. A long-time journalist, he contributes articles to many travel magazines.*

Clare and Connemara are two of the most popular tourist regions of Ireland. Geographically they comprise a stretch of spectacular rugged scenery, a combination of gray limestone and blue heather and a range of mountains that descends to fjords leading to the Atlantic Ocean. The area is bounded by the River Shannon in the south and the Twelve Pins to the north of Clifden.

MAJOR INTEREST

Rugged scenery
Irish culture
Luxury castle hotels
Fishing

Clare
The Cliffs of Moher
The Burren's lunar landscapes

Limerick City

Galway City Area
Influence of ancient trade with Spain
Shopping
Singing pubs

Aran Islands day trips
Tower at Thoor Ballylee (Yeats home and
  museum)

Connemara
Wild beauty of mountains and the sea
Celtic cultural revival
Shopping for Irish craft goods
Clifden's setting above the sea
Medieval Cong Abbey

For the purposes of planning a trip, Country Clare should be divided into three areas: first, cultural orientation in the Shannon region, near the airport; then the drive to the sea to the Cliffs of Moher; and lastly the Burren, before driving up the shores of Galway Bay to Galway City, capital of the West, and on to Connemara.

THE SHANNON REGION
OF COUNTY CLARE

Whereas most of Ireland is a plush green, Clare is predominantly gray. In places such as the Burren, a plateau of limestone rock covering more than 100 square miles in northern Clare, the land has a lunar quality. Between May and October—but especially early spring—is the best time to visit the Burren, when the rocks come alive with a beautiful carpet of wild flowers and heather. To the botanist the Burren is one of nature's wonders. To the casual visitor the wonder is how man has survived in these small rocky fields. As Cromwell said when he banished the Irish "to Hell or Connacht," there wasn't enough in this most westerly of Ireland's provinces to feed a snipe. But the people did survive, and today they retain an individuality from those in other parts of the country. When the Dublin businessman says he is getting away from it all, he is most likely heading for Clare. A 30-minute flight to Shannon International Airport and a short drive and he is in a different world.

Air travellers arriving in this part of Ireland generally come through Shannon Airport, on the north side of the River Shannon west of Limerick City, if they make the transatlantic crossing or come in via Britain. Shannon is a modern bustling terminal famous for its duty-free shops,

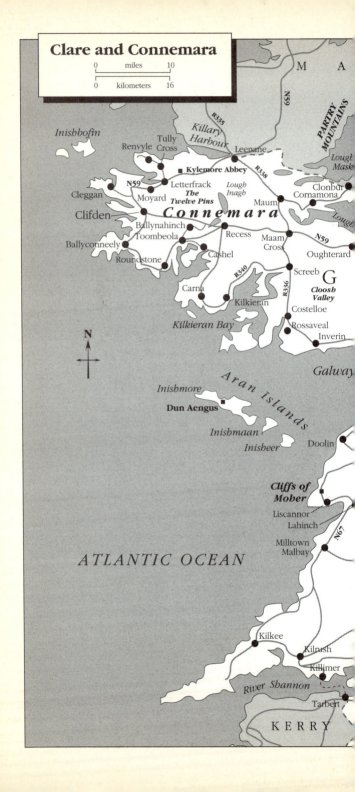

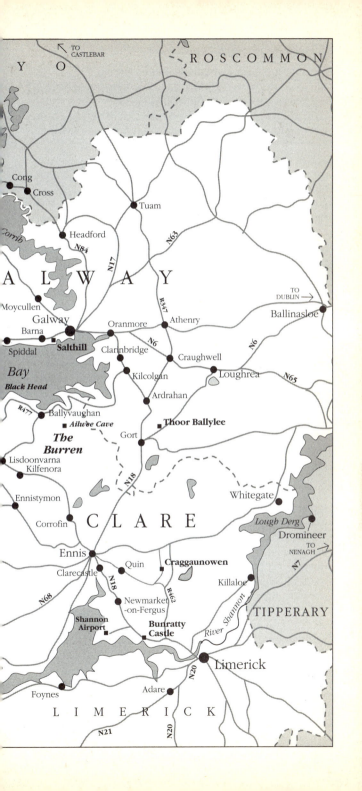

the oldest in Europe (but only visitors leaving the country can make purchases). Irish coffee is no longer mandatory, but it has wonderfully insulating qualities on a chilly morning, just as it once warmed the cockles of flying-boat passengers in the pioneering days of transatlantic aviation in the 1930s.

For those wishing to make hotel reservations, hire a car, or plan an itinerary, the arrivals terminal at Shannon has a wide selection of major car rental firms and a very good tourist information center. There are many bus tours available here, but the most leisurely way to see Clare is by car. But don't leave the airport area without shopping at the **Ballycasey Craft Centre**, which offers an unusually wide range of Irish handcrafted products, including embroidery, gold and silver jewelry, leather and suede garments, pictures, prints and frames, pottery, quilting, and wood turning.

Carrygerry House, a 200-year-old manor house elegantly restored to its former glory, is a good base in the Shannon area; it's about 5 km (3 miles) north of the airport. The hotel's surrounding woodlands overlook the estuaries of the Shannon and Fergus rivers. Rooms are *en suite,* and the chef features locally produced food prepared in the traditional Irish manner.

Another good base from which to explore the Shannon region is the **Shannon Shamrock Inn**, just 10 km (6 miles) east of the airport in Bunratty. It has an excellent kitchen, great ambience, and is very popular with international clientele flying from Shannon. In the shadow of the inn is **Bunratty Castle**, the first of many castles you will see dotted all over Clare. Like most of them it was owned at different times by the two great families that ruled this county, the O'Briens and the McNamaras. It is said that the boy William Penn was lowered in a basket from one of the turrets of Bunratty and so escaped the wrath of Cromwell. He went to America, where he would later found the state that bears his name. The present castle has been tastefully restored and is an excellent example of modern tourist amenity development. Medieval-style banquets featuring minstrels and their ladies who sing and dance are held in the Main Hall every evening throughout the tourist season.

A more literary version is held at two other castles—**Dunguaire** and **Knappogue**—where the script draws less on ballads and more on the writings of Yeats, Shaw, Wilde, and O'Casey to convey in pageant the story of

Ireland. Knappogue is near Quin, off route N18 from Limerick, and Dunguaire is in Kinvara, on the south shore of Galway Bay. Reservations for any of these banquets must be made in advance, through your hotel or Shannon Castle Tours; Tel: (061) 617-88.

For more private dining there is **MacCloskey's**, situated in an old converted cellar of Bunratty House, one of the old manor homes in the area. The decor is Old World discreet; Gerry and his wife, Marie, do all of the cooking, and they have won a deserved reputation for excellent cuisine among the many visiting businesspeople who fly in and out of the Shannon industrial zone nearby. Reservations are suggested; Tel: (061) 36-40-82. Closed Sundays and Mondays.

Those who might prefer less formal dining at lower prices should make a reservation (Tel: 061-617-88) for the **Shannon Ceili**, a dinner held in the Bunratty Barn, part of the **Folk Park**, which is a re-creation of the 19th century using cottages taken from various parts of County Clare. The furnishings are original, and local women prepare food and bake griddle bread just as in the days of their grandmothers. The meal itself is a delicious Irish stew served with wine and tea, with dessert of hot apple pie and cream. The entertainment is traditional music and dance, guaranteed to send you off with happy memories. Then you are ready for **Durty Nellys**, a very convivial local pub that seems never to be empty and serves an excellent pint. The Folk Park and Durty Nellys are both very near Bunratty Castle.

THE LIMERICK CITY AREA

Limerick City, 16 km (10 miles) east of Bunratty, is the gateway to the east and south, the place to cross the River Shannon, and a great base for those interested in fishing, boating, water sports, and hunting. The surrounding lush, green countryside is one of the best for breeding great hunters, and many a Derby winner has come from this area as well. The city is the third oldest in the Republic: It was fought over by the Norse, who built a fort here in the ninth century, then by the Normans and the English. Today's battles are more likely to be about rugby, as there are five clubs in the city, all rivals who have supplied some top players to Ireland's Triple Crowns. The city is also the hometown of film star Richard Harris and the BBC's Terry Wogan.

The visitor will find Limerick an easy city to walk around. The tourist office is located in the **Granary**, a beautifully restored 18th-century warehouse in Michael Street. While you are browsing or picking up literature on what's going on, including lists of the best entertainment, drop into the charming **Viking Coffee Shop**. A short walk north, across Thomond Bridge, are **King John's Castle** (circa 1200)—imaginatively restored and incorporating a new visitor building—and **St. Mary's Cathedral** (1172). This is the old city. The cathedral has some of the best Medieval carvings in Ireland and some fine antiquities; there is a sound and light show on Sundays.

Today's city, on the south side of the river, includes the wide expanse of O'Connell Street, with side streets that feature some great old Georgian town houses and squares. **O'Mahoneys** in O'Connell Street is a good bookstore for browsing. The staff is very helpful, and the historical material on the Limerick area here is hard to beat.

Top-quality accommodations include **Jury's Hotel**, the **Limerick Ryan Hotel**, and the **Limerick Inn**, all on the Ennis road. They offer private rooms with bath and in-house entertainment throughout the season, and their staffs will be glad to arrange special parties for golfing, fishing, or hunting. The first two are within a short distance of the city center; the Limerick Inn is 10 km (6 miles) out on the Ennis road. The inn has excellent dining, swimming, and sauna facilities.

For pubs and entertainment, students from the city's University, one of the best third-level institutes in Ireland, tend to gravitate toward **Willie Sexton's** in Henry Street or the **Shannon Arms**, which is next door. Good traditional music is available nightly at **Nancy Blake's** (Denmark Street); **Larry Murphy's** (Wolfe Tone Street); **Malibu Bar** (Cecil Street); and **Glen Tavern** (Mallow Street). Cabaret is provided nightly at the **Two-Mile Inn** (Ennis road) and at the **Brazen Head** in O'Connell Street. For the disco set there is the **Speakeasy** in O'Connell Street, and dancing at the Glentworth hotel. Literary types doing what they refer to as the "Stations of the Cross" (pub crawl) tend to forgather in the **White House** in Glentworth Street or at **Tom Collins** or **Foley's** pubs in Cecil Street.

Theatergoers should check in with the **Belltable Arts Centre**, which puts on a wide range of play performances during the year. **St. John's Square Museum** houses art exhibitions from Dublin and London.

Adare, 16 km (10 miles) southwest of Limerick on the N 21, is the social center for most of the hunting season. The village is maintained to picture-postcard perfection with the thatched cottages just as they were when they were built by the lords of Dunraven many centuries ago. The lords' ancestral home, **Adare Manor**, is now a luxury hotel similar in style to Dromoland Castle or Ashford Castle (see below). Adare Manor is set in 840 acres of woods and parkland and offers great fishing, hunting, and shooting. All rooms are luxuriously furnished, and rates are reasonable considering that you are staying in a historic castle. Should you wish to hunt with the famous Scarteen Black and Tans, the man to contact is Chris Ryan, master of the hunt, who lives at Scarteen, Knocklong; Tel: (062) 531-95. Or you can make contact in Adare through Brian Murphy, manager of the Dunraven Arms Hotel, himself no mean horseman. The Arms is the meeting place for the hunts, but be warned: If you are not an experienced horseman or woman, stay put and enjoy the hot toddies—following the "Tans" is not for amateurs.

The towns of **Killaloe**, north of Limerick City on the L 12, and **Dromineer**, in County Tipperary just outside Nenagh on the L 152 via the N 7, are excellent centers for yachting, fishing, sailing, or water-skiing.

COUNTY CLARE
OUTSIDE SHANNON

From Limerick there are two routes into Clare. You can travel along the southern shore of the River Shannon through the little town of **Foynes**, formerly the base for flying boats before Shannon Airport was developed. (There is an aviation museum in the former terminal building.) From there head on to **Tarbert**, where there is a ferry crossing of the river to Killimer, which brings you into the southern part of County Clare, with access to seaside beach resorts such as **Kilrush** and **Kilkee** on the N 67. These are of interest primarily for family-style vacations, with golf, sailing, and fishing.

The other route goes more directly from Limerick: the N 18 north to Ennis, the capital of Clare. En route is the little village of **Newmarket-on-Fergus**, and close by is **Dromoland Castle**, one of Ireland's leading luxury hotels. It belonged to the O'Briens, but was sold in the 1960s to an Irish-American entrepreneur, Bernard McDonough, who lavishly restored it. The view from the Long Gallery is worth the price of morning coffee, but if you have the time and can afford the high price (about £265 a day) for a suite in peak season (£220 in off-season), then this is one of the great baronial experiences of Ireland. Dromoland Castle is now run by an American syndicate, as is Ashford Castle at Cong, County Mayo (discussed in the Connemara section below). The castle-hotel has its own 18-hole golf course, year-round tennis courts, croquet, and bicycling. Nearby there is horseback riding and snipe and duck shooting in season, as well as access to deep-sea fishing and sailing, all of which will be arranged for you.

For those on a smaller budget there is the motel-style 121-room **Clare Inn**, situated in the seclusion of the trees near Dromoland and within easy access of Shannon Airport. From Dromoland you can make a series of day trips to Killarney and Dingle in Kerry, the Burren in County Clare, and even Blarney Castle in Cork (see also the Southwest chapter).

After Newmarket-on-Fergus the road continues through Clarecastle to **Ennis**. Ennis is a genuine Irish Medieval town of narrow streets, old abbeys, and good hotels. The old religion survived the Reformation here into the 19th century; the **Ennis Friary**, a Franciscan abbey, was by turns church and courthouse. Today it is back in the hands of the friars and worth seeing as a fine example of Medieval architecture. Ennis's **Old Ground Hotel**, part of which dates from the early 18th century, has big log-burning fires, a good restaurant, and a cabaret every evening in the tourist season.

Eamon de Valera was first elected to Dáil Eireann (the Republic's Parliament) by the people of Ennis, and the Nationalist tradition is still alive here. So is the good tradition of *fleadh,* the folk-music festivals that are held in many parts of the county in summer. (The precise dates vary; details can be provided by the local tourist office.)

Around Ennis there are a number of venues for what can be classified as specialty interests that you may wish to pursue. Fishermen can sample more than a hundred lakes in the county. Indeed, they are to be found almost everywhere, even in the Burren (see below). The best golf is at **Lahinch**, about 30 km (19 miles) northwest of

Ennis via N 85. The course here—laid out against the seacoast—is considered one of the most testing in Ireland. Lahinch is also a beach resort, ideal for swimming and sailing and with facilities for children. **Milltown Malbay**, south of Lahinch via N 67, is a similar beach resort.

Quin, a small village about 10 km (6 miles) southeast of Ennis via R 469, was a monastic site in the old days, and as such had a famous school. The restored **Quin Abbey** is a good example of what has been done in the area to recreate the everyday life of the Medieval monks. The effect is heightened by taped music and readings that allow you to get an insight into the monks' daily lives. Everything is tastefully and realistically done.

Craggaunowen, east of Quin, is a re-creation of a Bronze Age lake dwelling, called a crannog. On the grounds of the dwelling is a ring fort, a reconstruction of a farmer's house as it stood some 1,600 years ago. A more modern relic here is the *Brendan,* the hide boat that author Tim Severin sailed from Ireland to North America to prove that Saint Brendan the Navigator could have made the discovery of the New World long before Columbus.

From Ennis take the N 85 northwest to Ennistymon and from there on to Lahinch and Liscannor on the coast. This route will bring you up the coast to the **Cliffs of Moher**, one of the most breathtaking sights in Western Europe. The cliffs rise like a great natural cathedral almost 700 feet from the Atlantic Ocean and stretch for miles along the coast. The best view is from O'Brien's Tower, on the headland above the cliffs. To get a glimpse of the great variety of wild birds that nest on the ledges, visitors can use a number of walks that have been provided along the top. Care must be taken, however, especially in bad weather.

From the cliffs continue north on the coast road to **Doolin**, where there is a ferry service out to **Inisheer**, the smallest and least inhabited of the three Aran Islands. If the crossing intimidates you (the seas are seldom mirror-calm), save yourself for the daily 20-minute flight from Galway City to Inishmore or Inishmaan, the neighboring Aran Islands (see Aran Islands in the Galway section). The sea crossing to Inisheer from Doolin takes about 40 minutes.

There are some great singing pubs in Doolin. **Gus O'Connors** is especially worth a visit. The blond woman in the corner is most likely Swedish and her friend Dutch or Swiss; the reputation of Doolin for folk music has spread well beyond Ireland.

A few miles inland is **Lisdoonvarna**, which is famous for its spa waters and singing pubs. It is also a center for one of Ireland's leading summer schools: the Merriman Festival. This festival combines, as only the Irish could, learned papers given by distinguished academics with seemingly interminable pub talk. It is not for the weak of liver and should be taken in slow draughts.

Leaving Lisdoonvarna, take the scenic coast road to Ballyvaughan via Black Head or head inland directly toward Ballyvaughan via N 67. This latter road goes through **the Burren**, a landscape of gray rocks, a reminder of what the last Ice Age inflicted on Ireland. In springtime it becomes a sea of splendid colors, covered with wild flowers and heather. Botanists come here to study the unique mixture of Arctic, Alpine, and Mediterranean plants. The whole area is rich in antiquities, pre-Christian burial mounds, and the ruins of ancient abbeys. The **Burren Display Centre** at Kilfenora, about 8 km (5 miles) southeast of Lisdoonvarna by R 476, uses film and music to illustrate prehistoric life in Clare and to explain how the geology and botany of the Burren developed.

Ailwee Cave, well signposted off the Ballyvaughan road as well as along the route from the Cliffs of Moher, is one of the few stalactite caves in Ireland (it was only discovered in 1944). There's an excellent luncheon restaurant at the site, as well as a bookstore and crafts shop that sells beautiful pottery in addition to good quality knits and paintings by local artists. Tours are conducted regularly for a small fee.

The most luxurious accommodation in the area is at **Gregan's Castle Hotel**, 5 km (3 miles) from Ballyvaughan on the site of an ancient castle; some of the ruins are still visible. The hotel is recommended for its lovely ambience, exceptional menu and food prepared by the owner/chef Peter Hayden, and for the splendid views of the Burren Hills standing out against the green lowland valley where the hotel is located. After a night's hospitality with the Haydens you will be ready to drive up the shores of Galway Bay to the capital of the West.

Those on a more limited budget might try family-run **Hyland's Hotel** in Ballyvaughan. Dating back to the 18th century, Hyland's offers good, fresh home cooking with excellent seafood, and has in-house entertainment during the tourist season.

The itinerary suggested here is but one of many that can be taken, and if you wish to spend more time here and want more scientific information on the Burren we suggest *Burren Journey,* by George Cunningham, a guide available at any of the tourist offices. It comes with detailed maps and illustrations.

GALWAY CITY

Galway City, north of Ballyvaughan across Galway Bay, is the political and commercial capital of the West of Ireland. It was once the major trading port on this coast, when Ireland had strong links with Spain. Today most of its industrial wealth comes from overseas subsidiaries of multinational companies who have been attracted to Ireland in recent decades because of tax incentives and have set up in industrial zones or estates, of which Galway is one.

As a university town, Galway has a permanent floating population; when the students move out in the summer, the tourists take over. There is, therefore, a wide range of accommodations, from five-star hotels to guesthouses and bed-and-breakfasts. Particularly recommended are the **Galway Great Southern Hotel**, a luxurious accommodation in a 19th-century edifice on Eyre Square in the middle of town, with an excellent dining room, the **Oyster Room**, famous, as you may guess, for its seafood, and extensive facilities and amenities (such as an indoor swimming pool and health complex); the modern, 96-room **Galway Ryan Hotel**, on the Dublin road, not as close to the city center but comfortable and with all modern conveniences; and a local favorite, the **Ardilaun House** at Taylor's Hill, a very charming hotel housed in a former mansion and set on lovely grounds, reasonably priced and situated close to Salthill and its beautiful oceanfront west of the city.

Ireland West Tourism, the body responsible for promoting travel to the West, is located in Aras Fáilte, just off Eyre Square. Their office is worth a visit: In the same building you can rent a car, make hotel reservations, or book for the Medieval banquets at **Kinvara Castle** on Galway Bay. A very useful little book, *Tourist Trail of Old Galway,* lays

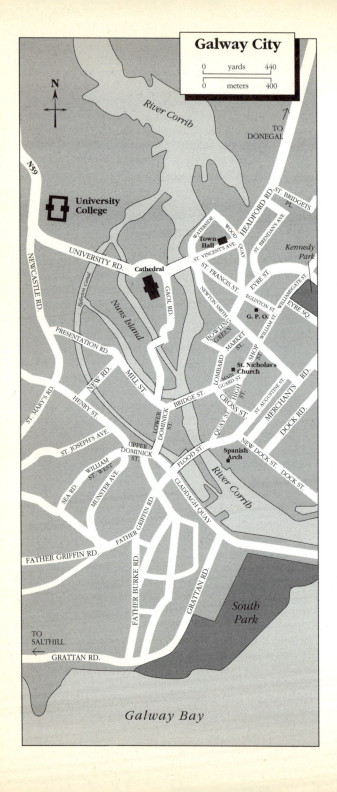

out a series of short walking trips around the old quarters of the city.

Most of these areas are not readily obvious because of the modern buildings, but they are worthy of your attention. For example, on Market Street you'll find **St. Nicholas's Church**, where it is claimed Columbus stopped off on his voyage of discovery, and on the riverbank south of the church is the **Spanish Arch**, a relic of the days when galleons tied up at the pier. The old **Claddagh District**, a short walk west from Eyre Square, was a state within a state up until the last century. Claddagh residents still see themselves as somehow separate. Today some of the city's best seafood restaurants are to be found here, such as **Old Galway Seafood** on High Street. The place also gave its name to the famous Claddagh ring, designed for lovers, though in terms of jewelry Galway offers a lot more than the Claddagh ring.

Galway City has one of the greatest ranges of stores and shopping malls outside of Dublin. Because of the tourist influx there is an abundant display of tweeds, linens, lace, crystal, and china. But if you are planning a trip out to Connemara, leave yourself some spending money; Connemara has genuinely great buys in knitwear and tweeds. With this caveat, therefore, these are some of the leading shopping centers in the city area, all centrally located, mostly on William Street close to Eyre Square: **Stephen Fallers**, for jewelry and china, Williamsgate Street; **Dillons Jewellers**, William Street; **Treasure Chest**, for the widest range of china, crystal, and the like, William Street; **Moons**, William Street; **O'Mailles**, for tweeds, Dominick Street; **Anthony Ryans**, for drapery and such, Shop Street; **Stephen Pearce**, for pottery and ceramics, Church Street. **Galway Irish Crystal** has a shop on the Dublin road open seven days a week; another shop offering crystal and other high-quality goods, **Royal Tara** at Mervue, offers daily tours for visitors.

Kenny's Bookshop and Art Gallery on High Street is one of those places that's hard to leave. The pictures are, for the most part, by contemporary Irish artists. The bookstore is divided between rare books for collectors, with a strong emphasis on Irish works, and a general selection of hardcover and paperback titles. The place is peppered with busts of some of the greats in Irish writing, and if you accidentally hit on a wine party, it is just one more Irish writer being launched. The brothers Kenny who run the business will be happy to take the time to find a rare book or advise you on Irish writers, and if you want a purchase shipped home they can arrange for that as well. As with any great bookstore, if Kenny's doesn't have it they'll get it.

Just across the street from Kenny's is an upmarket bookshop, **Sile na Gig** (The Galway Bookshop); the two women who run the store will remind you that "there is no cheap junk sold here." They stock the best in university publishing. Close by is another good general bookstore, **Hawkins House,** and when you are done here you can walk across to Bowling Green and see the house where **Nora Barnacle,** the wife of James Joyce, was born. The house is maintained by Sheila Gallager as a museum; for £1 you can go in and read some of the letters Nora wrote Joyce and see the bed she slept in as a young woman before heading off for Finn's Hotel in Dublin, where she met the Dubliner himself. The museum is open daily except at lunch and is worth a visit.

Good eateries abound in Galway, such as **The Park House** and **Eyre House** on Foster Street and the **Great Southern Hotel** on Eyre Square. **The Fountain, The Bentley,** and **Paddy's,** all on Eyre Square as well, all serve an excellent lunch. For great grub with atmosphere try **The Old Malt** off High Street, **The Quay's Pub** and **McDonaghs** on Quay Street, **McSwiggans** on Wood Quay, and **Naughtons** on Cross Street. Galway is compact, and all of these pubs are within walking distance of the city center; anyone will give you directions.

Evening entertainment in Galway City is mostly in singing pubs or good discos. Singing pubs include the **King's Head,** on High Street; the **Crane and the Clogs,** on Dominick Street; and the **Pucan,** in Eyre Square. The **Lion's Tower** in Eglington Street is a good disco. There is also a wide variety of nightly entertainment, dances, discos, restaurants and pubs in **Salthill,** a holiday resort on the bay on the western outskirts of the city that comes alive during the summer season. For the over-35 set choices include **The Salthill Hotel** at the end of the Promenade (for dinner and dancing), **Twiggs,** and **The Holiday Hotel.** The younger set tends to gather at **The Oasis, The Castle, The Promenade,** and **Rumours.** All feature a bar and dancing with a small cover charge. The resort is within a short drive or bus journey from the city center.

Theater in Galway is limited to the **Druid** (in Druid Lane), which puts on the classic Anglo-Irish playwrights, and **An Taibhdhearc** in Middle Street, which has produced such greats as the actress Siobhan McKenna. They put on musical theater with special emphasis on traditional music and folk presentations. Reservations— essential for both theaters—can be made through your hotel or directly.

University College, Galway, is a sprawling campus west of Eyre Square with a central Neo-Gothic quad. Summer courses for overseas students are held here annually in July and August, and the university is a base for the study of Celtic languages worldwide, under the sponsorship of UNESCO.

The annual races at **Ballybrit**, a kind of local Mardi Gras, should be taken in if you are anywhere in the proximity of the city at the end of July. (Ballybrit is on the eastern outskirts of Galway, about a half mile from the city center.) Accommodations in Galway must be reserved in advance, as demand is high then. The races form the fringe of a week's singing and entertainment that are special to the Irish racing calendar. Another noteworthy event is the **Oyster Festival**, held in Galway and at **Clarinbridge** (southeast of the city) toward the end of September. The festival marks the opening of the oyster season with two days of feasting. The center of activities is generally at the Great Southern Hotel. For horse lovers, two great traditional Irish fairs in the general area are the **October Horse Fair** in **Ballinasloe** in east Galway and the **Pony Show** in **Clifden**, at the western end of Connemara, in August.

The Aran Islands

No visitor to Galway should miss out on the Aran Islands. There are modern links by air and sea to the mainland, but once you arrive you will see that few other concessions to modernity have been made here. Life on this most westerly of outposts is much as it was when Oliver Cromwell's soldiers landed here in the 17th century. The largest of the islands, **Inishmore**, contains one of the greatest prehistoric stone forts in western Europe, **Dun Aengus**. The fort, thousands of years old, reaches out of the Atlantic at the very edge of an immense cliff, the last landmark before Boston.

Indeed, it is to America rather than to Ireland itself that the Aran people have always turned. There is a long tradition of emigration from the islands to America; today many islanders spend most of the year in the United

States and return home for the summer. They are a warm people who still speak the native Irish as well as English, and they have a repose and resourcefulness that fascinates the artists, writers, and ordinary visitors who come here.

The landscape, which can seem lunar, is a maze of small fields divided up by stone walls. In many places the soil was carried inland from along the shore on the backs of donkeys or men in order to have enough in which to grow potatoes. This is a place to walk near-empty roads, where if you run across someone you will be greeted with the traditional "God be with you"; or you might be invited to a dance in a cozy pub or to go deep-sea fishing with the trawlermen in search of lobster.

Culturally, the Aran Islands are a mixture of ancient pagan and Christian traditions. The people live by fishing, mostly in trawlers, although they still use the long beetle-shaped curraghs made of timber laths and canvas. The islands are very popular with artists, who are drawn to the seclusion and peace. John Millington Synge lived on **Inishmaan** for some time and thereby was inspired to write two of the classics of the Irish theater: *The Playboy of the Western World* and *Riders to the Sea*. The latter play captures some of the hardships of the islanders' lives, especially before they acquired some of the modern amenities. The famous Aran sweater originated here; according to tradition every family had its own special weave to facilitate identification if one of its members were lost at sea.

Accommodations on the islands are pretty much in guesthouses, and the entertainment is in pubs, where tourists gather to meet the local people and join in an evening's dance and sing-along. Island life is not without its complexities and frustrations, however, as portrayed in the contemporary novel *The Rock Garden,* by Leo Daly, who lived on the islands for many years. His insights contrast with the outer appearances seen by casual visitors. Good accommodations on the islands are **Gilbert's Cottage** on Inishmore, **Mrs. Faherty's** on Inishmaan, and the **Hotel Inisheer** on Inisheer.

There are daily flights from Galway City's airfield out to Inishmore, Inisheer, and Inishmaan. There is also boat service from Doolin (in County Clare) to **Inisheer**, the smallest of the three islands. A more leisurely way, if the seas are calm, is to take a day ferry from Galway or

Rossaveal on the Connemara shore. Details are available from the Galway tourist information office.

Around Galway City

Before leaving Galway and moving on to Connemara, visitors with a literary interest might like to visit Coole Park and Thoor Ballylee in the small town of **Gort**, about 40 km (25 miles) southeast of Galway on the N 18. Both places are associated with Lady Gregory and the poet William Butler Yeats.

Only ruined walls and stables remain of the Lady Gregory home in **Coole Park**, but the woods and gardens where she entertained the literary giants of the day are still here. If you take the time you can pick out the initials of the following on the autograph tree: George Bernard Shaw, Sean O'Casey, John Masefield, Augustus John, Oliver St. John Gogarty, and Douglas Hyde, who became the first president of Ireland. Close by are the lakes with the swans that inspired some of Yeats's best lyric poetry.

The **Tower at Thoor Ballylee** dates back to the 16th century; Yeats had it restored in 1917 and lived here for about ten years. It is now a Yeats museum (open to the public daily from May to October), where you can see some of the first editions of the poet's works. There is also an audiovisual presentation about Yeats and his place in Ireland's literary and political history.

On your way back to Galway you might drive northeast through **Craughwell**, a little village on the Dublin road (N6) where film director John Huston lived for many years and where he led the famous Galway Blazers Hunt. While you're in Craughwell stop in at **The Blazers Bar**, an excellent pub run by Donal Rafferty.

CONNEMARA

West of Galway City lies Connemara. A glance at the map shows that it is bounded on the east by Lough Corrib and, farther north, Lough Mask. On the west is the Atlantic Ocean. Galway Bay and Galway City link the Atlantic with Lough Corrib.

People who have never been to Ireland think of Connemara as that beautiful, wild, mountainous country that was depicted by Paul Henry in his popular paintings: the mist on the mountain, the stack of peat against the thatched cottage, and the lonesome little donkey somewhere in the foreground. Well, the thatched cottage is gone and replaced for the most part by modern, well-designed, one-story bungalows. The peat, the mist, and the mountains remain, but the air of loneliness is well dispelled. Connemara today is a community that has developed a genuine folk culture in the best possible sense. It has become a place where the Irish go to find themselves, to renew their own roots, to rediscover their identity.

At the turn of the century the search for identity was largely tied in with language. Yeats sought the Irish soul in the Celtic myths. The revolutionaries of 1916, founders of the modern-day nationalist movement, traced that soul to the Irish language. Padraig Pearse, the leader of the 1916 Easter Rising, had a cottage in Connemara. He believed that the essence of the Irish psyche lay in the simplicity of the Connemara lifestyle. The Irish language is still spoken in Connemara today; young schoolchildren and some adults, too, spend summers here to gain a facility in Irish. The area has its own Gaelic radio station.

But more than the language matters these days. Connemara has seen a great revival of local community centers, which in turn has brought a new outpouring of the visual arts, music, and sculpture. The products are to be seen in places like the **Crafts Centre** in Spiddal, where highly skilled artisans produce fine Irish handmade goods. Other fine shops for Irish goods are **Miller's** in Clifden, **Joyce's** in Letterfrack, **Michael Keogh** in Maam Cross, and **Pollycraft** in Kilraines near Spiddal. During Clifden Arts Week in September (September 20 to September 29), poets, writers, scholars, and artists—some Irish, most of them from overseas—come together to celebrate what Ireland means to them.

In addition to giving rise to its culture, Connemara is like a great Irish national park, comprising such outdoor activities as mountain trekking, boating and cruising on Lough Corrib, deep-sea angling off Galway Bay, golfing, shooting, and fishing.

The lasting pleasures of Connemara are only absorbed in silence. However, the silence of Connemara is not that of the vast, wide-open plains of the American West or of the Australian Centre, but the silence of awe at the beauty of the natural landscape and the genuine, caring friendliness of the people. In Connemara you will never be disturbed if you don't wish to be.

Around in Connemara

Many bus tours of Connemara are available, some booked in advance as part of an Irish tour, others departing from Galway. You can find out details from the West Tourism Office in Galway. The *Galway Guide,* available from the local tourist office, suggests tour options other than the ones we suggest here. Tel: (091) 630-81; Fax: (091) 652-01.

One possible itinerary includes a drive out to Clifden and the surrounding area. Take the N 59 out of Galway through Moycullen to Oughterard and stop for coffee in the **Connemara Gateway Hotel**. From Oughterard go on to Maam Cross (don't forget to visit Michael Keogh's shop here) and then on to **Ballynahinch**, the birthplace of Richard Martin, the duelist known as "Hairtrigger Dick" but rechristened "Humanity Dick" because he founded the Royal Society for the Prevention of Cruelty to Animals. The fishing for salmon and sea trout in the lake here is world renowned. Then continue through the scenic Inagh Valley and the Twelve Pins mountains and on to Clifden for the night.

Clifden, perched in an Alpine-like setting above an inlet of the Ardbear Bay, is a lovely spot for families and an excellent base for touring the surrounding countryside. The little town really comes alive in the summer months, so be sure you have booked ahead for rooms. (Clifden hosts the Pony Show each August.) There is an abundance of hotels, guesthouses, and restaurants here; to sample the local color, try the **Alcock & Brown Hotel** or the **Abbeyglen Castle**. Both have good dining facilities, but if you will only be in Clifden for one night you should go instead to **O'Grady's Seafood**, a lovely, large bar and restaurant that serves local lobster and steamed clams. Downstairs there is musical entertainment, or you might want to drop into **Mannion's Bar**, where there are nightly sessions of traditional music and singing all summer.

Several good side trips can be made from Clifden. From the center of town you can go northeast on N 59 to Killary Harbour and the Partry Mountains and on to the South Mayo border. This area is dominated by the mountain range known as the **Twelve Pins**. There is good fishing in myriad small lakes in the region, notably at Ballynahinch, discussed above. Sir William Alcock and Sir

Arthur Whitten Brown made their famous soft landing in a bog just outside Clifden after flying across the Atlantic nonstop from Newfoundland in 1919. A memorial marks the spot close to the ruins of the Marconi radio station.

Kylemore Abbey, also northeast of Clifden via N 59, is now a Benedictine convent. It was formerly the home of a British member of Parliament. In the Great Hall is a flag captured by the famed Irish Brigade at the Battle of Fontenoy. Visitors are welcome at the restaurant/pottery showrooms within walking distance of Kylemore; they have a very good selection of tweeds, linen, and china. **Connemara National Park** at **Letterfrack** near Kylemore Abbey has an audiovisual center that gives a good introduction to the geology and botany of the area. The park features several suggested walks for backpackers and mountain climbers.

The village of **Renvyle**, out on a peninsula north of Clifden and west Kylemore, is home to **Renvyle House Hotel**, once the summer residence of Oliver St. John Gogarty, Joyce's model for Buck Mulligan in *Ulysses*. Yeats and Gogarty used to hold séances here; proprietor Hugh Coyle will be happy to show you the Ghost Room. The hotel has great facilities for children, good tennis courts, and sailing in the sheltered bay just out front.

From Clifden you might take the coast road southeast through **Ballyconneely**, where there is an excellent golf course at which visitors are always welcome, then on to Roundstone and back along the northern shore of Galway Bay on the R 336 to **Spiddal**. Spiddal, just 12 km (7 miles) west of Galway, is in the heart of the Irish-speaking area. Its **Crafts Centre** offers weaving, pottery, stone carving, screen painting, and jewelry—all the finest available. **Staunton's** is a high-quality store here with great buys in knits and sweaters. The village also boasts one of the area's best fresh seafood pub-restaurants—**Boluisce's**, a place where the fishermen cook their catch.

If you have the time, there are several other attractions in this area. **Inishbofin**, a large inhabited island off Cleggan, northwest of Clifden, can be reached by a trawler that leaves daily from Cleggan. (Most of the many small islands off the coastline have no residents.) On Inishbofin you will find peace and tranquillity; should you wish to stay overnight, there are two good hotels: **Day's Hotel** and **Doonmore**.

Cong, on the northern shores of Lough Corrib and

actually in County Mayo, is one of the oldest monastic sites in Ireland. The famous Cross of Cong, now in the National Museum in Dublin, was originally at **Cong Abbey**, now in ruins, which was built about 1123 by Turlough Mor O'Conor, king of Connacht. Roderick O'Conor, the last high king of Ireland, spent the last 12 years of his life here following his failure to defeat the Normans; he died here in 1198.

The natural beauty of the countryside in the Cong area was used by John Ford in his film *The Quiet Man*. Perhaps Cong's greatest claim to fame today is **Ashford Castle**, originally built by the Norman family De Burgo (Burke) in 1228. Later it was owned by the Guinness family. Now refurbished, it operates as a luxury hotel resort like its sister hotel, Dromoland Castle in Clare. The rooms look out on Lough Cong and Lough Corrib, two of the most scenic lakes in the West of Ireland. There are tennis courts and a golf course on the grounds and cruising and fishing on the lakes. It is now a major center for conferences, and when Ronald Reagan visited Ireland he stayed here. The dining room is truly baronial, with a menu to match; before you leave Ireland, you really ought to try it.

GETTING AROUND

Passengers arriving at Shannon Airport who have not already booked a tour package with their travel agent should consult the Shannon Castle Tours counter at the airport. There is a wide variety of tours offered by coach with guide. Tours range from one day to five days and more.

There is air commuter service, up to three flights daily, by Aer Lingus from Dublin Airport to Galway City. The trip is about 40 minutes, and the aircraft returns to Dublin after a 35-minute ground turnaround at Galway.

Irish Rail makes the trip between Dublin's Heuston Station and Galway City four times a day (three times on Sundays); there is usually a buffet car. The trip takes about three hours.

ACCOMMODATIONS REFERENCE

The telephone country code for the West is 353. When dialing telephone numbers in the Republic from outside the country, drop the 0 in the area code. The rate ranges given below are projections for the low and high seasons in 1992; for up-to-the-minute rate information it is always wise to telephone before booking. Unless otherwise indicated, rates are per person sharing and do not include meals or service.

▶ **Abbeyglen Castle**. Sky Road, **Clifden**, County Galway. Tel: (095) 212-01; Fax: (095) 217-97. Closed January. £33.50–£45, breakfast and service included.

▶ **Adare Manor**. **Adare**, County Limerick. Tel: (061) 39-65-66; Telex: 70733; Fax: (061) 39-61-24; in U.S., (201) 379-6286. £45–£115.

▶ **Alcock & Brown Hotel**. The Square, **Clifden**, County Galway. Tel: (095) 210-86 or 210-06; Fax: (095) 218-42. £17–£24.50, breakfast included.

▶ **Ardilaun House**. Taylor's Hill, **Galway City**. Tel: (091) 214-33; Telex: 50013; Fax: (091) 215-46. £30–£40, breakfast included.

▶ **Ashford Castle**. **Cong**, County Mayo. Tel: (092) 460-03; Telex: 53749; Fax: (092) 462-60; in U.S., (800) 346-7007. £52.50–£87.50.

▶ **Carrygerry House**. **Shannon Airport**, County Clare. Tel: (061) 623-39 or 621-37; Fax: (061) 621-23. £23.50–£29, breakfast included.

▶ **Clare Inn**. **Newmarket-on-Fergus**, County Clare. Tel: (061) 711-61; Telex: 72085; Fax: (061) 716-22. £31.50–£47.

▶ **Day's Hotel**. **Inishbofin Island**, County Galway. Tel: (095) 458-29. £15–£17, breakfast included.

▶ **Doonmore**. **Inishbofin Island**, County Galway. Tel: (095) 458-04. Open Easter through September. £14–£18, breakfast included.

▶ **Dromoland Castle**. **Newmarket-on-Fergus**, County Clare. Tel: (061) 711-44; Telex: 70654; Fax: (061) 36-33-55; in U.S., (800) 346-7007. Double room, £52.50–£77.50; suite, £220–£265.

▶ **Galway Great Southern Hotel**. Eyre Square, **Galway City**. Tel: (091) 640-41; Telex: 50164; Fax: (091) 667-04; in U.S., (800) 44-UTELL. £42–£48.

▶ **Galway Ryan Hotel**. Dublin Road, **Galway City**. Tel: (091) 531-81; Telex: 50149; Fax: (091) 531-87; in U.S., (800) 44-UTELL. £35–£45.

▶ **Gilbert's Cottage** (**Mr. S. Dirrane**). Oatquarter, Kilronan, **Inishmore**, County Galway. Tel: (099) 611-46. £10–£15, breakfast and service included.

▶ **Gregan's Castle Hotel**. **Ballyvaughan**, County Clare. Tel: (065) 770-05; Fax: (065) 771-11; in U.S., (800) 223-6510. Open Easter through October. £40–£70, breakfast included.

► **Hotel Inisheer.** Lurgan Village, **Inisheer,** County Galway. Tel: (099) 750-20. Open Easter through September. £12–£17, breakfast and service included.

► **Hyland's Hotel. Ballyvaughan,** County Clare. Tel: (065) 770-37; Fax: (065) 771-31; in U.S. and Canada, (800) 223-1588. Open Easter through October. £19.50–£23.50, breakfast included.

► **Jury's Hotel.** Ennis Road, **Limerick City.** Tel: (061) 32-77-77; Telex: 70766; Fax: (061) 32-64-00; in U.S., (800) 843-6664; in Canada, (800) 268-1133; in London, (081) 569-5555 or (071) 937-8033; in U.K., (0345) 01-01-01. £40.

► **Limerick Inn.** Ennis Road, **Limerick City.** Tel: (061) 515-44; Telex: 70621; Fax: (061) 32-62-81; in U.S., (800) 223-0888. £35–£45.

► **Limerick Ryan Hotel.** Ennis Road, **Limerick City.** Tel: (061) 539-22; Telex: 70720; Fax: (061) 32-63-33; in U.S., (800) 44-UTELL. £35–£45.

► **Mrs. Faherty's.** Creigmore, **Inishmaan,** County Galway. Tel: (099) 730-12. £12, breakfast and service included.

► **Old Ground Hotel.** O'Connell Street, **Ennis,** County Clare. Tel: (065) 281-27; Telex: 70603; Fax: (065) 281-12; in U.S., (800) CALL-THF. £30–£45.

► **Renvyle House Hotel. Renvyle,** Connemara, County Galway. Tel: (095) 435-11; Fax: (095) 435-15. Open March through November, Christmas, and New Year's. £31–£45, breakfast included.

► **Shannon Shamrock Inn (Fitzpatricks). Bunratty,** County Clare. Tel: (061) 36-11-77; Telex: 72114; Fax: (061) 612-52; in U.S., (800) 221-1074. £44.

THE NORTHWEST

DONEGAL, SLIGO, AND MAYO

By Bernard Share

At the turn of this century the western seaboard of Ireland was densely populated. In the wild and rocky landscape of that region, thousands of people lived in poverty: large families in small thatched cottages, scraping a life from the thin soil or from a bit of fishing. Donegal and Mayo had been hit harder than most regions during the potato famine in the 1840s. The catastrophes of the 19th century had reduced the people of the West to a state of almost total social despair. Every penny that might come from selling a few vegetables went to pay the rent. Children went as seasonal workers to the farms of the wealthy lowlands of Ulster so that the rest of the family might survive. What lay ahead for the youth was three to ten months' feudal labor, often very far from home. When a boy was old enough he headed for Scotland or England for seasonal work picking potatoes. And, of course, thousands left in search of better lives in America or Australia—many because they could no longer pay the rent and were evicted. At Glenveagh, in Donegal, an entire valley was cleared and the homes razed. The story of those times is well told in contemporary fiction and folk histories widely available in the tourist centers and small bookshops of the region.

Culturally and historically, then, the western seaboard is something of a unit. One hundred years ago most of the area was Irish speaking, but the institutional machinery was beginning to impose the English language. (Brian Friel's play *Translations,* which explores the transition, is worth seeing or reading.) The collapse of the Irish language was an event that traumatized the entire area, though Irish has survived, and the traveller will hear it spoken freely in shops and public places, especially in west Donegal.

But what about Sligo? A visitor to that elegant town at the turn of this century would have found none of the despair pervading Donegal and Mayo at the time. Rather, among the literate, English-speaking shopkeepers, he would have encountered a culture altogether different from that which existed 50 miles on either side of the town. He might even have spied Mr. Yeats in a soft hat and flamboyant cravat leaning over the bridge at the River Garavogue dreaming of swans, lakes, or the heavens' embroidered cloths.

Sligo Town is a different country. In the mid-17th century Oliver Cromwell, the scourge of Ireland, allotted huge tracts of land in this county to his officers and soldiers in lieu of wages. Within a few years the old Sligo families—O'Connors, O'Dowds, O'Garas, and McDonaghs—had been replaced by Coopers, Wynnes, Ormsbys, and Gores. The town thus became more Anglo-Irish than Gaelic: A Protestant grammar school catered to families such as the Pollexfens and Middletons (Susan Pollexfen married Yeats's father in St. John's Church of Ireland in 1863).

The Anglo-Irish element did not always find favor among those who shaped the new republic; but now, under the burden of recent troubles, there is a growing pluralism and an acceptance that the island has more than one tradition. There is a new confidence in the Anglo-Irish heritage alongside that of Gaelic Ireland, and the interesting cultural contrast from Donegal to Sligo is well worth discerning. Of course, once the notion that Ireland is not merely Gaelic is accepted, the door is wide open for recognition of other tribes who make the Irish what they are: the Scots in Donegal, the wider European influences in Mayo.

So in the Northwest you will find an Irish-speaking community still flourishing and rich in tradition and literature, yet one laced with the complex strands of Anglo-Irish culture: in architecture, social mores, and literature. On the other hand, you may just wish to seek the solitude

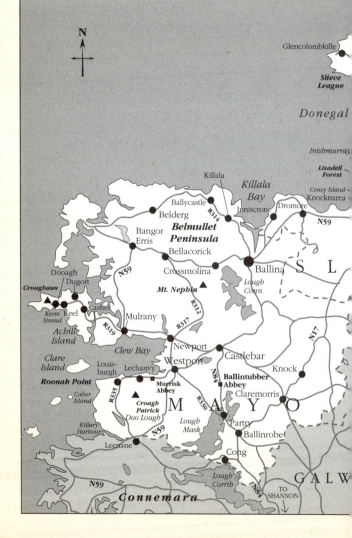

ATLANTIC OCEAN

N

Glencolumbkille

*Slieve
League*

Donegal

Inishmurray

*Lisadell
Forest*

*Coney Island ~
Knocknarea*

Killala

*Killala
Bay*

Ballycastle

Belderg

R314

Inniscrone

Dromore

N59

Bangor
Erris

**Belmullet
Peninsula**

S L

Bellacorick

Crossmolina

Ballina

Dooagh
Dugort

N59

Mt. Nephin ▲

▲

*Lough
Conn*

Croaghaun

▲

*Keem Reel
Strand*

Cashel

Mulrany

R312

R317

N17

*Achill
Island*

R319

Newport

Castlebar

*Clare
Island*

Clew Bay

Louis-
burgh

Lechanvy

Westport

Knock

Roonah Point

**Murrisk
Abbey** ■

**Ballintubber
Abbey**

*Caher
Island*

R335

▲
*Croagh
Patrick*

M A Y O

Claremorris

N84

*Killary
Harbour*

Doo Lough

*Lough
Mask*

R330

Partry

Leenane

N59

Ballinrobe

Cong

*Lough
Corrib*

N84

G A L W

N59

Connemara

TO
SHANNON
↓

of the mountains, or take long walks on deserted beaches, desolate moorland, or remote rock and let their magic call out of you that question that in this particular part of the world seems to come so naturally: Why is it that man is, and why is it that he is endlessly alone?

We cover the Northwest starting with County Donegal, heading south to Sligo, and then on to Mayo, leaving off just to the north of Connemara and the Galway area.

MAJOR INTEREST

Beautiful, wild scenery of mountains and sea
A mix of Irish and Anglo-Irish culture

Donegal
Letterkenny Folk Festival
Inishowen and Fanad peninsulas
Glenveagh National Park
Tory and Arranmore islands
Handweaving and knitting

Sligo
Yeats country
Sligo Town
Carrowmore megalithic remains
Lough Gill scenic road

Mayo
Achill Island and Croghaun cliff face
Clare Island
Westport Town
Croagh Patrick mountain, Celtic pilgrimage site
Fishing

COUNTY DONEGAL

The landscape of Donegal would make you think that the Ice Age happened last night. Little has changed the fierce mountains and rocky plateaus since then, except for a drop in the sea level that has left the seaboard with endless miles of beach. Add to this the relentless wind and raging Atlantic forever beating against the coast; Donegal is nothing less than spectacular.

It is better not to visit Donegal with half a heart. You may find yourself wandering country roads in a mist so thick you can scarcely see the front of the car—and there is a lot of mist in Donegal. But, as someone once said, rain is not bad weather in Donegal. The rain here is an extraordinary soft texture of cloud that drenches the landscape with stunningly gentle, melancholy blues and grays. And it clears as suddenly as it arrives, leaving the eye almost aching from the dazzle of the sun on glistening rock, white beach, and the white walls of the houses. Donegal requires a little stamina and energy, which will be well rewarded.

Its inhabitants are, like the landscape, equally tough and tender. Women here say of an attractive man that he is "a fine hunk." They like big men, in every sense of the adjective, and you won't go far without meeting the likes. To survive this territory or to gather fish from its ferocious seas requires physical strength and great courage. The people of Donegal bring the same energy and vitality to their recreation, music, and conversation.

To reach Donegal from Dublin, take the N 3 via Cavan and Belturbet. The route to Donegal Town (230 km/145 miles) then passes briefly through Northern Ireland (A 509) and thence along the beautiful southern shores of **Lower Lough Erne** (A 46) to **Ballyshannon**, a steep little town with strong associations with the poet William Allingham, an early influence on Yeats. As an alternative to the direct road from Ballyshannon to Donegal Town (N 15), take the coast road to **Rossnowlagh** (two interesting restaurants en route: **Giovanni Archetti** and **Danby Restaurant**) and stay for a night at the **Sand House Hotel** there, a coverted 19th-century lodge a very gentle stone's throw away from two golden miles of sand beach where the surfing is probably the best in the country.

Donegal Town, the gateway to the rest of the county, is built around The Diamond, in the center of which stands a memorial to the Four Masters, the clerics who produced the first extant history of Gaelic Ireland in the early 17th century. The remains of their **friary** (built in 1474) stand on the banks of the River Eske, south of the town. Also on the Eske riverbank are the ruins of **Donegal Castle**, completed in the 1470s and once the stronghold of the O'Donnells; the castle is closed temporarily for renovation. There is an excellent craft center about 2 km (a little more than a mile) south of the town offering a wide range of goods produced by craftsmen and women working on the spot. In Donegal Town itself, **Magee's**, purveyors of handwoven Donegal tweed, should not be missed. After suiting yourself, enjoy a snack and a glass of wine in the store's restaurant. The family-run **Hyland**

Central Hotel on The Diamond in town is convenient and reasonably priced.

Just north of Donegal Town on the N 15 is **Harvey's Point Country Hotel** (signposted on the left). Picturesquely situated on the shores of Lough Eske, the hotel has 20 deluxe rooms and a wide range of amenities, including tennis, golf, fishing, equestrian activities—and an on-site helicopter service. There's also a lodge on the grounds that offers simpler accommodations.

Back on the N 15, the road continues through the bleakly impressive Barnesmore Gap; **Biddy O'Barnes**, a quaint pub at the entrance to the pass, provides warm turf fires and equally warming sustenance. The cliff-hanging track of the narrow gauge County Donegal Railways—the entire system now alas vanished—can still be discerned around here.

Letterkenny (51 km/31 miles north of Donegal Town) is dominated by the Roman Catholic cathedral of St. Eunan, erected in the late 19th century. The town is built on a steep hill, and the shops are small, old-fashioned, and friendly. The **Donegal Shop** invites you to "pick your wool and pattern and we will have it knitted for you." **McGinley's**, at 25 Lower Main Street, is an attractive split-level pub with stone walls, open fires, and a view of the surrounding countryside.

Letterkenny is a wonderful place at the end of August, when the **Folk Festival** brings musicians and dancers from every corner of Europe and beyond. Most of the dancers spend the long weekend of the festival in colorful costume, dancing along the streets and entertaining in the hotels in the late evening. To check current happenings or to find a place to spend the night, try Donegal's first public-access Minitel. In the window of the First National Building Society, it provides computerized accommodations booking and tourist information over a wide area.

From Letterkenny the N 13 will take you northeast toward the **Inishowen Peninsula**, an area of unspoiled beauty and strongly entrenched folk tradition, at the apex of which is Malin Head, the most northerly point in Ireland. Eleven kilometers (7 miles) south of the waterside resort of Fahan, near **Lough Swilly** between Letterkenny and Malin (try **St. John's Restaurant** for good fish dishes in Fahan), is the **Grianán of Aileach**, a well-preserved circular stone mountaintop fort dating from 1700 B.C. that once was the residence of the O'Neill kings of Ulster. **Fort Dunree**, north of Fahan on Lough Swilly, has an imaginative military/naval museum and one of the best panoramas in the country.

Alternatively, take the Rathmelton road (R 245) north from Letterkenny and thence (R 247) to **Rathmullan**, a picturesque little village on the opposite (west) shore of Lough Swilly (try the **Water's Edge** restaurant). It was from here, in 1607, that the earls of Tyrconnell and Tyrone, with their friends and retainers, took ship for France—an event known as "the Flight of the Earls" that marked the virtual end of the Gaelic Order in Ireland and made way for the plantation of Ulster with British colonists. The imaginatively conceived **Heritage Centre** on the harbor tells the story.

Rathmullan House here was built by the Batt banking family of Belfast in the 1830s as a summer place. At the time of the First World War there were five girls in the family, and the Batts went bankrupt holding expensive parties in an attempt to marry them off to the officers of the British Navy, which was then using Lough Swilly as a base. Robin and Bob Wheeler have been running Rathmullan House since 1963 as a country-house hotel. The gardens are beautiful, the setting idyllic, and the accommodations themselves (superior, standard, and family rooms) breathe the genteel ambience of a more leisurely age. The food is also exceptional, and the Egyptian Baths (salt water) will ease away any excesses. The hotel is both a haven in itself and an ideal point from which to explore the upper reaches of the **Fanad Peninsula** to the north. The Fanad Drive (signposted) is a true "sky road," skirting the cliffs with an awe-inspiring drop to the sea. The **Lighthouse Tavern** at the Head itself (pub grub) is the last refuge before Reykjavik.

When you must move on, take the road back to Rathmelton (look out for **Chez Michel**, a good seafood restaurant just up the hill on the Milford road) and then go by back roads (well signposted, but Ordnance Survey Sheet 1 will be useful) to **Church Hill**. Not far from the village, and well signposted, is the **Glebe Gallery**, donated to the nation together with the adjacent house and its fascinating contents by the painter Derek Hill. Set on a spit of land projecting into Lough Gartan, the gallery is housed in an old stable above which the painter used to have his studio, and the building has been very sensitively converted into a modern gallery exhibiting works from Hill's own collection (mainly Irish, British, and European painters of the 1950s and 1960s), as well as some outside shows. The adjoining house, a former rectory that had become a fishing hotel, was bought in the 1950s by Hill, who furnished it with excellent pictures (Landseer and contemporary Irish and European artists) as well as with objets d'art ranging from William Morris wallpapers and hangings to French theater posters and chinoiserie. The gallery is open at Easter and from May to September.

From Church Hill take the road to **Glenveagh National Park** (signposted; about 8 km/5 miles), which comprises 25,000 acres of mountains and lakes, wild deer, a castle, and woodland gardens to laze about in the whole day long. There is something about Glenveagh that gathers to itself the ages of Irish history. With Mount Errigal in the distance and the Derryveagh Mountains all about, it is not difficult to imagine those early settlers of prehistory, the Tuatha De Dannann (people of the goddess Dana) settling about the River Owencarrow, hunting fish and animals in the surrounding mountains. But looking the other way, at the castle and its 50 acres of splendid gardens, you reflect on more recent times as well: The notorious John Adair, who bought the property in 1850, built the castle and was responsible for the savage eviction of tenants. His wife, the daughter of General James Wadsworth, eminent in the American Civil War, survived him by 30 years or more and was known as a more compassionate person. Henry McIlhenny, the American millionaire art collector, restored the entire property between 1940 and 1970 and then, in a most generous moment, bequeathed it to the nation.

From Glenveagh, turn west on R 251 out of the park; then make a right turn, following the signs through Muckish Gap to An Fál Carrach (in English, **Falcarragh**). Most signposts in this area are in Irish, as this is a fiercely individualistic Irish-speaking area, or Gaeltacht. An English-Irish map (available locally) is useful. Maheraroarty pier in Falcarragh is the departure point for **Tory Island**. For the most adventurous, a trip to Tory could be the highlight of anything else seen or experienced in Ireland. Bound up with the legend of the giant Balor of the One Eye, his tower, his daughter, and his terrible death at the hands of Lugh, the island is primitive, pagan, and terribly beautiful. It is a good distance (seven miles) out into the Atlantic, but ferries travel in the summer season (see Getting Around at the end of this chapter).

An interesting local cheese, Errigal, is made by Bill Hogan in **Gortahork**, on N 56 just south of Falcarragh. **Mc Fadden's** small family hotel in Gortahork is popular with anglers and scuba divers. **Teach Leo**, a pub on the left side of the road between the villages of Croithli (Crolly) and Anagaire (Annagary), is the home of the internationally known folk group Clannad.

For island lovers a less demanding alternative than Tory Island, certainly in terms of time, is Arainn Mhór (**Arranmore**). Arranmore, reached by ferry from Burtonport, which is southwest of Gortahork off R 259, has a hotel (**The Glen**) in Leabgarrow, a youth hostel, and entertainment all night long. A dance might begin in the **Pier Bar** at midnight and go on into the early hours. There are fine, sandy beaches on which to recover. The walk of three miles to the lighthouse brings you to the farthest end of the island, over the hills where in 1798 more than 300 French soldiers died in battle with the British. The walk back affords a view of the winding coastline and the blue crown of Mount Errigal in the distance. For those who balk even at the short boat trip to Arranmore, the island of **Cruit**, 5 km (3 miles) north of Burtonport, is joined to the mainland by a causeway. **Donegal Thatched Cottages** on Cruit offer traditional accommodations with modern conveniences.

The route back from Burtonport to Donegal Town offers a number of appealing alternatives. You may go more or less directly via Glenties to the south (no route in Donegal, you will discover, takes a straight line to anywhere) or, if time permits, travel west of Glenties through **Ardara**, where there are two good pubs—**P. S. Mac Giolla Dé** and the 200-year-old **Nancy's**. Then cross the Glengesh Pass out to the western remoteness of **Glencolumbkille**, the glen to which Donegal's patron saint, Colmcille (Columba), came in retreat from the world. There's a folk museum located here now, and a tea room, which sells homemade seaweed wine! Close by are the dramatic cliffs of **Slieve League**.

COUNTY SLIGO

From Donegal Town the N 15 takes you south through Ballyshannon to **Bundoran**, still in Donegal. The town itself is a poor man's Las Vegas, but there is a new eight-acre **Waterworld** on the seafront; a good, well-sited hotel, the **Great Northern**, dating from railroad days; **Conroy's** German-Irish restaurant, also on the seafront; and a spectacular **golf course** overlooking the sea. (For golfers, the Irish Tourist Board has selected five Donegal and Sligo courses as the Atlantic Challenge: at Rosapenna, North West, Murvagh, and Bundoran in County Donegal, and at Rosses Point in County Sligo.)

An alternative is to continue farther south and then to take a right at Creevykeel crossroads for the coastal village of Mullaghmore. From here the more adventurous can go by boat to **Inishmurray** (difficult in poor weather; inquire locally), an island peculiarly rich in Celtic monuments. Inishmurray has no visitor facilities and no drinking water.

From Bundoran to Sligo Town is an easy morning's drive, with the sea to the right and the flat-topped escarpment of Ben Bulben to the left. Passing through the village of **Grange** (with its **Horse Holiday Farm**—tours on horseback for experienced riders—and **Sligo crystal factory shop**) you reach **Drumcliff** and the churchyard where William Butler Yeats is buried. It is worth stopping here, just 6 km (4 miles) north of Sligo Town, because of the importance of the poet to his language. His often-quoted lines "Cast a cold eye on life, on death, / Horseman, pass by" are etched in the modest stone above his grave, and to stand in the shadow of the mountain Ben Bulben and read them is an unforgettable experience. Just west of Drumcliff in Carney is **Urlar House**, where Mrs. Healy provides simple and traditional bed and board in her Georgian farmhouse.

Sligo Town

The town of Sligo will present many other opportunities to think of Yeats. The **Sligo County Library and Museum** on Stephen Street has an interesting collection of Yeatsiana, and there's a boat excursion (from the riverside in town) to **Lough Gill**, which embraces the lake isle of Innisfree. But there is more to wandering about this beautiful town than its associations with the poet. This is an Anglo-Irish place, and a fine one at that. The street names and public buildings are all rich with a particular history. John Wesley preached here. Long before that, in 1245, Maurice Fitzgerald, earl of Kildare, built a castle here (the town having been burned by the Vikings in 807), and in 1252 he built a Dominican friary, the ruins of which survive under the name of **Sligo Abbey** (Abbey Street). Sligo Abbey is the burial place of kings and princes, including O'Rourke, king of Breffni, who died in 1418.

Sligo boasts few other buildings of real note, but some of the old shop fronts are worth a second look, and pubs such as **D. McLynn** on Old Market Street and **James Carroll** in Stephen Street preserve a traditional atmosphere and decor. The **Cygnet** restaurant of the Silver Swan hotel, atmospherically sited on the bridge over the Garavogue, is a good place for lunch; it also has a parking lot, and Sligo is a narrow-streeted, one-way town in which a car can prove something of a hassle. You might also try **Gulliver's** on Grattan Street, or **Hargadon's** on O'Connell Street, a traditional pub. Michael Quirke on Wine Street doubles as butcher and sculptor, and **Cosgrove & Son**, an old-style delicatessen on Market Street, sells original Irish whiskey marmalades and mustards. **The Hawk's Well**, the most important theater in the northwest, is located near the tourist office on Stephen Street.

Outside Sligo Town

Although all the names in this region seem to invoke Yeats, most are well worth visiting for their own sake: Rosses Point, Knocknarea, and Lissadell, the home of the Gore-Booth sisters ("...both / Beautiful, one a gazelle"), which is open to the public. (For Yeats aficionados Sheelah Kirby's *The Yeats Country* is recommended.)

Rosses Point, about 8 km (5 miles) northwest of the town via R 291, boasts two fine beaches, championship golf links, seaside pubs, and an intimate restaurant, **Reveries**, where you may dine, with luck, to the accompaniment of a memorable sunset (open for dinner only). Just off the point lies **Coney Island**, after which, so it is said, Coney Island, New York, was named by Peter O'Connor, captain of the Sligo vessel *Arethusa,* who observed similar quantities of rabbits as inhabited the Irish original (the Irish word *cóinín* means "rabbit"). The island is accessible by causeway at low tide.

Three kilometers (2 miles) southwest of Sligo Town (leave by John Street) is **Carrowmore**, a low hill that features the largest group of megalithic remains in Ireland: dolmens, stone circles, and sepulchral chambers. (The interpretive center at the site hosts an audio-visual presentation.) Three kilometers farther on is the **Hill of**

Knocknarea, on the summit of which is a cairn known as *Miscaun Meadhbh* (Maeve's mound), said to commemorate the queen of Connacht who flourished in the first century A.D. The area, rich in legend, held a particular fascination for Yeats.

The Yeatsian connotations of **Lough Gill** have already been alluded to, but it stands in its own right as a rival to Killarney in terms of natural beauty, surrounded on three sides by wooded mountain slopes and well worth the circuit by road. Take the N 16 from Sligo Town and, after leaving the town limits, turn onto the R 286. The 17th-century **Parkes Castle**, on the riverbank past the village of Dromahair, was formerly the site of Breffni Castle, from which Dervorgilla, wife of Tiernan O'Rourke, was abducted by Dermot MacMurrough, king of Leinster, setting in train the events that resulted in the Anglo-Norman invasion of Ireland and all that flowed from it. The abduction (some say she arranged it) took place in 1152, and O'Rourke got her back the following year. MacMurrough nursed his desire for revenge until 1166 when, threatened with defeat by O'Rourke, he took ship for England on his way to France to persuade the French/English King Henry II to help him against his rival. Henry agreed—and the rest, as they say, is history. Parkes Castle has been magnificently restored as an interpretive center for Leitrim, Sligo, and south Donegal.

COUNTY MAYO

Heading south from Sligo by the Dublin road (N 4), turn right at **Ballisadare** onto the N 59. Take a right at Dromore West for the coast road via **Inniscrone**, where you may sample the unusual and restorative seaweed baths.

Continue south to **Ballina**, an important angling center. The 52-room **Downhill Hotel** on its own lovely grounds about 1 km (less than a mile) outside Ballina, with a swimming pool and tennis and squash courts, caters to the sporting type. The **Belleek Castle** hotel and restaurant is a thoroughgoing restoration of a 17th-century original complete with armor and four-poster beds. Daniel Veillard's **Swiss Barn Restaurant** specializes in fondue.

From Ballina the R 314 takes you north and west on a circuit of the wild and beautiful northern Mayo coast, through **Killala**, where the ill-fated French expedition landed in 1798. Farther on, between Ballycastle and

Belderg, Professor Seamus Caulfield has been excavating a 5,000-year-old settlement known as the **Céide Fields**, home to a thriving Early Stone Age community of 10,000 people. (There's an interpretive center at the site.) The road continues to the remoteness of the **Belmullet Peninsula**.

Alternatively, take the N 59 due west from Ballina to Crossmolina. A left turn at the entrance to the town brings you to the shores of **Lough Conn**, a famous fishing lake, and **Enniscoe House**, described as "the last great house in County Mayo," and now run as a delightful and moderately priced country-house hotel by Mrs. Susan Kellett, a direct descendant of the family that built the place in the 1750s. The house is notable for its very fine plasterwork, beautiful fireplaces, and spacious, high-ceilinged rooms, with canopy beds in the suites. The clientele is cosmopolitan, and the cooking is in the best Irish country-house tradition. A particularly interesting cheeseboard exploits to the full the striking developments in Irish farmhouse cheeses in recent years. The Enniscoe mansion also houses the **North Mayo Heritage Centre**, with displays of restored farm machinery and other rural artifacts, and a family-history research service for those interested in identifying Irish forebears. Fishing can be arranged through **Clonmoye Fishery** (Barry Seagrave; Tel: 096-311-12), which provides a comprehensive service.

From Crossmolina the N 59 continues west to Bellacorick, location for a peat-fired power station that exploits the vast deposits of the area. The countryside here is dominated by the bulk of **Nephin Mountain**, often dramatically veiled or half-veiled in clouds. Depending on your inclination you may continue on N 59 west to Bangor Erris and thence south to Mulrany, or take the mountain road, R 312, south past Nephin to R 317, which goes southwest to meet N 59 at Newport, east of Mulrany. Distances are similar and the scenery equally spectacular.

Achill Island

The last train to Achill ran through Mulrany in 1937, carrying the bodies of ten migrant workers who had been burned to death in a fire in Scotland. It was the end of an unhappy century for this island's people. Even before the potato famine in the middle of the last century it was noted as a poor land. Achill, now connected to the mainland by a road (R 319) running west from Mulrany, offers a landscape that allows the visitor to reflect on the struggle for survival set against the enduring nature of sea and mountain and stone: It is a place of such beauty—and so warm are its people—that it is sometimes difficult to credit its unfortunate history.

Achill, the largest offshore island in Ireland, is a majestic expanse of heather-covered mountain and towering cliffs rimmed by fine golden beaches, and is rich in lore and legend. Corrymore House, near Dooagh in the western part of the island, was the home of the hated Captain Boycott, who gave a new word to the language; basking sharks are visitors to nearby Keem Strand; and Minaun Heights, in back of Keel, is one of the best hang-gliding locations in Ireland.

Dugort, on the north side of the island, offers comfortable accommodations (the **Slievemore Hotel**, in a secluded setting at the foot of the eponymous mountain) and an excellent beach. At the eastern end of the strand lies a small plot of wild moor, peppered with uninscribed stone slabs, known as *Cillín na Leanbh* ("the little church of the children"), the burial place for unbaptized infants. The custom of burying unbaptized babies in useless, unconsecrated ground was at one time widespread in Ireland. The landscape out here features very centrally in the work of Paul Henry, one of Ireland's foremost 20th-century painters: A look at his work, even in book form, before the visit would add an interesting flavor to the real thing. North of the town of **Dooagh** there is a deserted village—complete, ordered, and silent—around which the visitor may amble and wonder about the past.

Continue on to **Keel**, the island's main resort town, where you'll find **The Bervie**, a friendly and distinctive family-run hotel. The Bervie serves old-fashioned afternoon teas, and many of the bedrooms have magnificent views of sea and cliffs. The road continues on a steep cliffside ascent and descent to Keem Bay, a fine bathing spot and former site of a shark fishery. Still farther on is **Croaghaun**, the highest cliff face in Europe.

Achill is a popular tourist area offering a good range of accommodations—bed-and-breakfast, self-catering, and camping facilities as well as hotels—but early booking is advisable in the summer months, and current lists should be obtained in advance from the Irish Tourist Office. The island is just as attractive in spring and autumn, though, when the prices are lower and the beaches, mountains, lakes, and the deserted village are quiet, except perhaps for the lone cry of a golden eagle.

From Achill take the N 59 east and south to Newport. The 19-room **Newport House**, a gracious Georgian country-house hotel and restaurant overlooking the Newport River, offers a wide range of sporting facilities, including fishing, golf, riding, and shooting. It was a particular favorite of Princess Grace of Monaco.

Westport, a few miles to the south, is a little gem of a seigneurial town on Clew Bay built around a central octagon. Among Westport's interesting small shops is **M. Mulloy, Ironmonger & Grocer**, founded in 1762. Westport Quay and its substantial warehouses—testifying to a lively port traffic before the coming of the railway—has become the location for a number of good, small restaurants. The **Asgard Tavern** on the quay has won awards for its pub grub. In a more traditional style, try a drink in **O'Grady's**, a pub and general store in town. On the right as you approach the quay is the entrance to **Westport House**, a seat of the marquesses of Sligo. The house is open to the public, and there is a range of entertainment for young and old on the grounds, including a children's zoo, a miniature railway, and a variety of trailer and self-catering accommodations. The house, designed by Richard Cassells, was built in the early 1730s on the site of a castle of Grainuaile (Grace O'Malley, the pirate queen) and, apart from the chillingly authentic dungeons, is a treasure house of good silver, furniture, and paintings. The marquess of Sligo's book, *Westport House and the Brownes* (the family name), provides a lively account of the house, its inhabitants, and their relationship with their neighbors since the 16th century.

Clare Island

The R 335 out of Westport takes you west to Louisburgh (22 km/14 miles); a ferry from Roonah Point, to the west of town, serves Clare Island. Clare is a large island, quiet and ideal for a few days' real relaxation, but people also visit for its excellent water sports. The fishing includes blue and porbeagle shark, common skate, and conger. The **Bay View Hotel** on the island provides services for those wishing to take things really seriously and go shark fishing. The beach near the hotel is attractive and safe, and there is a choice of pubs that rarely shut their doors. Island weaving is available at the **Cliara** craft shop.

The island is closely associated with the life and adventures of Grace O'Malley, who had three husbands, established herself as the terror of the western seas, and was received at the court of England's Queen Elizabeth I. She is buried in the small **Monastery of St. Bridget** on the island. Day-long safaris conducted by Peter Gill's Historical Safaris include a visit to her castle; Tel: (098) 250-48. There is something careless about the old monastery ruins: The wall paintings, or what remains of them, are left exposed to the wind and salt, eroding more from year to year. Somewhere on the wall may be seen the O'Malley coat of arms and motto: "Invincible on land and sea." It's a sturdy walk from the hotel, but well worth it for the view of Clew Bay and Croagh Patrick (see below), and for those who don't like doing things by halves the road continues about the same distance again to the far side of the island over beautiful bog to the deserted lighthouse and the cliffs. All about is the sea and the beautiful landscape of Mayo. Walking anywhere on Clare Island you are struck by the manner in which the land flows down the steepest hills in wrinkles of man-made furrow, a testimony to overpopulation and the poor times in the last century.

Clare Island is the kind of sanctuary that attracts individuals: It is remote and yet has every comfort. Over the years it has attracted many international writers and artists. Tony O'Malley, one of Ireland's leading contemporary painters, who works half the year in the Bahamas, comes frequently. (But then, why wouldn't he? His cousins all live here.) It seems strange to say of an isolated island off an isolated coast, but Clare is the kind of place where you meet a lot of interesting people.

Toward Connemara

If you look south from Clare you can see Caher Island, once a holy place of pilgrimage but now a deserted heap of stones in the sea. And on the mainland southwest of Westport there is the towering peak of **Croagh Patrick**, where Saint Patrick was said to have prayed and fasted for 40 days in 441; it's a place of pilgrimage not just since the earliest days of Christianity but far into the pre-Christian past. On the last Sunday in July, the day of Crom Dubh, an ancient Celtic mythic figure, people still ascend the mountain to worship close to God's heaven. The only difference is that while pilgrims of olden days made the ascent in the dark in order to observe dawn from the peak, in recent years the church authorities have banned the night vigil out of concern for attendant alcoholic abuses. The mountain may, of course, be climbed any time, weather permitting (pay attention to local advice, as sudden mists can be treacherous). The best approaches are from Lechanvy or the 14th-century Murrisk Abbey on the Westport–Louisburgh road. **Campbell's** pub, on the road between Westport and the mountain, is a good place to prepare for the ascent—or to watch others prepare.

From Louisburgh a magnificent mountain road (R 335) takes you south past **Doo Lough**, a brooding stretch of water that lives up to its name—black lake—in overcast weather, to the fjord-like Killary Harbour and Leenane, and so into Connemara. The **Delphi Adventure Centre** on this road offers a wide conspectus of outdoor pursuits; Tel: (095) 422-08. Alternatively, return to Westport from Louisburgh and take the R 330 southeast to Partry, where a turn to the left on the N 84 brings you (8 km/5 miles) to **Ballintubber Abbey**, founded in 1216 by Cathal O'Connor, king of Connacht, and in uninterrupted religious use to the present day, though it has been extensively restored. From here you may head for Shannon via Cong and Galway or for Dublin via Ballinrobe. **Ballinrobe** is the center for excellent brown trout angling on loughs Mask, Carra, and Corrib; there's an angling information center at **Cushlough**, not far from Ballinrobe. If time permits, take in the **Lough Mask Drive**, which is signposted off the Westport–Partry road. From Ballinrobe continue toward Dublin via Claremorris and Knock.

In 1879 **Knock** was a poor town in a poor county. One night, at the end of August, something happened here that was to have enormous repercussions. A small gathering of believing church people experienced an apparition of the Virgin Mary, Saint Joseph, and Saint John. This event gathered the support of deep, communal belief and over the years began to draw large numbers of pilgrims. But it was a small town and a small church, and the pilgrims were not more than country people from other parts of Ireland. Then along came James Horan, parish priest and visionary. Through his blend of simple faith and business sense Knock became a major international Marian shrine. Today it has a basilica capable of holding thousands, a glass cover for the sacred gable wall of the old church, and an airport with a runway capable of handling jumbo jets. More than anything else Father Horan inspired the people of the West of Ireland and gave them new confidence.

GETTING AROUND

There is regular air service, connecting with international flights, from Dublin to Sligo Town, Knock, and Derry Town (for Donegal). Dublin is connected by rail to Sligo, Westport, Ballina, Derry, and intermediate points. Letterkenny, Bundoran, Sligo, Westport, and intermediate points are linked to Dublin by bus.

Ferries link Arranmore and Burtonport (passengers and cars); advance booking is advisable; Tel: (075) 215-32. A mail boat to Tory runs from Bunbeg approximately twice weekly; passengers only. Contact Mr. Doherty at (075) 317-24. Fishermen's boats are available at Maheraroarty pier in Falcarragh. Contact the Tory post office; Tel: (074) 355-01.

ACCOMMODATIONS REFERENCE

The telephone country code for the Northwest is 353. When dialing telephone numbers in the Republic from outside the country, drop the 0 in the area code. The rate ranges given below are projections *for the low and high seasons in 1992; for up-to-the-minute rate information it is always wise to telephone before booking. Unless otherwise indicated, rates are per person sharing and do not include meals or service.*

▶ **Bay View Hotel. Clare Island,** County Mayo. Tel: (098) 263-07. Closed October through April. £18, breakfast included.

▶ **Belleek Castle. Ballina,** County Mayo. Tel: (096) 220-61; Fax: (096) 225-25. £37–£41, breakfast included.

▶ **The Bervie. Keel,** Achill Island, County Mayo. Tel: (098) 431-14. Closed November through February. £14–£18, breakfast included.

▶ **Donegal Thatched Cottages. Rosses Point,** County Sligo. Tel: (071) 771-97. £120–£400 per week; call for weekend rates.

▶ **Downhill Hotel.** Sligo Road, **Ballina,** County Mayo. Tel: (096) 210-33; Telex: 40796; Fax: (096) 213-38; in U.S., (212) 684-1820 or (800) 221-1074. £34–£50, breakfast included.

▶ **Enniscoe House.** Castlehill near Crossmolina, **Bal-**

lina, County Mayo. Tel: (096) 311-12; Fax: (096) 317-73; in U.S., (800) 223-6510. Closed November through March. £35–£40, breakfast included.

▶ **The Glen. Arranmore Island,** County Donegal. Tel: (075) 215-05. Open Easter to October. £14, breakfast included.

▶ **Great Northern Hotel. Bundoran,** County Donegal. Tel: (072) 412-04; Telex: 40961; Fax: (072) 411-14; in U.S., (305) 566-7111 or (800) 521-0643. Closed January through March. £35, breakfast included.

▶ **Harvey's Point Country Hotel.** Lough Eske, **Donegal,** County Donegal. Tel: (073) 222-08; Fax: (073) 223-52. £25–£45, breakfast included.

▶ **Hyland Central Hotel.** The Diamond, **Donegal,** County Donegal. Tel: (073) 210-27; Fax: (073) 222-95. £30–£40, breakfast included.

▶ **Mc Fadden's. Gortahork,** County Donegal. Tel: (074) 352-67. £23, breakfast included.

▶ **Newport House. Newport,** County Mayo. Tel: (098) 412-22; Fax: (098) 416-13. Open March 19 to September 30. £49–£53, breakfast and service included.

▶ **Rathmullan House. Rathmullan,** County Donegal. Tel: (074) 581-88; Fax: (074) 582-00; in U.S., (212) 696-1323, (800) 372-1323, or (800) 223-6510. Closed November through February. £42.50–£57.50, breakfast included.

▶ **Sand House Hotel. Rossnowlagh,** County Donegal. Tel: (072) 517-77; Fax: (072) 521-00; in U.S., (800) 223-6764; in Canada, (800) 531-6767. Open Easter to mid-October. £40–£45, breakfast included.

▶ **Slievemore Hotel. Dugort,** Achill Island, County Mayo. Tel: (098) 432-54 or 432-24. Closed October through May. £17, breakfast included.

▶ **Urlar House. Carney,** County Sligo. Tel: (071) 631-10. Closed November through February. £13–£15, breakfast and service included.

THE BORDER COUNTIES

FERMANAGH, TYRONE, AND DERRY—WITH A DIP INTO CAVAN AND MONAGHAN

By Colm Toíbín

Colm Toíbín was born near Dublin and works there as a journalist and broadcaster. He has edited both of Ireland's current affairs magazines and is the author of a novel, The South, *and a travel book,* Walking Along the Border.

The border counties in Northern Ireland are dominated by water—rivers and lakes that offer some of the best and the widest range of fish and fishing facilities in the country. The political divide itself is full of anomalies: A boat can cross the border on Lough Erne without the slightest interference from the security forces, for example, and yet some of the official road crossings have fortress-like checkpoints.

There are huge differences as well in the quality of the land in these counties. Large estates of good pasture stand side by side with 30-acre holdings of poorly drained land, just as scenery that is hauntingly desolate, where narrow roads wind through bogland and lakeland, can be found only a few miles away from major motorways.

MAJOR INTEREST

The Ardhowen Theatre
Blake's of the Hollow public house in Enniskillen
Lough Erne cruising
The Marble Arch Caves
Roskit House at Lough Melvin
Monaghan County Museum
The Ulster *Fleadh Ceoil*
The Ulster American Folk Park
The Ardboe High Cross
The Walls of Derry Town

Many of the smaller border roads are now sealed, although it is still possible in certain areas for a car to cross and recross the line that divides the North of Ireland from the Republic without drawing the attention of the security forces. At most border crossings, however, there is a British Army checkpoint. A red light warns the driver to stop until a soldier can check the license number of the car on a computer. Normally he asks for identification, and he may also ask where you are going. The soldiers are usually polite, and in general crossing the border is not a problem.

Most people in the border areas genuinely welcome tourists, although the clientele in certain bars in some towns and villages may be less than forthcoming (the local economy on both sides of the border depends on smuggling, and some people are wary of strangers). However, most locals will be extremely helpful when asked for directions—which is fortunate, because the signposting in this part of Ireland is truly appalling; even when signs exist, they may point the wrong way.

The hotels in the border area often offer the only restaurant facilities. Lunch is generally available for less than five pounds in most hotels, and soup and sandwiches can be had in the bigger and more modern public houses and lounge bars. There is no particular style of cooking or type of fare available in these towns to make them different from anywhere else in Ireland. Most menus will include roast beef, chicken, and some common type of fish both for lunch and for dinner; some will offer fresh vegetables, although most of the food will come from the freezer. For this reason Franco's restaurant in Enniskillen and the Sheelin in Bellanaleck stand

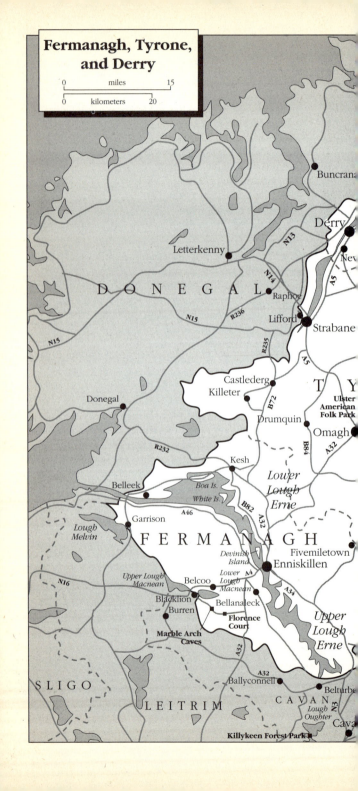

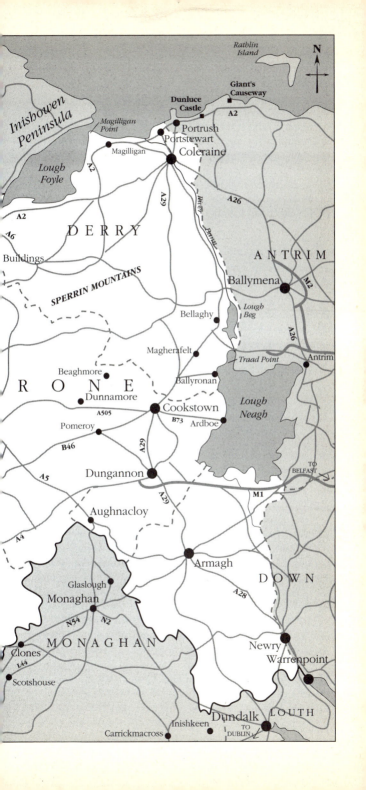

out as the only two restaurants in this whole area that can be wholeheartedly recommended.

This section details the three counties that make up the western half of Northern Ireland. First we explore Fermanagh, the northern county whose border touches five counties in the Republic—Monaghan, Cavan, Sligo, Leitrim, and Donegal; then we move north through County Tyrone, bordered on the west by Donegal, and the most sparsely populated of the six Northern Ireland counties, up into Derry, which forms the northwest corner of Northern Ireland.

COUNTY FERMANAGH

Fermanagh is the most developed and the most interesting of the border counties. The center of Fermanagh is Enniskillen, which has all the signs of a garrison town rather than a border town. The difference is important: A border town depends on trade and the economy of its hinterland. Thus, most border towns in recent years have become synonymous with depression, particularly in the South. Irish towns such as Dundalk, Clones, and Lifford have been badly affected by border tensions, by the loss of their natural hinterland, and more so in recent years since many products have become cheaper across the border in the North.

Enniskillen

Oddly enough, however, the border towns on the Northern side, such as Newry, Castlederg, and Strabane, have the same air of depression. Architecturally these towns all have a ramshackle appearance. Although each has individual buildings of distinction, there is no harmonious streetscape, no legacy of planning, no sense of money—things that distinguish Enniskillen and make it a sort of capital for the border counties.

The best place to stay is the **Killyhevlin Hotel**, about 2 km (a little more than a mile) south of town near the River Erne, which connects Upper and Lower Lough Erne. In addition to the usual rooms, the hotel has more than a dozen small wooden chalets right on the bank of the river, which, unlike many rivers in the border region, is full and strong-flowing, even in the summer. These accommodations are meant for fishermen but are available to other guests as well. The chalets have been carefully designed to blend in with the landscape and, because they can be heated in winter, are open year round. All have cooking facilities, but guests can also avail themselves of the hotel's dining room. Rates for rooms in the hotel and those for the chalets (which each sleep up to six people) are reasonable.

Between the Killyhevlin Hotel and Enniskillen is the recently built **Ardhowen Theatre**, a simple construction of steel and glass that manages to reflect the vast expanse of water in front of it—a bend in the River Erne—and the sky above. The theater's program is eclectic, ranging from local bands that specialize in American country-and-western music (which is extremely popular here) to touring drama groups.

The program for the Ardhowen and other information on local events and accommodations are available at the excellent visitors' center opposite the bus station in Enniskillen. The center also has information on local fishing facilities and stocks any fishing permits and licenses that may be necessary.

Beyond the bus station on the banks of the river is the leisure center, which contains a heated swimming pool and other sports facilities. Nearby is the dock from which the *Kestrel* leaves every day between July and September for cruises around the islands in Lough Erne. In May and June this trip is available only on Sunday afternoons.

Enniskillen has one of the best public houses in Ireland and one of the best restaurants in the border area. The bar, **Blake's of the Hollow**, stands in the town's main shopping street almost exactly opposite the Church of Ireland. It is, first of all, an extremely friendly bar and a good place to find out about local events and sights. More than a hundred years old, it has a beautifully carved wooden ceiling. Most Irish public houses are smoky and dark; Blake's, on the other hand, is opulent and bright. If most Irish pubs are churches or chapels, then Blake's is a cathedral. In cold weather there is a fire in the downstairs snug (a small closed-off area of a bar offering a certain amount of privacy); up a few steps there are more tables and chairs and another snug, and there's a pool table in the back room.

If you go down the lane across the street from Blake's and then turn right, you'll find **Franco's Italian Restaurant**, which serves particularly fine fresh seafood as well as excellent pizzas and Italian dishes. Should pheasant be on the menu, you've come on a good day and are in a for a particular treat. The wine list is also good.

Enniskillen is full of small pleasures like Blake's and Franco's, and also boasts a good bookstore, **Hall's**. For crafts in Enniskillen, visit **Fermanagh Cottage Industries** at 14 East Bridge Street, where handmade crochet work and local linen are sold. Enniskillen is a solid town, prosperous during business hours and quiet, almost empty, after six in the evening. There is no strong British Army presence here; instead, the town is patrolled by the local police. It is the perfect place to spend a few days before getting to know the lakes.

The Lough Erne Area

The best way to enjoy the lakes is to rent a power boat; a car journey around the shores of Lough Erne can give you only a vague sense of what is hidden away on its small islands. The cruisers, comfortable and easy to manage, range in size from two berths to eight berths. They are available virtually year round, and can navigate the lakes from Belleek near the border with the Republic's County Donegal in the northwest down to Belturbet across the border in County Cavan at the south.

Even in high summer there is a great stillness on the lakes, and it is always possible to tie up at one of the numerous islands without meeting another boatload of sailors. The jetties are well maintained without being too obtrusive. Even when the weather is bad there is a steely gray splendor about the lakes and the islands that makes this trip a unique experience.

It is easy to get a sense of Lough Erne on a two- to three-day trip. There are numerous places on the lake where boats can be rented, the most popular probably being at **Kesh**, north of Enniskillen, but the tourist office in Enniskillen can sort this out for you. Also at Kesh can be found the **Ardress Craft Centre**, run by Dorothy Pendry. She spins her own wool from her own sheep and runs a crafts shop where work by local people is shown and sold. She also runs courses in various crafts.

The islands are clearly marked on the detailed map provided with each boat. Three of the islands in the Lower Lough should definitely be visited, as they contain fascinating monuments from the 10th, 11th, and 12th centuries; all three—White, Inishmacsaint, and Devinish—have jetties for cruisers. The seven stone figures on **White Island** date from the 10th century and have been placed under a shelter within the ruined 12th-century church. The first one on the left is a *sile-na-gig,* a traditional female fertility figure; the other six are clerical figures holding religious objects. It could be said that some of them look distinctly glum in the presence of the fertility figure.

To come across these strange figures suddenly in the middle of an old ruin on a lonely island is a good reminder that Lough Erne was once inhabited by monks, and that early Christian sites have been found on most of the islands. If you keep the cruiser away from the main mooring places and tie up instead on one of the smaller islands, you will be able to sit up on deck and watch the sky darken over the dim outline of the islands all around and know that almost nothing has changed in this landscape since the time of the monks.

The second island in Lower Lough Erne is **Inishmacsaint**, which has a very stark and beautiful 14-foot-high 10th-century cross, as well as the ruins of a 12th-century church. The third island, **Devinish**, is included on the daily *Kestrel* boat tour from Enniskillen, and is by far the most popular in Lough Erne. Its most prominent feature is a 12th-century round tower more than 80 feet high, which can be ascended by a series of wooden ladders. There are also a number of interesting early Christian ruins on the island. Devinish Island is just north of Enniskillen. From the cruiser you can see Portora Royal School in Enniskillen (on the hill to the left as you approach the town)—the alma mater of both Oscar Wilde and Samuel Beckett.

Upper Lough Erne, on the south side of town, is narrower than the Lower Lough and more desolate. ("Upper" means farther from the outflow, so in this case it means the southern part of the lake.) The **Sheelin Restaurant**, in a thatched cottage just beside the jetty at **Bellanaleck**, southwest across the lake from Enniskillen on the A 509, is open for lunch and dinner six days a week in the summer (it's closed for dinner on Mondays), but it is important to book in advance (Tel: 0365-822-32). Saturday night is gourmet night, when the duck and salmon are particularly good. The Sheelin can also be reached by road; stop off first at **Cathcart's Supermarket** across the road and buy some of its excellent brown bread. (If you're on a boat with children, the Sheelin will find you a baby-sitter while you have dinner.)

The Upper Lough is navigable as far south as **Belturbet**

in County Cavan in the Republic. During this stretch the cruiser will cross the border several times, although there will be no line, mark, notification, or, indeed, customs control. If you're going as far as Belturbet, however, it's important to have Irish currency. The **Diamond Bar** in Belturbet's main square is worth a stop. Fishing in the waters around Belturbet is excellent, and visitors come back to the town year after year. There are a number of adequate bed-and-breakfast houses in the town, but nothing exceptional.

Several other sights in the Enniskillen area should not be missed. The first of these is the Janus-faced red-sandstone **Boa Island Figure** on an island in Lower Lough Erne that can be reached more easily by car than by boat. It's a short drive north from Enniskillen to Kesh and then to Boa Island, which can be reached by a bridge. The trip can also be made by taxi, readily available in Enniskillen and quite cheap—50 pence per mile, as opposed to a pound per mile in the Republic. A list of taxi drivers can be found in the local telephone book.

Once on Boa Island, be aware that the signposting is not clear. Look for a wooden sign on the left that says "Caldragh Cemetery." The Figure, which dates from the pre-Christian period, squats in the graveyard, almost hidden by gravestones and tall grass. One side has been slightly damaged, but both faces still manage to look somewhat menacingly at the unwary and wary alike. Most such statues are kept in museums, so it is extraordinary and refreshing to come across this image from pagan times on a plinth in the middle of a cemetery in a remote part of the country. There is a replica of the Figure and other ancient artifacts in the museum at Enniskillen Castle.

On the way back to Enniskillen, but still on Boa Island, there is a sign on the right for **Lusty Beg**, a small island on Lough Erne. In the summer you can telephone from the mainland for a ferry boat to pick you up and take you over to the **Lusty Beg Chalets and Restaurant**. The island is small enough for guests in the chalets to be constantly aware of the lake all around. In addition to providing the novelty of sleeping on a small island, the accommodation offered is useful as a base for fishing on Lough Erne.

There are also ten log cabins known as the **Ely Island Chalets** on Ely Island, which can be reached by taking the A 46 from Enniskillen toward Belleek and turning right 8 km (5 miles) outside of Enniskillen. The cabins, which have recently been completed, are very comfortable and tastefully decorated, and sleep five or six people. The owners rent boats and equipment for water-skiing and fishing. The island is extremely popular, so it's advisable to book well in advance.

Around Enniskillen

Southwest of Enniskillen there are two interesting sights. One is **Florence Court**, an 18th-century mansion that was once the home of the earls of Enniskillen; it's famous today for the sumptuous Rococo plasterwork on the ceilings. The house is open to the public each afternoon except Tuesdays. To get there take the A 4 and then the A 32 for roughly 6 km (4 miles) south of Enniskillen, then turn right. Florence Court is clearly marked on the road that leads to Blacklion in County Cavan in the Republic.

Farther west toward Belcoo, on the same road as Florence Court, are the **Marble Arch Caves**, open from Easter to the end of October. It is important to telephone in advance (Tel: 0365-82-88-55) to reserve a place on the guided tours of this complex and elaborate underground system, which has only recently been opened to the public. (If there's been a lot of rain, the caves are closed.) The tour consists of a boat journey along an underground river and a trip along a "Moses Walk" cut through an underground lake, as well as a tour of caverns. (A Moses Walk is a passage cut through a pool or lake whereby cement is placed on the bed of the pool and walls are constructed to the same height as the water, thus making a pass through the water that seems to defy logic. As you pass through, your feet are at the same level as the bottom of the pool; you are protected from the water by the walls, but your face, say, is at the same level as the water.)

Tullyhona House, a bed-and-breakfast close by the Marble Arch Caves, can be recommended for its hospitality and general air of warmth as well as its excellent breakfasts. It's located on the right-hand side of the road as you drive toward Belcoo from Florence Court. There is a sign at the entrance to the long avenue that leads to the new two-story farmhouse. An evening meal is also served here (there is an à la carte menu); the prices are extremely reasonable.

In addition to Lough Erne there are three other lakes close to Enniskillen worth exploring. The first is **Lough Melvin**, which straddles the border between Donegal and

Fermanagh southwest of Belleek. The landscape around this lake is rugged and remote, resembling the rough terrain of the West of Ireland more than the softer landscape of Fermanagh. The fishing in Lough Melvin is very good, and it is easy to hire a boat with a boatman who knows the lake. There are no hotels in the lakeside village of Garrison, but there is a hostel, the **Lough Melvin Holiday Centre**, that has none of the discomforts usually associated with such facilities; there is no curfew, there are carpets on the floors and duvets on the beds, and the building is adequately heated. The hostel has a family room as well as a number of dormitories, a room for drying out wet clothes, and a dining room. The Centre also organizes a great number of water-based sports activities, such as wind surfing, sailing, and canoeing, and its restaurant, open all day until 8:00 P.M., serves dishes prepared with fresh fish from the lake, among its other selections. There is also a serviced campsite and caravan (RV or trailer) park attached to the hostel, which is open between April and September.

An even more felicitous option is to stay at **Roskit**, a house on a small island in Lough Melvin, run by Mrs. Moody. The island is joined to the mainland by a causeway that leads from the road that goes west from Garrison to the border (the road is little used now, as the border is sealed at this point). The land around Lough Melvin is poor, the roads are narrow, and most of the houses are modest. Roskit is different. Though medium in size, it is beautiful—carefully decorated and surrounded by superbly kept gardens. There is a boat on hand for fishing for guests staying at the house, and full board is available. The rates are very reasonable indeed, considering the amount of comfort and care given. The lake beyond the garden is famous for two rare types of trout, the gillaroo and the sonaghan. For anyone needing a rest in comfortable, tasteful surroundings with good food, this island haven in one of Ireland's best fishing lakes is perfect. Understandably, Roskit is often booked, so Mrs. Moody requires at least two days' notice. Usually guests stay for several days; it is hardly worth trying Roskit for one night.

Another lake, **Lough Macnean**, is close to the Marble Arch Caves and Florence Court. Between the Upper and Lower lakes of Lough Macnean are the towns of **Belcoo** in the North and **Blacklion** in the Republic; a short bridge links the two. Both towns are close to the **Ulster Way** and the **Cavan Way**, trails that have been built and cleared for intrepid walkers and hikers. The area around Blacklion—where the two Ways in fact converge—is of great interest because of the sheer concentration of ancient monuments. With a good map (an Ordnance Survey map can be purchased from most large news agents) it should be easy to explore the chamber tombs and gallery graves (dating from the early Iron Age to the late Middle Ages) in nearby **Burren**, the cairns in **Legalough**, and the ringforts in **Moneygashel**—all within 6 km (4 miles) of Blacklion and along the 17-km (11-mile) Cavan Way.

While the Cavan Way runs south from Blacklion in the Republic, the Ulster Way runs exclusively through the North and can be picked up at any point. It is 500 miles long and is clearly signposted all of the way. It can be started, for example, near Blacklion and continued across South Fermanagh to Lough Erne. It can also be taken up just below Fivemiletown, which is near the border between Fermanagh and Tyrone, continuing into Antrim and Down. There is an extraordinary variety in the type of landscape in these regions, and the Ulster Way reflects this. Most of the time it keeps away from main roads and offers the walker a trail through a wild rural landscape, full of small hills and forests, with the tributaries of Lough Erne all around.

Walking anywhere in the border area is richly rewarding, not only because most local people will stop and talk, but also because there is a large number of small hills and ridges from which the surrounding countryside can be surveyed. This is particularly the case with the route of the Ulster Way through counties Fermanagh and Tyrone. The tourist office in Enniskillen has brochures on each stage of the Ulster Way; the route is also marked on the Michelin map of Ireland. Full details on the Ulster Way are also provided in a series of well-illustrated pamphlets from the Northern Ireland Tourist Board in Belfast (Tel: 0232-23-12-21).

Upper and Lower Lough Macnean are famous for their heavyweight pike; boats can be hired on either side of the border by those who want to do battle with these monster fish. Another excellent fishing lake is **Lough Oughter**, in County Cavan in the Republic, south of Belturbet and west of Cavan Town. The lake is surrounded by **Killykeen Forest Park**, where 20 self-catering chalets—the **Killykeen Forest Park Chalets**—have been built. There's a tennis court on the site, a golf course nearby, and a beach beside the lake; chalet guests can also take boats out to the lake islands. The chalets themselves, which sleep up to six people, are beautifully designed, though they resemble Scandinavian houses more than any native Irish model. Weekly rates are quite reasonable, even in the high summer season, and the chalets can be rented year round, for a weekend or a few midweek days, as they have central heating and double glazing as well as solaria and balconies.

The latest addition to visitor facilities in the Cavan area is the 150-room **Slieve Russell Hotel**, which can be reached by taking the N 3 from Cavan to Belturbet and then continuing toward Ballyconnell. The excellent indoor sports facilities include a large swimming pool, a gym, squash courts, and two tennis courts. The restaurant is generally very heavily booked, so visitors would be well advised to telephone in advance; Tel: (049) 264-44.

COUNTY MONAGHAN

In the adjoining Republic county of Monaghan to the northeast of Cavan, there are two buildings worth visiting in Monaghan, the principal town. The **Monaghan County Museum** in the main square is one of the best of its size in Ireland, having among its exhibits examples of local traditional arts and crafts, archaeological finds, and the 12th- to 13th-century Cross of Clogher. There are also displays of clerical vestments and an assortment of prehistoric artifacts.

The other building, also on the square, is the **Market House**, which dates from 1792 and is noted for its fine stonework and woodwork. Recently restored, it now houses the tourist office and an exhibition space and is one of the venues for the **County Monaghan Arts Festival**, which is held every September in Monaghan Town, Clones to the west, and Carrickmacross to the south. Musicians, actors, writers, and painters from all parts of Ireland join together in the festival's program.

In November at **Carrickmacross** there is a festival called Kavanagh's Yearly, which celebrates the life and work of the poet Patrick Kavanagh, who died in 1967. He was born at Iniskeen in the eastern part of County Monaghan, where his birthplace is open to the public. For more information on the Arts Festival or Kavanagh's Yearly, contact Bernard Loughlin (Tel: 047-540-03).

In the month of July there are two events in the border

area that are worth finding out about and attending. The first is known as the **Ulster Fleadh Ceoil**. *Fleadh Ceoil* is Gaelic for "festival of music." Normally, the Ulster Fleadh Ceoil is held in one of the towns on the Republic's side of the border, but several years ago it was held in Warrenpoint in the North. Musicians and traditional singers come from all parts of Ireland for the events, but most of the participants are from the North.

The best music can be heard at informal sessions that begin casually when two or three musicians who know one another go into a pub and start playing. During the Ulster Fleadh (there are also fleadhanna in other provinces, as well as the All-Ireland Fleadh) there are sessions going on in most bars and, if the weather is good, in the streets as well. The public houses are open until the early hours of the morning, and there is a sense of wild abandon in the main streets and squares before dawn arrives. The phone number, in Dublin, for information on dates and venues is (01) 280-0295.

The other major event of the month occurs on July 12, the anniversary of the Battle of the Boyne (1690), in which the Protestant King William defeated the Catholic King James. Twelfth of July marches take place all over the North. In certain regions the celebration has very serious sectarian overtones, and in other places it is just a pleasant day out for the family.

Of all the places to stay in the border area, one house stands out for its luxury, hospitality, and good food. This is **Hilton Park**, beside the village of Scotshouse just south of the border on L 44, 6 km (4 miles) southwest of Clones. Home of the Madden family since the 18th century, Hilton Park is a huge house, having been added to and refurbished repeatedly during the past two centuries. The shutters on the ground-floor windows are made of steel and have small apertures for rifles should the need arise to defend the house. Most of the guest bedrooms have enormous four-poster beds and overlook beautifully landscaped gardens, which include oak trees grown from the acorns brought here more than a hundred years ago as wedding presents by ancestors of one of today's incumbents. In the evening before dinner there is usually a big roaring fire in the drawing room. The owner and host, Johnny Madden, is a great source of information on local events and the history of the area. His wife, Lucy, is a marvelous cook; most of the food, including the cheeses, comes from the estate. The house is close enough to the

principal towns— less than 24 km (15 miles) from Monaghan Town or Enniskillen—to be used as a base for
touring.

The North is full of big houses, small cottages, and
hardly anything in between. One of the largest of the
estates belonged to the Leslie family, who still live at
Castle Leslie at **Glaslough** (on R 185) north of Monaghan
Town. However, their lands, once 80,000 acres, are now
much reduced. The Leslies now run an equestrian center
on the estate, and horses are available for trekking. One
of the gate lodges to Castle Leslie was designed by Nash;
the house itself was built in 1878.

The **Pillar House** is a good, small, inexpensive hotel at
one of the entrances to the Leslie estate. The village of
Glaslough itself was built and maintained by the Leslies.
The houses are stone-built, and the village is unusual for
its picturesque uniformity. About a kilometer (less than a
mile) to the southwest is an ancient site at **St. Donagh's
Church**, which has a Medieval High Cross that was found
in a bog in 1911 and erected in the graveyard.

COUNTY TYRONE

A quarter of a million Northerners emigrated to the
United States in the 18th century. By the time of the
signing of the Declaration of Independence, one-sixth of
the population of the 13 colonies was of Ulster origin.
Dotted throughout the North are the ancestral homes of a
number of American presidents, including that of Ulysses
S. Grant in Aughnacloy, on the border between Tyrone
and Monaghan, and the home of Woodrow Wilson's
grandfather in Dergalt, near Strabane.

The **Ulster American Folk Park** at Camphill, 8 km (5
miles) north of Omagh on the main Omagh-to-Derry
road (A 5), is dedicated to the preservation of the memory of the Ulster-American heritage. This open-air museum consists of various buildings that have been either
preserved or reconstructed, as well as a visitors' center
with an exhibition space and theater in which an audiovisual presentation tells the story of Ulster's emigrants to
America, such as the Mellons, forebears of the financier
Andrew Mellon. There is also a gift shop and a café.

Typical Early American houses, including a log cabin
and an elaborately furnished Pennsylvania long farmhouse, have been set well apart from each other on the

26-acre wooded site. There is also a forge, a Presbyterian meeting house, a schoolhouse, a weaver's cottage, and a covered wagon. In the summer, blacksmiths, weavers, spinners, and candlemakers in traditional costumes demonstrate their ancient crafts for visitors. This is interesting, if slightly corny; what is of real interest are the houses themselves and the furniture. The houses have been so well reconstructed that you get a genuine sense of being in another world.

Fermanagh, Tyrone, and Derry have a wealth of ancient historic and prehistoric sites, and more are being uncovered constantly in the bogland that abounds in these counties. These include passage graves, dolmens, and stone circles. Some of the most spectacular of the last are the **Bronze Age stone circles** at Beaghmore, northwest of Cookstown near Dunnamore, which were discovered in the peat-covered upland in the 1930s. Most of the stones here are small, less than a foot high; the highest is four feet. They have been cleared of peat, and seven circles can be distinctly made out. The site itself is interesting, with a spectacular view of the Sperrin Mountains to the north, and it is hard not to begin imagining a time when these stones were first put in place. Each stone circle would have been aligned with the other monuments in the area. The alignments within this particular system are intriguing and mysterious. They seem to correspond to the stone circles at Moymore, near Pomeroy, a couple of miles away.

East of Cookstown is **Lough Neagh**, the largest lake in the British Isles and Ireland. Although the lake is navigable, it has not been developed for leisure pursuits in the same way as Lough Erne. The rivers that flow in and out of the lake are very good for fishing, however. **Lough Beg**, north of Lough Neagh on the lower River Bann, has giant pike. There are several swimming and bathing spots on the western side of Lough Neagh, including Traad Point off B 18 near Ballyronan, which also has a marina.

The most interesting ancient monument in the area is the **High Cross** at **Ardboe**, on the lake 14 km (9 miles) east of Cookstown off B 73. Dating from the 10th century, it is more than 18 feet tall and has 22 carved panels. Although badly worn, they depict stories that can still be identified as Adam and Eve, the Sacrifice of Isaac, the Crucifixion, and other scenes from the Old and New Testaments. The High Cross at Ardboe was once a special place of worship, where the devout prayed and washed in the lake. In the corner of the churchyard is an old tree to which supplicants would hammer coins or other pieces of metal in the hope of having their wishes granted.

The bogland area of North Tyrone and South Derry, between Ardboe and the village of Bellaghy, north of Magherafelt, where many of Seamus Heaney's evocative poems are set, is full of hidden reminders of history and prehistory, and the past seems to hover over everything that happens, like a ghost.

West of Omagh, toward the border with County Donegal, the land is barren and lonely, the roads narrow. The small holdings, in general, are Catholic-owned. The British Army and the Royal Ulster Constabulary tend not to use these roads. Instead, they come in and out by helicopter.

There is a strong British Army presence in **Strabane**, which has one of the best and most comfortable hotels in the area, the **Fir Trees Hotel**. Outside town on the Sion Mills road, it offers good food and good service, but more important, perhaps, it is the *only* hotel in the area. Bed-and-breakfast houses are plentiful in the South but scarce in the North; there is nothing in a 15-km (9-mile) radius of Strabane on the northern side of the border besides the Fir Trees Hotel. Reservations should be made in advance to ensure accommodations.

Strabane, a predominantly Catholic town with the highest unemployment rate in western Europe, has been severely damaged by bombs during the past 15 years. One of the buildings that has survived from the 18th century is **Gray's Printing Shop**, on Main Street facing the bridge as you come into town from the Fir Trees Hotel. The shop, which has a Georgian front, is now in the hands of the National Trust. Among the many who served their apprenticeship here was John Dunlap, who would later print the first copies of the American Declaration of Independence, and James Wilson, grandfather of Woodrow Wilson, whose house at Dergalt, 3 km (2 miles) southeast of town, is open to the public.

Strabane and the town of **Lifford**, across the River Foyle, are joined by a short bridge. Lifford, however, is in County Donegal in the Republic. There is a British Army checkpoint on the bridge and a customs post on the Lifford side. The atmosphere in Lifford is strangely similar to that of Strabane—sleepy, untidy, and economically deprived. Its only hotel is now closed, but there are a number of houses in the center of town that offer bed and breakfast. One of the best examples of stone circles in Ireland is the **Beltany Stone Circle**, 64 Bronze Age stones close to Raphoe, not far from Lifford.

COUNTY DERRY

On many maps and some signposts, this county and its principal city are referred to as Londonderry, which is the name the Unionist population would give to Northern Ireland's northwest corner. But no one, Catholic or Protestant, calls the place Londonderry in everyday conversation. The word Derry, by the way, derives from the Gaelic *doire,* which means "place of the oak trees." The Sperrin Mountains, which also spill into County Tyrone, are the most imposing topographical feature in the southern part of County Derry, and its most northerly reaches form part of the Antrim coast. But it is the city of Derry, astride the River Foyle, that dominates the county.

Derry Town

Derry, Northern Ireland's second city, is deeply divided, and it is important to understand the divisions before setting out to explore it. The eastern bank of the Foyle is called the **Waterside** (the railway station—there is a rail link to Belfast—is on this side, as is the A 5, the main road to Strabane) and is inhabited mainly by Protestants. The western side of the river, with the exception of the small area in the center called the Fountain, is inhabited primarily by Catholics in a district called the **Bogside**. The two sides are connected by the Craigavon Bridge. Until the early 1970s, the Protestant minority ran the city through an elaborate system of gerrymandering, but the civil rights movement changed that, and there is now a Catholic majority on the City Council.

Derry Town, like Strabane, has suffered heavily from bombs, but its 17th-century walls still stand proudly and are one of the most interesting features of the city. Finished in 1618, they withstood three sieges, including the famous (or notorious, depending on which side you're on) Siege of 1688, which began when 13 apprentice boys seized the keys of the town and locked the gates against the approaching forces of the deposed Catholic King James II. (This event is celebrated by Protestants each August 12; because of the sectarian tensions it engenders, this is a poor time to visit Derry.) The **walls of**

Derry are a mile in length, the old cannon still peer over the ramparts—one a gift in 1590 from Elizabeth I—and, inside, four streets radiate from a center called the Diamond.

It is still possible to make a complete circuit of the walls, except for a short stretch close to St. Columb's that has been taken over by the British Army as a lookout post. Within the walls of Derry, the most interesting building is **St. Columb's Cathedral**, the city's Protestant cathedral, which dates from the early 17th century and was originally built for the early settlers by the City of London. It is full of plaques and memorials to three centuries of the city's rulers. In the chapter house of the cathedral there are relics of the siege, as well as old guns and paintings.

The **Creggan graveyard**, situated on a hill above the Catholic Bogside area, is a stark and powerful monument to the city's recent past. This is by and large a Catholic graveyard, but it is also used by the paramilitaries of the Nationalist side. The gravestones and monuments have elaborate inscriptions; the attendants are very friendly and usually will point visitors to the most interesting graves. There is a superb view of the city below and of the River Foyle as it curls out toward the sea.

As in Strabane, Derry's main hotel is outside the city, on the east side of the Foyle. The modern, well-run **Everglades Hotel** is on the right-hand side of the road as you drive toward the city from Strabane, past the oddly named village of New Buildings. The Everglades has a good restaurant, which visitors would be wise to frequent, as there is really nothing else of a similar standard in Derry Town.

During the past few years there has been a considerable amount of development in Derry, including the building of a **castle** on an old site at the entrance to Shipquay Street. It is the focal point for the gatherings of the O'Doherty clan, descendants of the Irish chieftain who led an attack on Derry in 1608. There is a new **railway museum** beside the main bridge that spans the Foyle; displays include many of the old engines and coaches that formerly were used on the lines from Derry to Donegal and from Strabane to Derry. There is an engine and coach in working order to take visitors on a short trip down to the river and back. The museum is open from 10:00 A.M. to 5:00 P.M. Tuesday through Saturday and Sundays from 2:00 to 6:00 P.M., May through September.

Over the past few years Derry has celebrated the festival of Halloween, the last night of October, with fancy-dress parades and much drinking and carousing, followed by a week-long arts festival. The impressive red-sandstone **Guildhall** on Shipquay Place, just outside the walls and close to the river, is the venue for the annual **Field Day** theater production at the end of August. Field Day is a theater touring group whose directors include the poet Seamus Heaney and the playwright Brian Friel, whose great play *Translations* was given its first production here. Each year the company puts on a production of a new Irish play at the Guildhall and then tours it throughout the country. Call the theater company's office in Derry for more information on Field Day; Tel: (0504) 360-196.

The **Orchard Gallery**, also in the center of the city, is one of the most energetic and exciting modern art galleries in Ireland. Similarly, the **Bookworm Bookshop**, just off the Diamond, is excellent; it's particularly good on local history, archaeology, and books of Irish interest, but also carries a fine general selection. It and Hall's in Enniskillen are the best bookshops in the border area.

Outside Derry Town

Derry Town is a mixture of the dreary and the dynamic. Like other towns in the North, it tends to close down after six, and the streets are often deserted in the evening. The area northeast of the city can be lively, however, particularly the seaside towns of **Portrush** (which is actually in County Antrim and is further discussed in that section, below) and **Portstewart**. Full of old-fashioned summer hotels and boarding houses, these places are a great escape from the troubled history that seems to hang over Derry. **Maddybenny Farm** is a traditional farmhouse run by Mrs. Rosemary White on the Loguestown road. The farm is still in use, and the house is close to the beach as well as to the town of Portrush. There's a new "Grade A" hotel in the town called the **Magherabuoy House Hotel**, built around an old house. The hotel's restaurant is quite good, the average dinner costing about £15. (East along the coast from Portrush are Dunluce Castle and the Giant's Causeway, for which see the Antrim section in the following chapter.)

In Portstewart the family-run **Edgewater Hotel**, at 88 Strand Road, is beautifully situated overlooking the strand. Also in Portstewart, Mrs. Vi Anderson runs a good

guesthouse called **Oregon** in one of the terraced houses
that are so common in Irish towns.

The six-mile-long Atlantic beach northeast of Derry
Town begins at Magilligan Point near the mouth of Lough
Foyle. This west end of the beach has a **Martello tower**
like the one in Sandycove in Dublin, where the opening
scene of *Ulysses* is set; the other end has the picturesque
Mussenden Temple, also circular but rather more ornate.
This Corinthian-columned temple was once the summer
library of Downhill Palace, now in ruins; it was completed
in 1785 and is kept in perfect condition by the National
Trust.

The sea here is good for fishing, especially for bass,
and there are several good golf courses, including the
outstanding **Royal Portrush Golf Club** (there are two 18-
hole courses at the club), which is open to visitors.
Greens fees range from £8 to £15, depending on the
season. The telephone number is (0265) 82-23-11. The
sport in Derry Town is rather less sedate. The Derry
soccer team has its own pitch in the Brandywell area of
the city. The club's supporters are without doubt the most
loyal and devoted in Ireland; thousands of fans travel with
the team to away games. The sense of local pride is
enormous. Another good venue from which to sample
the peculiar flavor of Derry is the **greyhound track** in the
Brandywell, where racing is a popular and reasonably
nonsectarian sport.

GETTING AROUND

The best roads from Dublin are the N 2 to Monaghan,
which crosses the border at Aughnacloy, the N 3 to
Cavan followed by the N 54 from Cavan to Clones; then,
after the border crossing, the A 34 from Clones to Enniskillen. The best road from Sligo is the N 16, which
crosses the border at Blacklion and Belcoo, and then
becomes the A 4 on the Northern side between the
border and Enniskillen. There are two ways in from
Donegal: The N 15 from the south of the county and the
N 14 from the north of the county meet at Lifford, from
where there is a border crossing into Strabane; the
other crossing is at the end of the N 13, which crosses
the border close to Derry. All these are official crossings,
manned by either Irish or British security forces, and are
the routes to and from these counties used by most
people, locals included.

Derry can also be reached by rail from Dublin and Belfast and by air from Dublin.

ACCOMMODATIONS REFERENCE

The telephone country codes for these accommodations vary, so they are listed individually. When dialing telephone numbers from outside the country, drop the 0 in the area code. The rates given below are projections *for 1992; for up-to-the-minute rate information it is always wise to telephone before booking. Unless otherwise indicated, rates are per person sharing and do not include meals or service.*

▶ **Edgewater Hotel.** 88 Strand Road, **Portstewart**, County Derry BT55 7LZ. Tel: (44) 0265-83-22-24; Fax: (44) 0265-83-33-14. £31 sterling, breakfast and service included.

▶ **Ely Island Chalets.** Ely Lodge, **Enniskillen**, County Fermanagh. Tel: (44) 0365-897-77; Fax: (44) 0365-893-28. £250–£350 sterling per week for six people.

▶ **Everglades Hotel.** Prehen Road, **Derry Town**, County Derry BT47 2PA. Tel: (44) 0504-467-22; Fax: (44) 0504-492-00. £38 sterling, breakfast and service included.

▶ **Fir Trees Hotel.** Melmount Road, **Strabane**, County Tyrone BT82 9JT. Tel: (44) 0504-38-23-82; Fax: (44) 0504-88-59-32. £30 sterling, breakfast and service included.

▶ **Hilton Park (Johnny and Lucy Madden). Clones,** County Monaghan. Tel: (353) 047-560-07. Open April to September. IR£42, breakfast and service included.

▶ **Killyhevlin Hotel.** Dublin road, **Enniskillen**, County Fermanagh BT74 7AU. Tel: (44) 0365-32-34-81; Fax: (44) 0365-32-47-26. £35 sterling, breakfast included.

▶ **Killykeen Forest Park Chalets (Jim O'Reilly).** Killykeen Forest Park, **Cavan**, County Cavan. Tel: (353) 049-325-41; Telex: 46809 KFP. A six-berth chalet costs IR£230 per week in June, £290 per week in July and August.

▶ **Lough Melvin Holiday Centre. Garrison**, County Fermanagh. Tel: (44) 0365-65-81-42. £6 sterling for a bed in the dormitory.

▶ **Lusty Beg Chalets and Restaurant.** Lusty Beg Island, **Kesh**, County Fermanagh. Tel: (44) 0365-63-13-42. £300–£400 sterling per week for six people.

▶ **Maddybenny Farm (Mrs. Rosemary White).** 18 Maddybenny Park, Loguestown Road, **Portrush**, County

Antrim BT52 2PT. Tel: (44) 0265-82-33-94. £15–£17.50 sterling, breakfast and service included (there is a discount for children).

▶ **Magherabuoy House Hotel.** 41 Magherabuoy Road, **Portrush,** County Antrim BT56 8NX. Tel: (44) 0265-82-35-07; Fax: (44) 0265-82-46-87. £32.50 sterling, breakfast and service included.

▶ **Oregon (Mrs. Vi Anderson).** 118 Station Road, **Portstewart,** County Derry BT55 7PU. Tel: (44) 0265-83-28-26. £13–£15 sterling, breakfast and service included.

▶ **Pillar House Hotel. Glaslough,** County Monaghan. Tel: (353) 047-881-25. IR£14, breakfast and service included.

▶ **Roskit (Mrs. Moody). Garrison,** County Fermanagh. Tel: (44) 0365-652-31. £35 sterling, breakfast, dinner, and service included.

▶ **Slieve Russell Hotel. Ballyconnell,** County Cavan. Tel: (049) 264-44; Fax: (049) 264-74. IR£37.50, breakfast and service included. Weekend rates are IR£80 for two nights' bed and breakfast and two dinners.

▶ **Tullyhona House (Mrs. Rosemary Armstrong). Florence Court,** County Fermanagh. Tel: (44) 0365-824-52. £13 sterling, breakfast and service included.

THE NORTHEAST

ANTRIM, BELFAST, DOWN, AND ARMAGH

By Sam McAughtry

Sam McAughtry, born in Belfast, is a short-story writer and former award-winning columnist for The Irish Times. *He is popular on radio and television north and south of the border.*

The Northern Ireland counties of Armagh and Down run northward from the border with the Irish Republic adjacent to the South's counties Monaghan and Louth. Armagh is bordered on the west by the North's County Tyrone and on the east by County Down, which runs north on the channel coast as far as Belfast, where it meets County Antrim. Antrim, which has one of Ireland's most beautiful coasts, lies on the eastern side of Northern Ireland all the way up to the northern tip of the island. The largest lake in Ireland, Lough Neagh, is located in the very center of Northern Ireland, its shores formed by parts of five counties: Antrim, Down, Armagh, Tyrone, and Derry.

Like the people in Northern Ireland generally, the residents of counties Antrim, Armagh, and Down are direct and plain in their speech and use fewer words through the day than the people of the rest of Ireland. If they do you a favor and you thank them, they will say "You're welcome." It was New World immigrants from Northern Ireland who put this nice phrase into everyday speech in the United

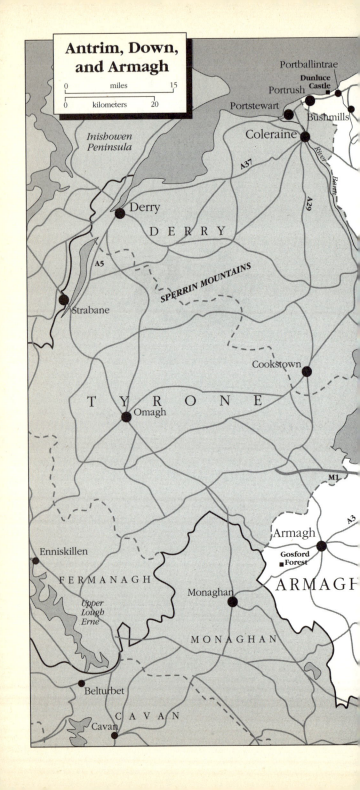

Antrim, Down, and Armagh

miles 0 — 15
kilometers 0 — 20

Inishowen Peninsula

Portballintrae
Dunluce Castle
Portrush
Portstewart
Bushmills
Coleraine
River Bann

A37

A29

Derry

D E R R Y

A5

SPERRIN MOUNTAINS

Strabane

Cookstown

T Y R O N E

Omagh

M1

A3

Armagh

Gosford Forest

Enniskillen

F E R M A N A G H

Upper Lough Erne

A R M A G H

Monaghan

M O N A G H A N

Belturbet

C A V A N

Cavan

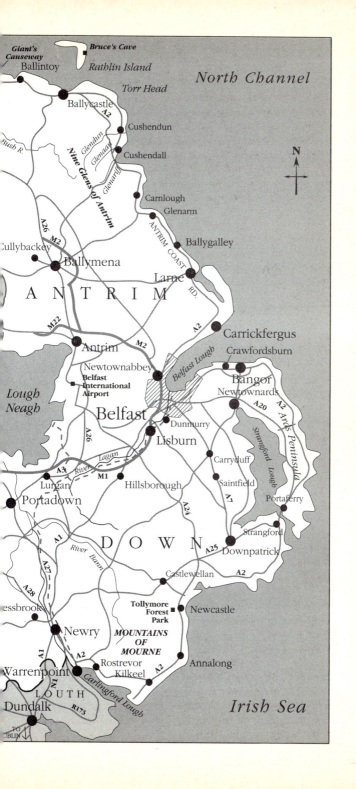

States. To visitors, the local people are shyly polite; they usually will not speak to strangers unless they are addressed first. Once the ice is broken, however, the visitor will be surprised at the friendliness of the people, who will go to great lengths to make strangers feel welcome.

Northern Ireland has 300 miles of unpolluted coastline, virtually all of it in County Antrim and County Down, offering some of the best sea fishing in Europe. Sea trout, skate, dogfish, halibut, bass, and mackerel abound. The coast around the Giant's Causeway, near Portrush in north Antrim, is an especially popular fishing ground with visitors, but the County Down coast, including Strangford Lough, offers equally exciting sport to the sea fisherman.

For freshwater fishermen there are more than 60 rivers and lakes available. It is not uncommon for a fisherman to have a long stretch of good trout water to himself. In the Glens of Antrim there are rivers where both salmon and trout can be caught; the lakes of County Armagh are stocked with rainbow trout and managed by the Department of Agriculture, but good fishing waters in Northern Ireland are, quite literally, too numerous to mention.

MAJOR INTEREST

Fishing

Antrim
Giant's Causeway
Dunluce Castle
Rathlin Island
The nine Glens of Antrim
Carrickfergus Castle

Belfast dining and shopping

Down
Saint Patrick's burial place
The Mountains of Mourne

Armagh
Navan Fort, ancient Celtic stronghold

To explore the three counties that make up the eastern half of Northern Ireland, we begin on the extreme northwest near County Antrim's border with County Derry and then follow the Antrim coast east and south to Belfast, the capital of Northern Ireland. From there, we take in the highlights of County Down, south and east of Antrim, and then move west to County Armagh.

COUNTY ANTRIM

There is a strong affinity for Scotland in the Northeast; only 13 miles separate them at one point. Because of this proximity, the people of Scotland have, for thousands of years, regarded the Antrim Coast as their own back yard. Hence there is a particularly strong Scottish influence in the speech and the way of life of the County Antrim folk. County Down shares this influence too, but to a lesser extent.

Antrim is the only one of Northern Ireland's six counties that is not contiguous with some part of the Republic. It is bordered on the west by County Derry, on the south by County Down, and on the east and north by the North Channel. Most people who explore Antrim beyond Belfast, its principal city, are drawn to the north coast, where the chief attractions are the Giant's Causeway and the Glens of Antrim.

Ancestral sites associated with two U.S. presidents are to be seen at **Cullybackey,** 7 km (4.5 miles) northwest of Ballymena, a home traditionally linked with Chester Alan Arthur, 21st president; and at **Boneybefore,** half a kilometer east of Carrickfergus, where there is a period cottage on the site of a similar one from which the parents of Andrew Jackson, seventh president, emigrated.

The North Antrim Coast

The **Giant's Causeway,** a vast promontory of basaltic columns formed by the volcanic action during the Cenozoic period 70 million years ago, is easily the most popular and most interesting geological sight in Northern Ireland and one of Europe's major tourist attractions. Many ancient myths are connected with this site on the west side of Benbane Head, including one that Finn McCool, Ireland's fabled giant, used one of the formations as a Giant's Chair.

The Giant's Causeway is located 13 km (8 miles) east of Portrush, near the Derry border. **Portrush** itself is a bright, breezy seaside resort and is particularly well known for its championship **Royal Portrush Golf Club** (Tel: 0265-82-23-11). One of the best-known stores outside Belfast is the **White House** on Main Street in Portrush. It stocks the best-quality Aran sweaters, Waterford crystal, fine china, and nearly everything else you might want. For those who find themselves overnighting in the Portrush area, the **Ramore Bar**, a pub with great atmosphere right on the harbor edge of town, serves very good meals, fish dishes being a specialty. Note that the Ramore Bar does not offer accommodation, however. The **Royal Court Hotel** at Whiterocks, just outside Portrush, is highly recommended, with 18 bedrooms each with private bath. The **Ballymagarry Country House** at 46 Leeke Road in Portrush is a small guesthouse with above average facilities. (See also County Derry in the Border Counties chapter, above.)

While you're in the Portrush area, visit **Dunluce Castle**, a substantial ruin on the edge of a cliff 5 km (3 miles) or so east of Portrush on the coast road. The castle was occupied first by Normans in the 13th century, then by Irish and Scottish chieftains until the 17th century. The Scots were everywhere in this part of Ireland for thousands of years; they were so proprietary that one of them, Sorley Boye MacDonnell, after a run-in with Queen Elizabeth's men, sent a note to the local garrison commander saying that the English had no right to be in Ireland. There are guided tours of the Dunluce Castle area, and in good weather a sea cave that was part of its defense can also be visited.

Rathlin Island, a small, boomerang-shaped bit of land off the north coast of Antrim, is a 50-minute trip by motorboat from **Ballycastle**, 25 km (15 miles) east of Portrush. While Sir Francis Drake was an ordinary sea captain in 1575, he helped massacre the MacDonnell population on the island while Sorley Boye MacDonnell, chief warrior of the clan, looked on helplessly from Fair Head across Rathlin Sound. The most famous feature of the island is **Bruce's Cave**, where Robert the Bruce stayed when he was outlawed from Scotland in 1306. It was here that he was reputed to have been so inspired by the will to win of a spider that it lifted his sagging morale, and he returned to Scotland and licked the English at the Battle of Bannockburn in 1314. Daily excursions to the island leave from Ballycastle from April through September. Torr Head, less than 16 km (10 miles) due east of Ballycastle, is the point in Northern Ireland closest to

Scotland—from here it's only 13 miles across the Channel to the Scottish coast.

It's a glorious drive from Ballycastle around to the west through Ballintoy, past the Giant's Causeway to **Portballintrae**. This road leads on southeastward to **Bushmills**— the world's oldest legal whiskey distillery—on the River Bush, famed for its salmon and trout. In olden times travellers restored themselves with a glass of whiskey here, for it has been distilled at Bushmills since 1608. The spirit can be sampled within reason in the course of a tour of the distillery and malt house.

For an overnight stay here, the medium-priced **Bayview Hotel** in Portballintrae is recommended. Accommodation is comfortable, and this small, family-run hotel specializes in home-cooked food and personal service. The **Auberge de Seneirl**, on the Ballyclough road in Bushmills, provides excellent accommodation and French cuisine. Just about any hotel in this area, though not luxurious, will be comfortable and friendly for an overnight stop.

The Glens of Antrim

If the Giant's Causeway is Northern Ireland's most intriguing scenic attraction, its most beautiful is without doubt the Glens of Antrim, nine lovely valleys—created by retreating glaciers—that stretch inland from the Antrim Coast road between Cushendall and Cushendun, two pretty little villages 20 km (12 miles) southeast of Ballycastle, and Larne, 34 km (21 miles) north of Belfast. If you want to see the glens properly, you'll need to set aside the best part of a day. With names like Glendun and Glenaan, Glenarm and Glenariff, and with their murmuring waterfalls and wind-rustled ferns, the Glens of Antrim could be dangerous for poets, the mixture is so rich.

If you have time for a meal while you're in the area, look for the **Londonderry Arms** on Harbour Road in **Carnlough**, about 20 km (12 miles) north of Larne, at the mouth of Glencoy, one of the smaller Antrim glens. The homemade wheaten bread, locally caught salmon, and trout (in season) are excellent. The Londonderry Arms is also a small, charming, family-operated hotel. The building itself is of some historic interest; it was once owned by Winston Churchill.

For those intending to spend some time exploring the Antrim coastal area, the **Ballygalley Castle**, right on the coast road about 5 km (3 miles) north of Larne, is both a comfortable and an interesting place to stop over. The castle was built in 1625 by James Shaw, according to an armorial escutcheon and a date carved above the door. Rooms and food here will meet all good expectations, and the manager will talk history for half the night if encouraged.

Another point of interest in Antrim is **Carrickfergus Castle**, a very well preserved 13th-century Norman castle overlooking the harbor. Carrickfergus, northeast of Belfast on the north side of Belfast Lough, is where King William III landed to do battle with King James in 1690, at the River Boyne, just over the border.

Also worth a visit is the **Lisburn Museum** in Lisburn, 11 km (7 miles) southwest of Belfast. John Wesley preached here in 1756; exhibits include records of the 1798 Rising in Ireland, in which Presbyterian insurgents in this area were active. Five kilometers (3 miles) east of Lisburn on the main Belfast road is the **Forte Crest Hotel**, which specializes in Irish salmon dishes and offers lodging as well. The accommodations here are well up to international standards. There are also a squash court and gymnasium.

BELFAST

A once-pushy Victorian city that grew more quickly than any other in Europe during the 19th century, Belfast is attractively situated at the mouth of the River Lagan where it enters Belfast Lough, with blue hills—particularly the peak of Ben Madigan to the north—providing a lovely, atmospheric backdrop in the distance. Once Belfast had the biggest shipyard in the world, and the largest ropeworks; recently, like so many European cities, the capital of Northern Ireland has had to come to terms with its reduced importance in the scheme of things. Today's Belfast is modest and the pushiness is gone, the only visible evidence left being the proud City Hall and some lovely, gracious buildings arranged in a high-sided square around it. About a third of Northern Ireland's 1.5 million population lives in the capital. Belfast folk are very friendly: If you look as if you're having a problem, passersby will stop to offer help.

The atmosphere in Belfast and the provincial towns is usually relaxed and normal. There are barrier gates, but traffic flows freely through these. Parades from both sides are held from early July through August. These cause some tension, but are routed through well-marked areas where visitors would not normally go even in happier times because, as a rule, they are away from shopping areas. Downtown stores seldom any longer search customers' purses, etc., upon entering. There is violence, but tactics on both sides are to attack individuals. For years there have been no cases of visitors being injured. The police are armed but are invariably polite. Army vehicles and soldiers will be evident but the activities that interest them mostly occur in small side streets where tourists never go.

The Lagan, which separates County Down from County Antrim, also bisects Belfast, so parts of the capital lie in both counties. There are three main bridges across the river in the heart of the city, over which traffic flows smoothly; though there may be some congestion at peak times, it clears quickly. Belfast's downtown district is the most modern in Ireland, with new shopping malls and excellent pedestrian facilities. The street layout is not complicated, and most places in the shopping area can be reached in the space of half an hour's walk.

The downtown area's most striking feature is the **City Hall**, which holds a prominent position in Donegall Square. Completed in 1906, this rectangular classical Renaissance building has four towers, one at each corner, and a magnificent copper-covered dome. The City Hall staff conducts tours of the building, which houses many mementoes of turn-of-the-century Belfast. The **Linen Hall Library**, on Donegall Square North near the City Hall, established in 1788, is still maintained by public donation and subscription. The library contains some very fine Irish collections and other rare books. Its first librarian, Thomas Russell, was executed in 1798 for rebellion, but the current librarian conspires only about ways and means to keep the Linen Hall's excellent reputation.

The **Grand Opera House**, on Great Victoria Street, is another of Belfast's best-known buildings. Pavlova danced here, Sarah Bernhardt trod its boards, and Orson Welles did his thing here in *Chimes at Midnight*. The Grand Opera House was allowed to fall into decay in the mid-1970s, but it was restored with help from the Northern Ireland Arts Council and reopened in 1980. Today it is considered to be one of the most stylish and evocative theaters in the British Isles and Ireland, its Victorian reds and golds, tassels and velvets as bright and warm as they were when it first opened in 1895. Leading British and

European performers appear here regularly in modern and classical drama productions and in musicals.

Just across the road from the theater is the **Crown Liquor Saloon**, another building rescued from dereliction by the Arts Council. This is the sort of pub that was commonplace before the Second World War: all brass and mahogany, with intimate "snugs" where small parties may drink together in privacy. It has been shown on television so many times that the regulars who drink here now stand at the bar as if they are acting in a classic Victor McLaglen or John Wayne film about Ireland.

Where the performing arts are concerned, Belfast is not nearly as well provided for as Dublin, but the **Lyric Theatre** on Ridgeway Street, near Stranmillis Embankment, and the smaller **Arts Theatre** in Botanic Avenue receive strong support from the Belfast public. The Queen's University English Society holds poetry and prose readings most Thursday evenings in a house adjacent to the university building or in the English lecture theater.

About 8 km (5 miles) east of Belfast on the Upper Newtownards road is the **Stormont Parliament Building**, erected in 1928 in beautiful parkland and woods to house a Northern Ireland parliament that no longer exists. During the guided tours of the impressive white stone building, visitors get a good short course in the history of Northern Ireland to date. The **Ulster Folk and Transport Museum**, off the Bangor road at Cultra, northeast of Stormont, is a 136-acre complex where cottages and other buildings and artifacts of Ulster social history are displayed.

On the wooded slopes of Cave Hill, 7 km (4 miles) north of the city, sits **Belfast Castle**. Built in 1870, it is now a restaurant, with a delightful panoramic view over the city and Belfast Lough to the east. This restaurant has a reputation for its wide choice of cuisine and for the peace of its surroundings.

Elsewhere, the 38-acre **Botanic Gardens**, on the Stranmillis road in the southern suburbs, is a fine example of Victoriana. An outstanding feature is the Palm House, one of the finest early examples of curvilinear glass and cast ironwork in Europe. It was built in the 1840s and was restored to splendid condition in the mid-1970s. The large variety of exotic plants in the Tropical Ravine nearby made it a setting much loved by the folk who lived here a hundred years ago—all Oriental, jungly gloom, and rustling mystery. It still works. The **Ulster Museum**, also on the grounds of the Botanic Gardens, is a major museum and art gallery. Among its displays is some of the Spanish treasure found in the sunken wreck of the Armada galleon *Girona,* which went down in a storm off the Giant's Causeway in 1588. There are also exhibits on the making of linen, once one of Northern Ireland's specialties.

Staying and Dining
in Belfast

Half a dozen leading hotels are located at or near the center of Belfast. The biggest and most expensive of these is the **Europa** on Great Victoria Street, which is only yards from the place where the bus from the airport deposits passengers. The Europa is the hotel favored by visiting press and television news crews. A number of good hotels are scattered around the edges of Belfast, including the **Culloden Hotel**, off the Bangor road at Craigavad. Graded "A" by the Northern Ireland Tourist Board, the Culloden Hotel has everything from sports facilities to a beauty salon. All rooms have private baths, and suites are also available. The moderately priced **Stormont Hotel**, east of Belfast on the Upper Newtownards road, is another top-graded hotel with an excellent view of the historic Parliament buildings opposite. The **Dunadry Inn** at Templepatrick is a large hotel and country club just 6 km (4 miles) from Belfast International Airport. Situated in a quiet, rural area, it's frequented by flight crews for its proximity to the airport as well as for the quality of its food and facilities.

Belfast has a number of very good restaurants. Most of these are intimate and fairly new as well, and are fighting for clientele in a competitive market, so prices tend to be quite reasonable. Hotels provide good food in pleasant surroundings, but the little bistros and restaurants have more inviting atmospheres. The area near Queen's University is particularly well served, with **Branigan's**, which has a good vegetarian menu, and **The Strand**, mentioned in all the good food guides, both on the Stranmillis road. Nearby are **Saints and Scholars**, on University Street, with a reasonably priced and varied bistro menu, and the more specialized **Roscoff**, at Shaftesbury Square, which features nouvelle cuisine. In central Belfast, near City Hall, **Restaurant Forty-Four** at 44 Bedford Street includes both vegetarian and meat dishes on its menu. Also in the city center, Great Victoria Street claims a wide range of restaurants and is close to the entertainment area of Belfast. The best of these restaurants is **La Belle Epoch**, with a French menu. Nearby, **Salvo's** offers Italian food, and is very popular with locals; bring your own wine if you wish.

New restaurants are opening all the time; the old Dockside area, which is being extensively redeveloped, promises to become a new center for entertainment in Belfast, and is worthy of further investigation. But these choices are not far from random, Belfast having so many good places.

Shopping in Belfast

Because prices for many goods are lower in Northern Ireland than in the Republic of Ireland, Belfast is well used to seeing visitors from the South looking for bargains in the city center. For many years it was the other way around, and the people of Belfast are now enjoying the city's shopping appeal and are always ready to help direct visitors to the best stores. Getting around the city is easy; cabs are plentiful and cheap—and the drivers are as talkative as New York cabbies. For those who come from the South by rail, the Central Station is only minutes from the main shopping areas of Belfast, and there is a bus service from the station.

It is impossible to go wrong as far as shopping in Belfast is concerned. The heart of the city has contracted and is now located north of the City Hall. The high dome of this building towers over the city. Stand with your back to the City Hall entrance and the shopping lies before you. **Parson's and Parson's**, 29 Wellington Place, stocks good-class menswear, as does **Anderson and McAuley** at 1 Donegall Place. **Rene Meneely**, at 5 Donegall Square West, sells fine gowns; **Jaeger's**, on nearby Royal Avenue, has both men's and ladies' casual wear.

For jewelry, **Fred J. Malcolm** at 18 Chichester Street is recommended. **Hogg's**, 10 Donegall Square West, is the top place to go for fine bone china, Irish crystal, and good-quality gift items, and **Smyth's Irish Linen**, at 14 Callender Street, sells fine embroidery and laces. Several of the main British department stores have large branches in the center of Belfast, one of the biggest being **Debenham's**, a prestigious clothing store for both men and women, in the new, impressive Castle Court shopping center in Royal Avenue. There may be security checks on entry to some stores, but these are quick and painless.

COUNTY DOWN

All across Northern Ireland there is a neat and tidy appearance to the countryside; the hedges are trim, the fields well managed—and in County Down this is especially so. Probably the best-kept town is **Hillsborough**, about a 45-minute drive southwest of Belfast. Hillsborough is something of a showpiece, very Southern English in appearance.

Between the famed Mountains of Mourne, which sweep down to the sea near Newcastle some 40 miles south of Belfast, and the Ards Peninsula, which curves southeast from the capital around Strangford Lough, County Down is a place of gentle hills and valleys very attractive to the eye. Its coast can be covered in two hours by car, but the numerous pleasant resort towns tempt travellers to tarry. And throughout the county traces of three outside cultures—Norse, French, and Scottish—are still strongly evident.

In the town of **Downpatrick**, some 40 km (25 miles) southeast of Belfast, a granite boulder marks the spot beside the **Church of Ireland Cathedral** where Saint Patrick himself is said to be buried. On Saint Patrick's Day pilgrims strew his gravesite with daffodils. Not many people outside Downpatrick know why; it's because the saint wasn't Irish at all, but Welsh—and the Welsh think highly of the daffodil. In Downpatrick, too, is a **museum** housed in the Old County Jail, built in 1796; the museum has a section devoted to Saint Patrick.

The **Abbey Lodge**, a reasonably priced 21-bedroom hotel on Belfast Road in Downpatrick, is a fine lodging. It also offers a high tea menu starting at £6 and an à la carte menu from £8. Downpatrick is also a good shopping town. The **County Corner**, in English Street, is recommended for ladies' wear, **H. W. Kelly** in Market Street is the main outlet for fine china and glassware, and **McGorrian's**, also in Market Street, is a quality jeweler.

The **Butterfly House** is an unusual attraction at Seaforde, 10 km (6 miles) southwest of Downpatrick, where visitors walk among more than 30 species of tropical butterflies. Take the A 25 from Downpatrick, which joins the A 24 at Clough.

In the southern part of County Down are the **Mountains of Mourne**, immortalized by the songs of Percy French. Slieve Donard (2,796 feet), their highest peak, provides an imposing backdrop for **Newcastle**, a small and hospitable seaside resort with an extensive sandy beach and one of the world's finest golf courses, the **Royal County Down**. Visitors are welcome, but advance bookings are recommended; Tel: (0396) 72-33-14. The club's informal **Centenary Bar** is also open to visitors. **Burrendale Hotel and Country Club**, on Castlewellan Road in Newcastle, serves a nice fresh salmon and scampi made with locally caught shrimp and offers rooms for overnight stays, with top-class facilities, including a swimming pool and sauna.

Forest parks are well laid out at **Tollymore**, 3 km (2 miles) west of Newcastle, and **Rostrevor**, 16 km (10 miles) west of Kilkeel on the north shore of Carlingford Lough near the border with the Republic of Ireland. Notable gardens are at **Castle Ward**, 3 km (2 miles) west of the village of **Strangford** at the bottom of the Ards Peninsula near Portaferry; **Mountstewart House**, 8 km (5 miles) south of Newtownards on Strangford Lough; and **Rowallane House**, at Saintfield, 18 km (12 miles) southeast of Belfast.

The **Glassdrumman House and Lodge** at **Annalong**, down the coast from Newcastle, is a restaurant and small hotel with a deservedly high reputation. It serves food grown on the premises and is popular for its home-cooked granary wheaten bread and walnut bread in particular. Beef and pork dishes are made from the stock reared here; seafood comes fresh from the port of Annalong, only yards away. The Kitchen Garden restaurant has a daytime menu starting at £5 and in the evenings an à la carte menu from £10. A seven-course meal in the Memories restaurant will run from about £25.

Farther up the coast, at **Portaferry** on the southern tip of the **Ards Peninsula**, is the **Portaferry Hotel**, run by John Herlihy. Seafood is the specialty here—through the window you may see fishermen bringing their catch to the restaurant. After extensive refurbishment, 14 suites are also available. Not far from the hotel is the **Northern Ireland Aquarium**. The only public aquarium in Ireland, it displays the variety of marine life in Strangford Lough.

If you plan to spend some time in County Down,

O'Hara's Royal Hotel, on the seafront at **Bangor**, at the top of the Ards Peninsula east of Belfast, is a good-quality establishment. Rooms at the front of the hotel cost more than those at the side because of the lovely views across the Irish Sea to Scotland, but special weekend rates are offered on all rooms. Five kilometers (3 miles) west of Bangor you will find **Crawfordsburn**, a beautifully preserved village; the **Old Inn** here, built in 1614, is well worth a stop for dinner or an overnight stay. **Cottage Crafts**, opposite, offers knitwear, Tyrone crystal, and local pottery.

COUNTY ARMAGH

County Armagh, characterized by gentle hills, is sometimes referred to as the Garden of Ulster, and **Armagh City**, 136 km (85 miles) north of Dublin and 59 km (37 miles) southwest of Belfast, is the religious capital of Ireland. The Catholic Primate has his palace in Armagh City, and nearby in town is the Anglican **Cathedral of St. Patrick**. The cathedral is reputed to be the burial place of Ireland's high king Brian Boru, who was killed in the Battle of Clontarf in 1014. The cathedral's library contains a copy of *Gulliver's Travels* corrected in Swift's own hand.

A striking feature of the city is **the Mall**, a tree-lined promenade flanked by gracious Georgian houses; cricket is often played on the Mall. The **Armagh Planetarium and Observatory** at College Hill to the northeast of the city center has exciting, computer-aided exhibits and displays; in the Star Theatre viewers travel through time, as the universe puts on its own show. The **Drumsill House Hotel** on Moy Road in town has a fine restaurant as well as comfortable accommodations.

Market and Scotch streets in Armagh City will meet most shopping demands in the area. **Whitsitt's**, on Market, has a wide range of fine china wares, while Scotch Street has a concentration of smaller fashion shops for women. For jewelry, try **Ewart** and **City Jewellers**, both on Scotch.

Navan Fort, or, in the Irish, *Eamhain Mhacha,* a huge elliptical earthwork mound about 3 km (2 miles) west of Armagh City, was the site of the chief stronghold of the Celtic kings of Ulster for a thousand years, until its destruction in A.D. 332. The mighty Cuchulain, one of the most heroic figures in Irish mythology—well known to readers of Yeats—practiced feats of arms below the palace in ancient times. Today it is a grassy 16-acre mound.

There is a fine forest park at **Gosford**, 10 km (6 miles) southeast of Armagh City, and another at **Slieve Gullion**, 8 km (5 miles) southwest of **Newry** and about 30 km (18.5 miles) southeast of Armagh City. Northwest of Newry off B 133 is one of the prettiest villages in County Armagh: **Bessbrook**, founded in 1845 by a Quaker, John Richardson.

In addition to its comfortable accommodations, the **Carngrove Hotel** in **Portadown**, 17 km (11 miles) northeast of Armagh City, operates a highly recommended restaurant. The **Silverwood Hotel** on Kiln Lane, Silverwood, Lurgan (near Portadown off the M 1), makes a good, comfortable headquarters from which to plan itineraries in County Armagh.

For golfers there is the **Portadown Golf Club** just 5 km (3 miles) southeast of Portadown town, on the M 1 motorway direct from Belfast at 192 Gilford Road. This is a standard scratch score 70, 70-par course. Visitors are welcome any day except Tuesdays and Saturdays; Tel: (0762) 35-53-56.

GETTING AROUND

Travelling by car is the most efficient way to see the Northeast. There are 70 miles of high-quality motorways, as well as divided highways and very good secondary roads right across Northern Ireland. All major road signs are in English, although in some areas smaller street names may be in the Irish language.

This is the greenest part of Ireland, so it is not surprising that it is also the rainiest. Summer and autumn can be idyllic, but the mist on the mountains that makes this part of Ireland so romantic also makes carrying a light raincoat a sensible idea.

Entry documents are not usually required at border crossing points, for either travellers from the Republic or visitors from Britain. For those coming from the Republic by road or rail there is usually no delay at entry points in Down or Armagh, but on the return south the customs and excise people may ask whether consumer goods such as TV sets or microwave ovens have been purchased during the run north. Prices for many things are about 15 percent cheaper in Northern Ireland than in the Republic.

Away from border districts, only sterling currency is

accepted in stores and places of business. In the vicinity of the border, however, Republic of Ireland pounds are accepted at gas stations, hotels, and stores.

Belfast International Airport is located inland, in County Antrim, about a 30-minute drive from Belfast. A bus service runs every 30 minutes from the airport to the city center. Travellers by rail from Dublin arrive at Central Station in the heart of Belfast. For those intending to visit Britain from Ireland and return, the fares from the North, both sea and air, are generally cheaper than those from the Republic. Train fares are cheaper in the North as well, running roughly 30 percent below those in the Republic.

Northern Ireland and Scotland are very close to each other along the Antrim coast; only 35 miles separate them at the port of Larne. There are two ferry companies operating from Larne to Stranraer in Scotland: Sealink Ferries, Tel: (0574) 736-16; and P & O European Ferries, Tel: (0574) 743-21. The scenic route to Larne is on the coast road through Carrickfergus and Whitehead. Upon entering the town, signposts direct you to the harbor. No reservations are necessary except during July and August.

Throughout Northern Ireland, banks are generally open from 10:00 A.M. until 3:30 P.M., and many have automatic cash dispensers. Cash is needed at smaller hotels and guesthouses, although Access, Barclaycard, and American Express credit cards are accepted more frequently now; Diners' Club cards are not quite as widely accepted.

ACCOMMODATIONS REFERENCE

The telephone country code for the Northeast is 44. When dialing telephone numbers in Northern Ireland from outside the country, drop the 0 in the area code. The rates given below are projections for weekday rates for 1992 in pounds sterling; for up-to-the-minute rate information it is always wise to telephone before booking. Unless otherwise indicated, rates are for double rooms and do not include meals or service.

▶ **Abbey Lodge Hotel.** Belfast Road, **Downpatrick**, County Down BT30 9AV. Tel: (0396) 61-45-11. £45.

▶ **Auberge de Seneirl.** 28 Ballyclough Road, **Bushmills**, County Antrim BT57 8UZ. Tel: (02657) 415-36. £18.50–£29. All rooms with bath; some larger rooms with sitting rooms are available.

▶ **Ballygalley Castle**. 274 Coast Road, **Ballygalley**, County Antrim BT40 Q2Z. Tel: (0574) 58-32-12; Fax: (0574) 58-36-81. £60.

▶ **Ballymagarry Country House**. 46 Leeke Road, **Portrush**, County Antrim BT56 8NH. Tel: (0265) 82-37-37. £35.

▶ **Bayview Hotel**. 2 Bayhead Road, **Portballintrae**, County Antrim BT57 8RZ. Tel: (0265) 73-14-53; Fax: (0265) 73-23-60. £28 per person sharing.

▶ **Burrendale Hotel and Country Club**. Castlewellan Road, **Newcastle**, County Down BT33 0JY. Tel: (03967) 225-99; Telex: 747377; Fax: (03967) 223-28. £64; £15 supplement per person sharing.

▶ **Carngrove Hotel**. 2 Charlestown Road, **Portadown**, County Armagh BT63 5PW. Tel: (0762) 33-92-22; Fax: (0762) 33-28-99. £44.

▶ **Culloden Hotel**. 142 Bangor Road, **Holywood**, County Down BT18 0EX. Tel: (0231) 752-23; Telex: 74617; Fax: (02317) 67-77. £135.

▶ **Drumsill House Hotel**. 35 Moy Road, **Armagh City**, County Armagh BT61 8DN. Tel: (0861) 52-20-09; Fax: (0861) 52-56-24. £55.

▶ **Dunadry Inn**. 2 Islandreagh Road, **Templepatrick**, County Antrim BT41 2HA. Tel: (08494) 324-74; Fax: (08494) 333-89. £90.

▶ **Europa Hotel**. Great Victoria Street, **Belfast** BT2 7AP. Tel: (0232) 32-70-00; Telex: 74491; Fax: (0232) 32-78-00. £110.

▶ **Forte Crest Hotel**. 300 Kingsway, **Dunmurry**, County Antrim BT17 9ES. Tel: (0232) 61-21-01; Telex: 74281; Fax: (0232) 62-65-46. £88; £55 per person sharing.

▶ **Glassdrumman House and Lodge**. 85 Mill Road, **Annalong**, County Down BT34 4RH. Tel: (03967) 685-85 or 684-51; Fax: (03967) 670-41. £65; large double, £75.

▶ **Londonderry Arms**. 20 Harbour Road, **Carnlough**, County Antrim BT44 0EU. Tel: (0574) 88-52-55; Fax: (0574) 852-63. £48.

▶ **O'Hara's Royal Hotel**. Seafront, **Bangor**, County Down BT20 5ED. Tel: (0247) 27-18-66. £58, side of hotel; £68, front of hotel.

▶ **Old Inn**. 15 Main Street, **Crawfordsburn**, County Down BT19 1JH. Tel: (0247) 85-32-55; Fax: (0247) 85-27-75. £77.

▶ **Portaferry Hotel**. 10 The Strand, **Portaferry**, County Down BT22 1PE. Tel: (02477) 282-31; Fax: (02477) 289-99. £55.

▶ **Royal Court Hotel.** Whiterocks, **Portrush,** County Antrim BT56 8NF. Tel: (0265) 82-22-36; Fax: (0265) 82-44-91. £100.

▶ **Silverwood Hotel.** Kiln Lane, **Lurgan,** County Armagh BT66 6NF. Tel: (0762) 32-77-22; Fax: (0762) 32-52-90. £46.

▶ **Stormont Hotel.** 587 Upper Newtownards Road, **Belfast** BT4 3LP. Tel: (0232) 65-86-21; Fax: (0232) 48-02-40. £96.

CHRONOLOGY OF THE HISTORY OF IRELAND

- **c. 6000 B.C.**: First known inhabitants cross from Scandinavia via Britain and settle in Derry and Offaly. Few archaeological remains apart from flints and kitchen middens.
- **c. 3000 B.C.**: Neolithic Age: rough tools and pottery. Houses and field patterns excavated at Lough Gur, County Limerick, and north County Mayo. Many passage and portal tombs (Newgrange, County Meath, Carrowkeel, County Sligo, etc.).
- **c. 2000 B.C.**: Bronze Age. Metalworkers and miners reach Ireland from Europe. Gold necklet (lunula) in National Museum, Dublin, c. 1800 B.C. Stone circles widely distributed.

The Celtic Era

- **c. 500–150 B.C.**: Celtic people from central Europe establish in Ireland. La Tène culture (named for Celtic site in Switzerland) produces gold torques and other fine ornaments (National Museum, Dublin). Irish language develops from Proto-Celtic roots.
- **c. A.D. 130–180**: Ptolemy, Roman geographer, makes map of Ireland.
- **297–c. 450**: Irish raids on Roman Britain.
- **431**: Palladius, first bishop to Irish Christians. Beginning of *Annals of Ulster*.
- **432**: Saint Patrick's mission (traditional date).
- **c. 526**: Death of Saint Brigid of Kildare.
- **546**: Foundation of Derry by Saint Colmcille.
- **574–578**: Foundation of Clonmacnoise by Saint Ciaran.

- **c. 590**: Saint Columbanus begins Irish mission on Continent.
- **c. 650–750**: Ossory group of High Crosses.
- **c. 750–800**: Book of Kells and St. Gall illuminated manuscripts.

Viking Period

- **795**: First Viking raids. Irish settlement in Iceland.
- **837–876**: Semipermanent Viking settlements.
- **841**: Viking settlement at Dublin.
- **853**: Olaf becomes first Norse king of Dublin.
- **914**: Viking base at Waterford.
- **978**: Brian Boru becomes king of Munster.
- **1002**: Brian Boru becomes high king of Ireland.
- **1014**: Irish defeat Danes at Battle of Clontarf. Brian Boru killed and buried at Armagh.
- **c. 1028**: Foundation of Dublin's Christ Church Cathedral.
- **1092**: Beginning of *Annals of Inisfallen* (to continue to the 14th century).
- **1127–1134**: Construction of St. Cormac's Chapel, Cashel.
- **1142**: First Irish Cistercian foundation, Mellifont, County Louth.
- **1152**: Diarmait Mac Murchada (Dermot MacMurrough) abducts Dervorgilla, wife of Tighernan Ua Ruairc (Tiernan O'Rourke).
- **1155**: Papal bull approves conquest of Ireland by English King Henry II.

Anglo-Norman Period

- **1169**: Anglo-Normans land at Bannow, County Wexford.
- **1170**: Waterford captured by Normans under Richard de Clare (Strongbow), who marries Aoife, daughter of Mac Murchada. Capture of Dublin.
- **1171**: Henry II receives submission of four Irish kings.
- **1174**: Henry II grants charter to Dublin.
- **c. 1188**: Geraldus Cambrensis (Gerald of Wales) writes *Expugnatio Hibernica,* first tourist guide to the island.
- **1207**: First national coinage carrying harp symbol.

- **1224**: Irish Dominican foundations at Dublin and Drogheda.
- **c. 1224–1230**: Irish Franciscan foundations at Youghal and Cork. Opening of Dublin mint.
- **1262–1263**: High kingship offered to Haakon IV of Norway in return for help in expelling English, but not accepted.
- **1315–1317**: Famine.
- **1348**: Black Death at Howth and Drogheda.
- **1395**: Irish kings submit to England's Richard II.
- **1422**: Proclamation for expulsion of Irish from England.
- **1431**: Establishment of St. Patrick's Cathedral choir in Dublin.
- **1478–1513**: Supremacy of Garrett Fitzgerald, eighth earl of Kildare ("the Great Earl").
- **1487**: First record of firearms in Ireland.
- **1539**: Dissolution of monasteries within the Pale.

The Tudor Conquest

- **1561–1567**: Rebellion of Shane O'Neill.
- **1571**: First printing in Irish in Dublin.
- **1580**: Papal force massacred by British at Dun an Oir (Smerwick).
- **1588**: Ships of Spanish Armada wrecked off Irish coast. Survivors massacred by Irish.
- **1590**: Foundation at Alcalá de Henares, Spain, of first Irish college on the Continent.
- **1592**: Incorporation of Trinity College, Dublin.
- **1595–1603**: Rising under Hugh O'Neill, earl of Tyrone.
- **1601**: Battle of Kinsale. Spanish force and allies Tyrone and O'Donnell defeated. O'Donnell leaves for Spain.
- **1606**: Foundation of Irish Franciscan college at Louvain, Belgium.
- **1607**: "Flight of the Earls": Tyrone and Tyrconnell lead exodus to European mainland.

Plantation and Colonization

- **1610**: Plantation of Derry by Scots and English settlers.
- **1632–1636**: Compilation of historical work *Annals of the Four Masters* at Donegal.

- **1642**: Catholic Confederation at Kilkenny.
- **1649**: Massacres at Drogheda and Wexford by Oliver Cromwell.
- **1660**: Robert Boyle enunciates Boyle's Law, which concerns the behavior of gases.
- **1681**: Execution of archbishop Oliver Plunkett in London.
- **1689**: Siege of Derry by James II of England.
- **1690**: Battle of the Boyne between James II and William III.
- **1691**: Treaty of Limerick (subsequently broken) allows Irish soldiers to follow James II to Europe.
- **1695–1709**: Penal laws against Catholics.
- **1713**: Jonathan Swift becomes dean of St. Patrick's, Dublin.
- **1728**: Oliver Goldsmith born in County Longford.
- **1729**: Irish Parliament's first meeting in College Green, Dublin.
- **1731**: Foundation of Royal Dublin Society.
- **1737**: First issue of *Belfast News Letter,* oldest newspaper in continuous publication in Ireland or Britain.
- **1742**: First performance of Handel's *Messiah,* Dublin.
- **1759**: Arthur Guinness establishes a brewery in Dublin.
- **1771**: Benjamin Franklin in Ireland.
- **1778**: John Paul Jones, American pirate, raids Belfast Lough.
- **1782**: Britain concedes parliamentary independence: Grattan's Parliament. John Field, composer and inventor of the nocturne, born in Dublin.
- **1785**: First meeting of Irish Academy (later "Royal").

The Struggle for Independence

- **1791**: United Irishmen founded in Belfast by Wolfe Tone.
- **1792**: Gathering of Irish harpers in Belfast.
- **1796**: Ambrose O'Higgins becomes viceroy of Peru. His son, Bernardo O'Higgins, was a leader of the forces that achieved Chile's independence from Spain in 1818.
- **1798**: Rising. Arrest and death of Lord Edward Fitzgerald; French force lands in Connacht and is

defeated; Tone is arrested and commits suicide in jail.

- **1801**: Union of Ireland with Great Britain.
- **1803**: Rising of Robert Emmett in Dublin. Emmett executed.
- **1808**: Christian Brothers teaching order founded in Wexford.
- **1829**: Daniel O'Connell ("the Liberator") enters British parliament.
- **1834**: First railroad in Ireland: Dublin–Kingstown (Dún Laoghaire).
- **1841**: J. P. Holland, inventor of the submarine, born in County Clare.
- **1842**: First issue of *Nation*, organ of Young Ireland movement.
- **1843**: O'Connell addresses monster meetings supporting repeal of Union.
- **1845**: Inauguration of Rosse telescope, the world's largest, at Birr.
- **1845–1849**: Great Famine follows failure of potato crops.
- **1847**: Bram Stoker, creator of Dracula, born in Dublin.
- **1848**: Young Ireland rising. Leaders transported to Tasmania.
- **1853**: Opening of Belfast shipyard: builders of *Titanic*.
- **1856**: Playwright George Bernard Shaw born in Dublin.
- **1858**: Irish Republican Brotherhood (IRB) founded in Dublin; Fenian Brotherhood founded in New York.
- **1865**: William Butler Yeats born.
- **1866**: Fenian raids against British in Canada.
- **1867**: Fenian rising in Ireland: leaders transported.
- **1873**: Home Rule League: constitutional independence movement.
- **1874**: Ernest Shackleton, Antarctic explorer, born in County Kildare.
- **1875**: Charles Stuart Parnell elected to British parliament.
- **1876**: Rescue of Fenian prisoners from ship *Catalpa*, West Australia.
- **1879–1882**: Land War. Irish National Land League (1879).

- **1880**: Parnell addresses U.S. House of Representatives. "Boycotting" of Captain Charles Boycott, County Mayo.
- **1884**: Gaelic Athletic Association (GAA) founded, Thurles.
- **1892**: Ulster Convention, Belfast, resolves against Home Rule.
- **1895**: First production of Oscar Wilde's *The Importance of Being Earnest.*
- **1896**: Irish Socialist Republican party: secretary, James Connolly.
- **1899**: Irish Literary Theatre, forerunner of the Abbey.
- **1906**: First issue of *Sinn Fein* ("We Ourselves"), editor Arthur Griffith. Samuel Beckett born in Dublin.
- **1913**: General strike in Dublin. Workers led by James Larkin. Ulster Volunteer Force established.
- **1914**: Publication of James Joyce's *Dubliners.*
- **1916**: Easter Rising. Fifteen leaders executed by British.
- **1919–1921**: War of Independence.

"A Nation Once Again"

- **1920**: British Government of Ireland Act sets up separate subordinate parliaments in Dublin and Belfast.
- **1921**: Northern Ireland parliament convened by George V.
- **1922**: Anglo-Irish Treaty. Civil war between pro- and anti-Treaty forces. Constitution of Irish Free State approved by Dáil Eireann (parliament). First publication, in Paris, of James Joyce's novel *Ulysses.*
- **1926**: Fianna Fail party launched by New York–born Eamon de Valera.
- **1932**: De Valera becomes chairman of League of Nations, Geneva.
- **1937**: Under new constitution approved by referendum, Irish Free State becomes Eire and severs links with British monarchy.
- **1939**: Ireland declares neutrality in Second World War.
- **1949**: Republic of Ireland declared, removing last British links.

- **1960**: Irish troops serve with United Nations in the Congo.
- **1963**: U.S. president John F. Kennedy in Ireland.
- **1968**: Clash between civil rights marchers and police in Derry: beginning of Northern confrontation.
- **1973**: Ireland joins European Economic Community.
- **1977–1982**: "Treasures of Ireland" exhibition of Irish art, 1500 B.C.–A.D. 1500, tours U.S. and Continental Europe.
- **1979**: Ireland joins European Monetary System (EMS) and breaks link with sterling. Visit of Pope John Paul II.
- **1981**: Death of ten IRA hunger strikers in Long Kesh (Maze) prison, Belfast.
- **1983**: First session of New Ireland Forum to seek solution to Northern situation.
- **1985**: Signature of Anglo-Irish agreement, allowing Dublin a voice in Northern affairs, particularly those relating to the Nationalist minority.
- **1990**: Ireland holds presidency of the European Community.

—Bernard Share

INDEX

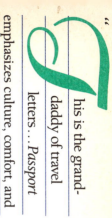

"This is the grand-daddy of travel letters... *Passport* emphasizes culture, comfort, and quality... it can glow with praise, or bite with disapproval."

Condé Nast Traveler

BUSINESS REPLY MAIL
FIRST CLASS   PERMIT NO. 45660   CHICAGO, IL

POSTAGE WILL BE PAID BY ADDRESSEE

PASSPORT
350 WEST HUBBARD STREET
SUITE 440
CHICAGO, ILLINOIS 60610-9698